82-433

W9-BHY-554

ARITHMETIC AND LEARNING DISABILITIES

Stanley W. Johnson
State University of New York at Plattsburgh

ARITHMETIC AND LEARNING DISABILITIES: Guidelines for Identification and Remediation

Allyn and Bacon, Inc.
Boston, London, Sydney

PRO
371.92 *3/82* *DIRECT*
JOH *Allyn and Bacon*

Library of Congress Cataloging in Publication Data

Johnson, Stanley W   1928-
  Arithmetic and learning disabilities.

  Bibliography: p.
  Includes index.
    1. Arithmetic—Study and teaching. 2. Learning disabilities. I. Title.
QA135.5.J69   371.9'2   78-21295
ISBN 0-205-06444-2
ISBN 0-205-06504-X pbk.

Printed in the United States of America

TO KAREN

Who Has Made So Many Things Possible

Contents

Preface

Such a great amount of the attention in learning disabilities work is focused on reading skills that many other important areas have suffered from neglect and underexposure. It is difficult to be sure why this has happened. Perhaps it is because so many children exhibit reading problems. Or perhaps it is because these problems have proven to be readily accessible to many different remedial strategies. Some have thought that it is because other problems have not yielded to attempts to construct meaningful remedial strategies and materials.

The actual reason remains hidden. But certainly there appears to be no intrinsic reason why arithmetic problems created or affected by learning disabilities should not be remedied with a concentrated approach. There is indeed a dire need for integrated systematic research. Theoretical knowledge about arithmetic behaviors—along with the necessary reservoir of empirically garnered research data—is not as abundant as in other academic subject matter areas. It is true that the work of a few notable pioneers and guides stands out. But the cumulative positive effects which come from the endeavors of the thousands of workers who come in contact with such problems everyday is lacking in this area. Problems in reading have been effectively reduced largely due to such effects. The area of arithmetic, and certainly the larger field of mathematics, deserves as much attention.

It is hoped that the ideas and procedures outlined in this text will help activate further research and practical application. It is not claimed that what is produced here is any "open sesame." Rather, it is hoped that this may serve as a stimulus for more and more attention to the problem, hopefully resulting in refinement and eventually in substantial progress.

As must be obvious, many individuals have contributed ideas, support, constructive criticism, and countless hours of hard work to the production of this material. All cannot be named, but at least these few deserve specific thanks. Ms. Billie Houghton offered enthusiasm and support for the original idea and was important in the early conceptual phases. Ms. Judy Dashnaw, as usual, was a bulwark against the storm of technical office problems. Ms. Joan Granoff helped check out many little details which, for the author, offer nothing but pain and torment. Three hard-working graduate students worked many hours helping present some of the ideas at conventions and workshops, thus assuring a flow of early feedback. These students, Mr. Rick Converse, Mr. Jon Gould, and Ms. Susan Kuemmerle, deserve special thanks. Ms. Mary Ann Mercier and Ms. Jackie Hessing worked long hours on details of diagnostic procedures and remedial activities, and their work is sincerely appreciated.

Finally, my wife, who should really have joint authorship, literally poured over curriculum outlines, textbooks, journal articles, and the most difficult reading in the world—an author's rough-draft manuscript. Her work and support has been absolutely vital. She deserves much more than the thanks I have given here.

And to the others—too many to mention—their encouragement is noted here and personally remembered.

SWJ
Plattsburgh, New York

Introduction

This is not a book about learning disabilities alone. Nor is it a book solely about elementary arithmetic. It is, instead, a book about how learning disabilities and elementary arithmetic activities interact. It deals with how a child's approach to and progress in learning basic arithmetic concepts and skills may be affected by the presence of several different specific learning disabilities.

This book is not written for the rare specialist who is disinterested in practical problems a child may experience in classroom learning. Nor is it written for the occasional elementary teacher who is so bound to a specific syllabus or subject matter that a child's more basic problems go unheeded. Rather, it is written for the more typical teacher and teacher-specialist who share the desire that every child should experience the joy of learning in any and all subjects; who endorse the proposition that the school system with its many accoutrement exists for the primary purpose of facilitating and expediting children's learning experiences; and for those who yearn for the key which might unlock the door for children who stand outside, still waiting to know normal learning experience.

The specific intent is to provide concepts and materials which may assist in identifying children who are experiencing some difficulty in learning arithmetic due to the inhibiting interference of a learning disability. And, once such children are positively identified, to assist school personnel (most frequently the classroom teacher) in the preparation and presentation of activities designed to increment learning in clearly defined deficit areas. Theory is presented only to the extent which is necessary to defend applied practice. Arbitrary stances, such as offering a firm and unassailable definition of learning disabilities, or the espousing of a polemic viewpoint of arithmetic conceptualization, are deliberately avoided in order to make the material serviceable from as many viewpoints as possible. The bias of the author's approach is obviously behavioristic, but not to the exclusion of all other approaches or orientations. Some might wish for an up-to-date description, discussion, and critique of the state-of-the-art of either field from research, development, and implementation viewpoints. Obviously, such a work would have value. But, the intent here, to provide a handbook-type text which facilitates *doing* by providing a pragmatic complement to such knowledge gained from more formal and theoretical orientation, precludes inclusion of most of such type data and discussion. However, though the approach is pragmatic, the author would not wish the reader to ignore important theoretical and technical considerations such as the need for established reliability and validity characteristics in diagnostic instruments. Consideration of such technical safeguards should be part of the standard approach of any careful worker in the field.

Since the book deals with the interaction of two separate fields, learning disabilities and arithmetic, it is necessary to introduce them separately and then subsequently explain how they may interact.

Part I contains five preparatory chapters. Of these, chapter 1 introduces the general field of specific learning disabilities. For the learning disability specialist, the first chapter will serve largely as review. For the classroom arithmetic teacher, it may provide some new basic concepts vital to subsequent steps. Chapter 2 relates some of the fundamental concepts, principles, and content of elementary arithmetic. Much of the material in the chapter may be new to the learning disability specialist, but present a generally familiar review for the elementary arithmetic teacher. Chapter 3 examines how the arithmetic curriculum of the pre-school and elementary years may be analyzed and categorized in a manner which facilitates problem identification and remediation procedures. This same chapter also introduces a scheme for grouping specific learning disabilities into a few major categories so they may be more easily conceptualized and applied to curriculum content areas. These two categorization schemes, one for elementary arithmetic curriculum content and one for specific learning disabilities, provide the framework for concepts and activities introduced in later chapters. Chapter 4 explains the reasoning and principles behind the general strategy for identifying children with arithmetic deficits due to the presence of an identified learning disability. Chapter 5 explains in a step-by-step fashion how to implement the strategy.

Part II includes four chapters for use as a handbook and referral source in identifying and remediating each of the possible interacting arithmetic-learning disability problem areas previously noted.

Chapter 6 presents and explains the various curriculum content areas selected for the three different levels. An outline and explanation of the eight learning disability areas used is also included in this chapter. Chapters 7, 8, and 9 present examples of problem-free behavior, sample tasks where the deficit child may display difficulty, do-it-yourself diagnostic activities, non-arithmetic situations where similar behaviors are required, remedial objectives for confirmed problems, and sample remedial activities for every interaction of a curriculum area with a learning disability type of each on the three levels.

PART I

PREPARATORY MATERIAL

Chapter 1

Introduction to Learning Disabilities (LD)

Thousands of elementary school children, otherwise normally developing and growing individuals, are deprived of the joy and elation accompanying successful school achievement due to their having handicapping learning disabilities. According to some estimates (Mackie, 1969; Lerner, 1976), learning disabilities represent the single largest category of exceptionality even when including such other common problems as mental retardation, speech handicaps, and crippling diseases. Some, such as Myklebust and Boshes (1969), indicate that typical school populations may contain as many as 15 percent learning disabled. Even by using much more conservative cutoff points, which ignore many borderline cases, as many as 7 percent apparently suffer restricted educational development due to learning disability deficits. The National Advisory Committee on Handicapped Children (1968), early in the developing recognition of this problem area, reported a "conservative" estimate of 1 to 3 percent.

Yet, despite these alarmingly high incidences, learning disabilities remain less clearly defined and recognized than many other problem areas. More often, these learning disabilities are overlooked and become a major problem for today's schools, teachers, and pupils. Application of what knowledge has been assembled to some curriculum areas, such as arithmetic, is sparse indeed.

Just what is a learning disability? How does a learning disabled child act? How can one recognize these behaviors which prevent accomplishment and set about eliminating them?

EARLY DEVELOPMENT

Identification and treatment of learning disabilities are modern phenomena. Rising out of special education and the work of several pioneers working in the fields of retardation and brain injuries (Strauss and Werner, 1942; Strauss and Lehtinen, 1947; Stevens and Birch, 1957), a number of different practitioners, representing a variety of professional fields, began in the 1940s and 1950s to recognize that many school children were displaying learning problems which did not fit earlier established classifications of exceptionality. These children displayed some of the symptoms of brain injury, such as high distractibility, yet evidenced no particular hard or soft signs of specific neurological damage. Many of these children struggled with basic elements of learning which, while simple for most, proved to be discouragingly and destructively difficult for them. Yet, their behavior in other areas belied any such categorization as *retardate* or *slow learner*. Some experienced so much frustration and disappointment in their school accomplishments that their interest and motivation dropped, their patience shortened with resulting displays of temper and poor emotional control, yet no aberrant personality structure or signs of emotional pathology seemed to be present.

Concern rapidly grew for this troubled segment of the school population, easily observed but mysteriously handicapped by learning problems not yet clearly established or identified. Some of the earlier practitioners struggled with problems of identification and description. Doll (1951) offered the term *neurophrenia* as a diagnostic classification. Johnson (1962), aware that these children uncertainly traveled the edge between borderline normality and disabilitating low achievement, called them *marginal children*. Johnson organized workshops of educators and psychologists, attempting to better explain and help these mysteriously low achieving children.

In the early 1960s the attention and concern of professionals and laymen began to yield results. Kirk (1962) for the first time included a definition of learning disabilities in a text dealing with exceptionality. In 1963, again with strong impetus from Kirk, the Association for Children With Learning Disabilities was formed. In the same year, several agencies of the United States government joined with the National Easter Seal Society to work toward establishing some meaningful definitions of the problem area which might better lead to preventive and remedial activities. Three years later, extensive lobbying by those interested in special education led to Congress establishing the Bureau for Education of the Handicapped, an important prerequisite for the significant Learning Disabled Act of 1970.

By the early 1970s the area of learning disabilities was clearly established as a major problem worthy of attention. Professional organizations such as the Council for Exceptional Children established divisions devoted to special attention to the field.

PROBLEMS OF DEFINITION

Despite this quite recent growth in attention and focus, learning disabilities are still difficult to adequately define in any one, simple, clear, concise, and unequivocable statement. No single consensually established definition exists even for professionals trained in the field. Professionals' technical definitions vary largely, based primarily upon the approach and the orientation of the user. Yet another difficulty encountered in defining learning disabilities is due to the reality that few, if any, specific problem behaviors can be said to exist purely as the sole result of learning disability. Most inadequate learning behavior arising from a learning disability might as easily be caused by other difficulties as well. Thus, an important step in practical remedial strategy is to determine if observed problems are actually LD-related or not. Inability to discriminate *3*'s from *8*'s, for example, may be due to either poor vision or inadequate perceptual performance or both. Other viable etiologies must in many cases be eliminated before proceeding with remedial programming for specific learning disabilities.

There is, however, no shortage of standardized definitions, consensual or not. For example, most federally funded programs use the following formal definition:

> Children with special learning disabilities exhibit a disorder in one or more of the basic psychological processes involved in understanding or using spoken or written languages. These may be manifested in disorders of listening, thinking, talking, reading, writing, spelling, perceptual handicaps, brain injury, minimal brain dysfunction, dyslexia, developmental aphasia, etc. They do not include learning problems which are due primarily to visual, hearing, or motor handicaps, to mental retardation, emotional disturbance, or to environmental disadvantage.

Although not really definitive and certainly not uniformly consensual, this definition and others, as Gearheart, (1973), Myers and Hammill, (1976), and Johnson and Morasky (1977) point out, do receive a substantial amount of basic agreement from the majority of workers in the field. Agreement centers around these five main points:

1 Some principle of discrepancy or disparity is involved.

2 There is no necessary assumption that central nervous system pathology is involved.

3 Primary physiological problems are excluded.

4 Some special problem areas are excluded.

5 Relevance of the problem to the learning process is important.

These are important areas of agreement since applied work in learning disabilities, the actual remediation of children's deficits, is largely shaped by these consensual points.

1 The principle of disparity (see Figure 1.1) states that there is a significant difference between the level at which an individual performs a specific educational task and the level at which he does other tasks of the same relative difficulty. The principle implies an important assumption about typical learning disability behavior. Individuals with a specific learning disability are not achieving in a given area up to their own natural ability. Thus, a portion of the individual's capabilities is being unused or overlooked—a portion which can be tapped by the proper educational program. Learning disability children are essentially normal individuals with physical integrities, capabilities, and potentialities in harmony with their own general overall level of behavior. A diagnosed learning disability represents a defined segment of learning

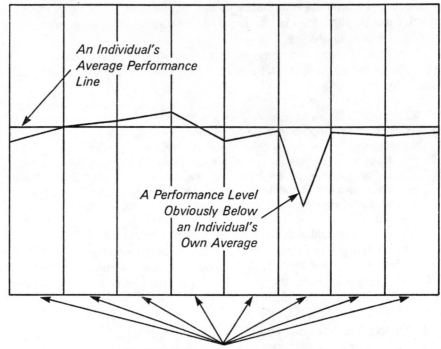

Identified Areas of Academic Behavior

Figure 1.1 *Principle of disparity**

* From Stanley W. Johnson and Robert L. Morasky, *Learning Disabilities.* Copyright © 1977 by Allyn and Bacon, Inc., Boston. Reprinted by permission.

behavior incongruent with an individual's total behavioral picture. The LD child is out of phase with himself—a concept more important for remediation purposes than being below grade, or sub-normal by some group standard.

2 Few if any professionals in the learning disability area are such dualists as to suggest that an individual can perform any act or deed without the nervous system being involved. However, it is *commonly* agreed that proof or absolute evidence of central nervous system dysfunction is not necessary for learning disability remediation to be successfully undertaken. Even when evidence of such involvement is firmly at hand, it does not seem to be of much practical help to the individual practitioner. So few examples of one-to-one brain structure damage or dysfunction and learning problems can be demonstrated that this approach is not generally considered profitable in either a diagnostic or prescriptive programming sense. Consequently, the focus of attention is upon remediation of problem behavior, removing behavioral disparity by building new skills, correcting inappropriate behaviors, or supplying needed experience rather than spending much time looking for why efficient learning initially broke down.

Much of the early struggle to have learning disabilities recognized as a separately viable field, distinctive and apart from other areas of exceptionality, has in part given rise to the third and fourth areas of consensus.

3 Primary physiological difficulties are rather easily isolated by comparison to more ambiguous learning problems. Hence, they should be initially considered as a possible cause of learning problems, and if present, be removed before concern for other types of inadequacies involve more detailed behavioral analysis. Such problems as vision and hearing deficits and speech pathology are excluded.

4 In the same vein, other nonphysiological entities causing learning problems (subject to specialized treatment) but not classified as learning disabilities are specifically excluded from current federal funding-related definitions. These include problems of learning stemming from cultural disadvantage, mental retardation, and emotional disturbance.

5 The final consensual point is particularly relevant to our concern about learning disabilities and arithmetic. The crucial point of focus must be the learning process. The intent is that study and remedial efforts related to learning disabilities be seen as focusing on those processes and behaviors necessary for effective educational performance. A learning disability is uniformly perceived as something which interferes with an individual's ability to adequately learn in a definable segment of the normal school experience. In the specific context of this book, learning disabilities will be examined as problems which hinder the school child from progressing normally through the arithmetic aspects of the early years of the elementary school curriculum. Remedial techniques and procedures will be viewed in terms of their usefulness in helping the deficit-performance child achieve parity between arithmetic and other learning abilities and behaviors of that particular child.

Despite such formal definitions as presented by the federal government endorsed study committee and the high amount of consensual support it evokes, it is still difficult for the developing professional, as yet largely unexposed to learning disabilities, to clearly see and understand what the field entails and what is involved. Part of the ambiguity is due to the common inadequacy of formal definitions which simply cannot clearly establish all the possible facets of behavior present in a designated problem area. And, part is due to the variety of actual problems subsumed under the learning disabilities label. The LD field is not a simple, homogeneous, cleanly clear-cut collection of problem behaviors. Indeed, the opposite seems to be the case with a wide variety of behaviors, subject matter areas, and skills being involved in any approach to learning disabilities.

PERCEPTIONS OF LD BY THOSE MOST INVOLVED

It may be initially more helpful for the student of learning disabilities to perceive the problem as seen by those it most often touches, rather than worry about some all-encompassing definition or a myriad of debatable detail. The varying perceptions of different groups of people are interesting. These include: pupils, parents, teachers, related professionals, and LD specialists.

The Pupil Looks at Learning Disabilities

The child afflicted with a learning disability most frequently is a youngster in the first three or four years of school, more often a boy than girl (though LD problems are common to both sexes), and who presents a very sad picture indeed. This type of child suffers from one of the most disabilitating types of experience possible. He sees himself as not capable of performing on a level with his peers (which in itself is frightening), but even more fear-producing, not performing on the level where he himself feels and expects he should be. The function of the principle of disparity is nowhere displayed more graphically than in the young child who has every reason to expect criterion-level behavior from himself based upon his own general level of behavior and experience, but instead finds his performance inadequate, below standard, and often glaringly obvious to others.

There seems to be something intrinsically reinforcing in successful learning, particularly for the young child. But the learning disabled youngster is denied the assurance and subsequent drive producing rewards which come from adequate performance. The negative results can be severe. Depending upon the situation and the individual's personality, the child may strike out in aggressive alternative attempts to achieve, or retreat by withdrawing into a passive protective shield against failure accomplished by refusing to try. The child is frightened, frustrated, insecure, and typically begins to have doubts about his or her own capability. Since schoolroom performance in harmony with that of peers is so important to the developing child, such failures to achieve apace with classmates magnifies the anxiety of sub-par performance. Nowhere is this more easily seen than in the arithmetic curriculum. Numbers and abstract manipulations can be strange and frightening and there is a great deal of comfort in finding that personal experiences, uncertainties, and accomplishments are shared by peers. Failure frequently becomes habitual, expected, and extremely disabilitating.

The world begins to take on a flat opaqueness as possibilities for success become increasingly obscure. The child's motivation suffers—a reality that further compounds the problem. Thus, the learning disabled child often is a fearful, unhappy child, desperately confused by his or her own unexplained inadequacies in certain learning situations. The result is a child whose emotional reaction to academic failure may largely preclude effort and therefore bar successes even in areas where no problems exist. The world of such a child is not a pleasant one.

Parents Look At Learning Disabilities

Parents, too, share the frustration of a child who, apparently without explanation, is unable to achieve in some particular learning area. Since such behavior is, strictly speaking, not representative of the child's overall productive capabilities, the contrast between past and present in the child's performance and between a child and his siblings is almost brutally apparent for many parents. Comments such as, "I can't understand it. He doesn't seem to have problems learning other things," are commonly heard from worried parents. They frequently ask questions about the possible presence of some mysterious progressive deterioration in learning ability, or worry about the probability of younger brothers and sisters developing similar problems. Concern over possible guilt is not infrequently present. Parents often ask, "What did we do wrong? Is it our fault?"

Even parents relatively naive to psychological implications will perceive and react to their learning disabled child's developing emotional response to the problem. Such terms as "immaturity" or "increasingly nervous" or "more and more distractible" are often used.

When parents do not react in a way constructive to mental health they may increase the problem by incrementing pressure to achieve, over-reacting to even small academic failures, or by adding to the child's suspicion of his own inadequacies through name calling or derogatory comparisons. On the other hand, parents can be legitimately involved in many positive phases of remediation and, in such roles, have important and constructive contributions to make. It should be emphasized, however, that even for perceptive parents, tuned to the needs and feelings of their children, having a learning disabled child in the family can be a trying and difficult experience, especially if responsible and knowledgeable help from educational professionals is not present.

Teachers Look At Learning Disabilities

Teachers' perceptions of learning disabled children have been the focus of much attention. As noted previously, a consensual point of definition is that learning disability problems have educational relevance. Hence, a large majority of learning disability research work has focused on the school, and the pupil and teacher together in the learning situation. One research team (Cowgill, Friedland, and Shapiro, 1973) studied traits which may successfully predict the presence of learning disabilities from the reports of kindergarten teachers. They found that in the trait areas of maturity-immaturity, attention span, impulsive behavior, motor control, and speech and language problems, identified LD children stand out as being significantly different from control groups in the eyes of kindergarten teachers.

Meier (1971), in a study of more than 3,000 second graders, found that over two-thirds of the learning disabled children had been checked by second grade teachers as having distinctively short attention span, being more easily distracted from their school work, slower readers (both aloud and silently), and displaying a tendency to substitute words which frequently distort the meaning of the written or read material, for example, *when* for *where*. This latter characteristic can easily be seen as a particularly disruptive influence in arithmetic problem solving.

Whether these identified traits accurately represent all or most teachers' perceptions of learning disabled children is uncertain. What is clear, however, is that teachers easily see deficit behaviors resulting from learning disabilities and are often sensitive to problem behavioral traits which may develop as a result of the child's emotional reaction to failure.

It should be pointed out that teachers also suffer the effects of frustration along with the learning disabled child and his or her parents. Traditional time-and-trial proven classroom techniques may fail to produce the desired criterion behaviors in learning disabled children. Teachers frequently seek the help of other specialists because of their concern over being ineffective with these children. The effects of the presence of such a child on his own peers is not overlooked by teachers either. Any emotionally aberrant behavior in the classroom does not operate in a vacuum, but instead has some interacting effect on all children in the class.

The concerns, worries, and fears expressed by the teachers of learning disabled children may be worded differently than those of others (being more related to educational contexts and activities rather than personal concerns) but they are just as real and important. They are encountered with equal frequency and, in too many cases, are severely disabilitating for the sincere teacher, as well as for parents or the child having difficulties.

Other Professionals Look At Learning Disabilities

Professionals related to non-educational disciplines also present characteristic views of learning disabilities. As Lerner (1976) points out, a large number of disciplines may at one time or another become involved in activities relevant to specific learning disabilities. She includes such major discipline areas as medicine, language, education, psychology, and a host of others including optometry, audiology, social service, physical therapy, genetics, biochemistry, guidance and counseling, and clinical administration.

Often the viewpoints of representatives of these different disciplines are inadequately integrated with the learning disability field. The resulting mix of ideas, perceptions, and approach is at best confusing and sometimes destructive to successful remediation. The wide divergence of professional orientations involved in some interrelationship with learning disabilities is evidence of how wide and far reaching the presence of learning inadequacies in a child may actually be. The poor academic performance of a learning disabled child has drawn the attention of almost every clinically-oriented profession. Too often, professionals may see aspects of learning disability behavior related to their own specialization, yet not perceive or ignore others. For example, psychologists may be overly concerned with emotional states, thereby neglecting perceptual problems that optometrists would naturally pinpoint. The myriad array of ideas and approaches presented by this full spectrum of professional interest in learning disabilities has been confusing and not particularly helpful to the individual practitioner. The need to make some type of sense out of the maze of professional opinions and biases has led to the efforts of some to facilitate interprofessional communication and action (Johnson and Morasky, 1977). This need has caused others to suggest that perhaps what is ultimately needed is a learning disability specialist (Kirk, 1969).

The worry and frustration of the individual specialist may not be as acute as those of child, parent, or teacher (perhaps due to less day-by-day and hour-by-hour contact and involvement). There is, however, considerable concern over the need to better understand the problem of learning disabilities and to be able to offer more firm and defensible suggestions for successful prevention and remediation. To this extent, learning disabilities are also seen as a frustrating and trying problem area for professional specialists representing many non-educational disciplines.

IDENTIFICATION OF SPECIFIC TYPES AND CATEGORIES

What do we know about specific learning disability behaviors and the children which display them that will help us in an initial definition of the area? Our knowledge seems to come from three broad aspects of the problem:

1 We have some fairly clear-cut ideas about differences between learning disabilities and some other problem areas.

2 Our attempts to resolve problems of categorization have led to some useful information about discriminative behaviors.

3 The varied interests and efforts of differently-oriented theorists and practitioners have helped pinpoint some different types of disabilities which are often subsumed without specifications under the overall label of specific learning disability.

CONFUSION WITH OTHER PROBLEMS

There are some other frequently encountered problem areas which bear superficial resemblance to learning disabilities, but which in reality have sufficiently separate characteristics as to be discriminately different. These are useful to note not only for the purpose of further defining learning disabilities, but also since confusion among the different categories is frequently faced by practitioners working with individuals untrained in learning disabilities, such as parents, professionals of other fields, aides, etc.

Mental Retardation

A very common misconception is to confuse learning disabilities with mental retardation. This is a most honest error since both frequently involve inadequate performance by school children. Confusion is also due to many professionals working in both mental retardation and learning disability fields at the same time. It is true that a great deal of what we currently know about learning disabilities can be traced almost directly to early work in retardation, especially the sub-area of exceptionality concerned with brain injury. Many of the early pioneers in the learning disabilities area (Bateman, Cruickshank, Kephart, Kirk, Myklebust, and others) have also made distinctive contributions to the field of retardation. Mental retardation and learning disabilities are not synonymous terms, however, and do not represent identical behavior patterns. As has been previously outlined, retardation problems are categorically excluded from the learning disability field in the definition used by HEW in all government work in the field.

Gearheart (1973) has rather clearly addressed the problem of differentiating the learning disabled child from the retardate:

> The learning disabled child behaves as he does due to forces beyond his control, and with proper attention has the potential for normal development and successful school achievement. This assumption removes the child from the ranks of the mentally retarded in perceived learning potential and social adaptability. The learning disabled child's condition is amenable to treatment and specialized instruction. This assumption proclaims that the condition is remediable and that there are persons with the knowledge and skill to accomplish this (Gearheart, 1973).

As Johnson and Myklebust (1967) have noted, the assumption is that the learning disabled child has integrities which are adequate or above, and that specifically in the intellectual area the child has capacity for normal productive behavior. One might take some argument with this prerequisite for normal intelligence by pointing out that a retarded individual can also experience a deficit area significantly below the average of other areas of his or her behavior. Thus, by the principle of disparity, the retardate may be portraying a learning disability. This seems to be proven true in practice, but the principle assumption that sufficient intellectual capacity is present for the individual to be able to perform at the desired criterion level is not violated. In the nonretarded individual the assumption of general intellectual normality is assumed and thus intelligence ceases to be an etiological factor. In the retarded individual experiencing an added learning disability problem, the assumption is that the deficit behavior is below that level reasonably to be expected, given the general demonstrated intellectual capacity of the person, regardless of what that level may be.

Behaviorally, this difference between retardation and learning disability is most frequently demonstrated in the unusual unevenness perceived in the production of the learning disabled child. Instead of a generally depressed or lowered level of accomplishment, the learning disabled child, especially early in the development of the problem, is apt to show areas of no particular problems alongside readily discriminable substandard performance areas. It is common to hear teachers of a learning disabled child say something like, "If only she could do that as well as she does other things!" Such remarks are obvious reactions to the unevenness of production—the disparity principle as behaviorally evidenced.

Emotional Disturbances

Distinguishing between learning disabilities and emotional disturbances is sometimes difficult, particularly in those cases where a child has experienced so much long-term frustration and failure as to begin to develop emotional reaction patterns to them. The discriminating basic differences seem to be twofold. First, emotional problems in reaction to learning disabilities do not seem to be of any particular deep-seated or involved types, and seldom if ever are portrayed along classic neurotic-psychotic syndromes. This is not to say that they are never intense, for learning frustrations can be powerful, long-lasting, and permeating to the personality structure. But, such problems tend to be specifically related to the learning context, and thus perhaps generalize to other situations less frequently, less easily, and more obviously than more basic personality difficulties.

Secondly, although the emotional problems which emerge from learning disabilities may yield to a wide range of typical therapeutic strategies, they also are commonly remitted relatively quickly and easily once the learning difficulty itself is alleviated. They are seen, therefore, to be rather clearly related to the failure to accomplish in the learning environment, and as such are a legitimate, fairly predictable reaction to the frustration-failure lowered self-concept experience. Since they are apt to be less basic than more involved personality pattern problems, they tend to be more easily and quickly removed, and often spontaneously remit once the deficit learning behavior is removed.

In some cases, more involved personality deterioration is observed. But most often, this is found to be an interaction of a learning disability and a more basic personality problem. Had the learning disability not been present, the problem would have emerged using some alternate route. In these cases, treatment must proceed along two lines: (1) removal of the emotional problem behavior, and (2) removal of the learning deficit as well. And, though the two cannot be said to be independent of each other, they are not necessarily parallel problems with removal of one directly affecting or alleviating the other.

Poor Motivation

Sometimes low motivational levels are confused with learning disabilities, though they are more apt to be simply a reflection of a more general personality problem or some other nonacademic problem, for example, sibling rivalry or a particular health problem such as hypoglycemia. Discrimination between this type problem and learning disabilities is not particularly difficult upon close observation and analysis. The disparity between different performance areas is almost always discriminable, and in the case of learning disabilities, removal of the deficit behavior areas often results rather dramatically in quickly incremented motivation.

LESSONS LEARNED FROM CATEGORIZATION ATTEMPTS

Even the early search during the 1940s and 1950s for the discriminative behaviors which comprise what we now call learning disabilities was involved with problems of labeling, categorization, and stereotyping. In his early remarks to the convention that was to later create the first national organization devoted to learning disabilities, Kirk said:

> I often wonder why we tend to use technical and complex labels, when it is more accurate and meaningful to describe behavior. If we find a child who has not learned to talk, the most scientific description is that he has not yet learned to talk. The labels of aphasia or mentally retarded or emotionally disturbed are not as helpful as a description and may, in many instances, tend to confuse the issue. Instead of using the term hyperkinetic we would understand the child better if the observer states that he continually climbs walls or hangs on chandeliers . . . I have felt for some time that labels we give children are satisfying to us but of little help to the child himself. We seem to be satisfied when we give a technical name to a condition . . . I would like to caution you about being compulsively concerned about names and classification labels . . . I would prefer that people inform me that they have a child that does not talk instead of saying to me their child is dysphasic . . . This approach has led me and my colleagues to develop methods of assessing children or describing their communication skills in objective terms . . . (Kirk, 1963).

Labeling almost always causes more problems than it solves as Hammill and Bartel (1971) reiterate:

1 The recognition of commonly shared behavioral learning characteristics of groups of children invariably leads to their being christened with a label.

2 No matter how neutral the label is intended to be, it will rapidly acquire a stigma.

3 Negative labels may reduce teacher expectations and demands from these students, thus further depressing their opportunities for achievement.

4 It is *easy* to use labels as causes for conditions that the label is supposed to describe—a kind of tautological thinking in which one can reason that the child is not learning to read because he has a learning disability, and he must have a learning disability because he is not learning to read.

5 These children differ so widely on intellectual, motor, perceptual, and behavioral traits that a common label—and more importantly, a common treatment—is meaningless and impossible.

Still, as pointed out by Johnson and Morasky (1977), descriptive data which is grouped appropriately under titles which have behavioral relevance can be useful in assembling materials, techniques, and personnel which may then best fit a given remedial strategy. As Bateman (1964) noted in an early article, there are three board descriptive dimensions to the field of learning disabilities which when properly used help us better assemble our resources. These are the dimensions of focus, orientation, and problem. Under focus, Bateman lists the alternatives of etiology, diagnosis, and remediation. Under orientation, she includes those of the major disciplines involved in the field—education, psychology, and medicine. Under problem types, she lists reading, communication, and visual-motor—a breakdown commensurate with approaches commonly used at the time the article was written. The contribution which such an analysis of description or labeling has made, is largely to sensitize the practitioner to the need to be aware of these three dimensions in ascribing importance to any particular set of materials, techniques, or theoretical contributions to the field. Focus, orientation, and problem type must all be congruent with the predetermined objectives of the practitioner if the approach is to work well.

For example, the focus of this work is primarily remediation with some attention to diagnosis. The orientation is a blending of education and psychology and the problem area is directly that of arithmetic criterion behaviors in elementary school years. Thus, this work differs distinctly from others which might represent, for example, an analysis of the cause of arithmetic problems.

ATTEMPTS TO LIST MAJOR TYPES

The major categories of learning disabilities are impossible to list with any degree of certainty of accurately representing what individuals may find while practicing in different situations within varying contexts. Such lists instead represent personal theoretical or practical biases with those interested in a particular type of problem tending to perceive it most often and to study it most thoroughly. This is not an unproductive feature of the field, for if one can disregard any specific advocate's assumption that his way is the "one and only" and the "single most important facet of the field," then one may assume that it is reasonable to suppose that with professional background and experience being equal, those most intensely interested in a specific area or areas may be expected to be most productive in that area(s). Rather, one can shop around in the academic-technique marketplace prudently buying or borrowing those techniques which seem to fit the needs of the situation most currently important to the individual practitioner. Such eclecticism should be carefully considered with forethought and planning just as one should avoid impulsive unplanned shopping in the market. Uncritical acceptance and assimilation in either context is apt to leave one both bankrupt and disappointed. It is important to shop and select with a basis of knowledge and forethought.

A survey of what is available yields an interesting array of isolated problem areas under the aegis of learning disabilities, some much narrower and specific than others. Thus, one may choose from such listings (accompanied usually by varyingly relevant remedial techniques) as these:

1 Dyslexia
2 Verbal communication disorders
3 Visual-motor integration problems (Bateman, 1964)

1 Disorders of motor activity
2 Disorders of emotionality
3 Disorders of perception
4 Disorders of symbolization
5 Disorders of attention
6 Disorders of memory (Myers and Hammill, 1976)

1 Gross motor development
2 Sensory-motor integration
3 Perceptual motor skills
4 Language development
5 Conceptual skills
6 Social skills (Valett, 1967)

Still others tend to group all problems under a single major heading such as developmental problems, perceptual motor skills, neurological integration problems, visual integration problems, and many others. Unfortunately for the practitioner, very few authors in the field attempt to relate their interests specifically to certain subject areas and there is a reason for this which is quite defensible. Many feel that most single academic subject areas do not represent behaviors sufficiently different from those of other areas, therefore, specific learning disabilities are not totally peculiar to and inherent in one area alone. Thus, there do not seem to be very many purely "spelling" learning disabilities or "reading" learning disabilities or "arithmetic" learning disabilities. This is not to say that focus on an individual subject matter is non-productive. Indeed, such an assumption would preclude a work such as this of being of any worth. Rather, it should be pointed out that a number of common learning disability behaviors can be seen to be operating in distinctive ways in different subject matter areas. Various remedial strategies may be applied in quite distinctive ways through different subject matters. Finally, there exist a number of clearly different ways in which the native material of a subject matter field may be used categorically to help alleviate deficit behaviors demonstrated in that subject matter by a learning disabled individual. This is the objective of this work as applied to the area of arithmetic.

EFFECTIVE USE OF PERSONNEL

To assist the developing professional in defining and understanding the field of learning disabilities, one final general area needs to be mentioned—the use and roles of various personnel. No amount of behavioral definitions, prescriptive categorizations, or therapeutic techniques can be useful without effective involvement of personnel in remedial and diagnostic activities. In later chapters, at least five different types of personnel or roles will be involved in the explanation and description of specific diagnostic and remedial strategies and activities applicable to the arithmetic learning process. These include that of the learning disabled individual, peers, parents, general educational personnel, and specialists.

The Learning Disabled Individual

This person is the focus of our entire study. It is vital that we be able to adequately observe and describe (1) those behaviors which this individual performs inadequately, (2) those behaviors which are performed in lieu of desired criterion behaviors, (3) the individual's own reactions to important environmental and prescriptive programmatic variables, and (4) the individual's discriminable progress toward more effective learning and personally satisfying behaviors. As simple and straightforward as these objectives may seem, they interrelate quite complexly with each other and with the roles of the various personnel involved. These separate role functions must be carefully delineated and studied if remediation is to be effective.

Peers

Often overlooked as an important component of the picture, one of the assumptions of this text is that peers can make positive contributions to help achieve adequate performance by the disabled child. Attention will be given to how such individuals may be involved and how their participation may be encouraged and measured as part of the regular remedial strategy.

Parents

Certainly no single group of involved individuals are better motivated to be of assistance to the learning disabled child than parents. Splendid opportunities are available for involving parents so that they may best understand and help their children, and at the same time satisfy their own needs for being positive catalysts in their children's quest for better academic performance. Specific attention will also be given to this group as aides in adequate diagnosis and support in school-based programs.

General Educational Personnel

The contributory roles of teachers, school psychologists, guidance workers, school health staff, and maintenance and support staff will also be considered. Opportunities for effectively using such personnel in remedial planning and programming are many and fit well into an attack on a specific subject matter such as arithmetic.

Learning Disability Specialists

There are times when the distinctive contribution of specialists must or should be sought. This is as true for arithmetic problems as any other and an attempt will be made to carefully delineate such instances. It is especially important that the distinctive role of the specialist be integrated with others so as to make most effective use of the focused expertise available without denigrating the contributions of others.

Overall, though, it is the assumption of this author that the single most important person on the remedial team is the individual classroom teacher. This is the individual most likely to be in touch with the important behaviors to be observed and studied. This is the individual most likely to be able to clearly spell out the criterion behaviors which are the objectives of any remedial programming. Finally, this is the individual who must of necessity be able to blend into and focus the distinctive contributions of others upon the task at hand, the successful accomplishment of the task of learning within the school environment.

The final consensual definition point mentioned earlier may be the most important of all. If it were not for the need for individuals to successfully learn in a normal school environment, there would probably be no such thing as learning disabilities. It is vital to remember that the deficit behaviors have ultimate educational relevance and that the overall purpose of any learning disability text, any program of training, any diagnostic strategy, any remedial programming is to help the individual produce more adequate behavior in the learning situation. This is, after all, the ultimate goal of all teaching, and hence, the direction this text takes toward helping the classroom instructor learn how to more effectively work toward remediating arithmetic learning disabilities.

Chapter 2

The Learning Disabled Child and Arithmetic

As early as the 1940s those working in the area we now popularly call "special education" were recognizing that highly standardized, traditional, patterned, rote approaches to dealing with arithmetic learning problems are not particularly effective. Strauss and Lehtinen (1947) wrote,

> Sufficient experiences with insight, rather than repetition of the formula, will bring about habituation. It is our experience that counting out answers, usually considered an error in the fundamentals, results not from much practice in counting but from lack of well developed concepts and knowledge of more mature methods.

Unfortunately, early recognition of the need for special treatment and remediation techniques did not quickly lead to creating or assembling a large body of useful information for those who wished to attack the problem in practical situations. As Bannatyne (1974) has pointed out, there is still a significant void in the literature pertaining to learning disability's role in arithmetic difficulties and it is only beginning to be filled. Despite the tremendous number of resources in math education which are now available and Reisman's (1972) careful delineation of five processes for diagnostic teaching of math (identifying strengths and weaknesses in arithmetic, hypothesizing possible reasons for them, formulating behavioral objectives, creating and trying corrective remedial procedures, and continued reevaluation of achievement) the practitioner still receives little specific help and guidance stemming from a meaningful blend of what is known about each of these areas, arithmetic learning and learning disabilities. Theoretical literature based upon organized, systematic, and well-designed research is even more sparse. As Brown (1975) has succinctly written in introducing special educators to some available resource areas,

> Instruction in mathematics for the child labeled learning disabled is an area about which little has been written except that, "little has been written. . . ." Few pages are allotted to it in special education methods books, and instructional personnel seem to be on their own when trying to evaluate children or to select methodologies and materials.

There seems to be no substantial explanation for this current lack of information and shortage of guidance. Much information has been gathered about arithmetic instruction viewed from a variety of theoretical orientations ranging from behavioral management to Piaget. Learning disabilities has come of age and it is increasingly possible to carefully pinpoint specific deficit learning areas and to proceed constructively toward removing these deficits in an individual's behavior.

To successfully attack arithmetic problems in a learning disabled child requires progressing through five steps. These are:

1 Identifying the actual arithmetic learning problem areas which seem to be commonly encountered in everyday school learning situations.

2 Outlining what learning of arithmetic involves behaviorally for children at different stages of traditional educational experience.

3 Establishing a relationship between specific learning disability areas and these arithmetic behaviors.

4 Constructing a cross-referencing system which allows the worker to quickly identify and understand these specific learning disability-arithmetic behavior relationships.

5 Assembling practical information and guidance for the three processes involved in effective preventive and remedial work, namely: screening, individual diagnostic analysis, and remedial program activity.

The remainder of this chapter covers the first two of these important steps. Chapters 3 and 4 deal with steps three and four, respectively. The remainder of the book covers in detail the information required for successful completion of the final step.

MAJOR PROBLEM AREAS

One can easily identify and list some major problem areas in deficit arithmetic* performances of school children. On the other hand, establishing a consensually acceptable list or one which will serve all orientations, curricula, and age levels is more difficult, perhaps nearly impossible. Still, despite the diversity of information provided by many people working in this field, some factors do stand out. While noting that arithmetic is an area which has not received much attention and also pointing out the generally limited contribution of a non-explanatory label like *dyscalculia*, Lerner (1976) broadly categorizes some of the problem areas of *dyscalculic* children. She includes:

1 Disturbances of spatial relationships.
2 Disturbances of visual-perception and visual-motor association.
3 Poor sense of body image as it may relate to lack of number sense.
4 Poor sense of time and direction.
5 Possible relationships between arithmetic abilities and social maturity and social perception.
6 Arithmetic problems caused or compounded by reading handicaps.

---

* The term *arithmetic* (instead of the more inclusive term, *mathematics*) is used deliberately since the behaviors examined are those which can be assessed directly in terms of "right or wrong" and thus more easily lend themselves to simple evaluation and, when necessary, remediation. It should be clearly noted that the typical elementary school curriculum includes the broader subject matter, concepts, and skills of *mathematics*; and that *arithmetic*, as used here, is indeed but an important subset of that larger segment of study.

The broad, general nature of these categories and the tentativeness with which some of them must be associated with learning disability-related arithmetic problems is symptomatic of the general problem a practitioner faces. Existing categories of problem areas give but general clues as to where to go or how to move in planning work with an individual experiencing arithmetic learning difficulties. Chalfant and Scheffelin (1969) grouped factors related to quantitative or arithmetic disability in a very broad sense. They included the factors of intelligence spatial ability, verbal ability, problem-solving ability, and neurophysiological correlates (largely suspected but unproved mediating variables). As the practitioner soon discovers, such broad categories are as helpful as calling a rose a rose. They don't really offer any practical solutions, new information, or guidance.

Some other lists, less broad, are more helpful. Johnson and Myklebust (1967) identify thirteen arithmetic deficiencies which may be found to varying degrees in school age children (see Figure 2.1).

Bartel (1975) outlines six general factors related to such problems:

1 Ineffective instruction
2 Perceptual disturbances
3 Directionality
4 Abstract or symbolic thinking
5 Memory
6 Reading

Bartel's list may be especially helpful, since it leads the user along a particular behavioral vector in search of answers: for example, modification of instructional strategies. It is interesting to note that other authors, such as Otto and McMenemy (1966), also cite the importance of considering ineffective instruction as a causal factor for deficit learning behaviors, an assumption not to be overlooked in planning remedial strategies.

Bartel carries the identification of specific problems an essential further step by noting a dozen more definite factors involved in deficit behavior (Figure 2.2).

In addition to the problems cited in Figures 2.1 and 2.2 (which represent the pattern of general problems most often mentioned by a number of writers) several other specific problems are cited by some. These include memory and reading (Johnson and Myklebust, 1967), general lack of pre-arithmetic readiness (Otto and McMenemy, 1966), problem solving difficulties (Cruickshank, 1948a, 1946), failure to learn how to filter out extraneous material (Cruickshank, 1948b), and inability to move beyond existing stimuli—a failure to discover, explore, or creatively generalize (Lerner, 1976). Inability to use arithmetic vocabulary in an expressive way or to comprehend it in a receptive fashion is mentioned or implied by many. It is related in both a direct and indirect way to reading difficulties independent of arithmetic skills.

1. Inability to establish a one-to-one correspondence. The number of children in a room cannot be related to the number of seats, nor an estimate made of how many forks to place on a table at which four people are to eat.
2. Inability to count meaningfully. Although numbers can be said in rote fashion, relationship between the symbol and the quantity is not established.
3. Inability to associate the auditory and visual symbols. It is possible to count auditorially but not to identify the numerals visually.
4. Inability to learn both the cardinal and ordinal systems of counting.
5. Inability to visualize clusters of objects within a larger group; each object in a group must always be counted.
6. Inability to grasp the principle of conservation of quantity. Some dyscalculics are not able to comprehend that ten cents is the same whether it consists of two nickels, one dime, or ten pennies, or that a one-pound block of butter is the same as four one-quarter pound sticks.
7. Inability to perform arithmetic operations.
8. Inability to understand the meaning of the process signs. In certain instances the deficiency is related to a perceptual disturbance (inability to distinguish the difference in the plus and multiplications signs). More important is failure to grasp the meaning conveyed by the signs.
9. Inability to understand the arrangement of the numbers on the page. Children learning to read must know that the sequence of letters within a word is significant. Those learning arithmetic must know that a specific arrangement of numbers also has meaning. Because of visual-spatial problems, this factor often interferes with computation abilities.
10. Inability to follow and remember the sequence of steps to be used in various mathematical operations.
11. Inability to understand the principles of measurement.
12. Inability to read maps and graphs.
13. Inability to choose the principles for solving problems in arithmetic reasoning. The dyscalculic can read the words and do the problems if he is given the principle (add, subtract, multiply, etc.) but without assistance he cannot determine which process to use.

Figure 2.1 *Arithmetic deficiencies found in varying amounts among school-age children**
* Johnson and Myklebust, 1967.

1. Inability to associate numbers with numerals.
2. Inability to match numerals with objects (counting).
3. Inability to recognize part-whole relationships.
4. Lack of understanding of measurement principles.
5. Inability to add, subtract, multiply or divide.
6. Difficulty with place value and the decimal system.
7. Inability to decide which process to use in problem solving.
8. Inability to learn the cardinal and ordinal sequences.
9. Inability to understand the meaning of the process signs.
10. Inability to visually recognize numerals.
11. Failure to learn to tell time.
12. Failure to learn the value of coins and inability to count change.

Figure 2.2   *Specific types of arithmetic disabilities**
* Bartel, 1975.

The identification of these general and specific behaviors by researchers and workers seems to indicate that development of some type of meaningful identification scheme is not an unreasonably difficult task, even though it has not as yet been fully accomplished.

GENERALIZATIONS DEVELOPED FROM OTHER AREAS

As is true of most of the learning disability field, much of the early categorization work was generalized from observations of the mentally retarded and other handicapped individuals. There is a defensible rationale for this since the retarded do present a readily observed profile of deficit behaviors and the size of the retarded child population and large number of special facilities and practitioners working in this area assure massive amounts of easily available information. Unfortunately, in the early days of recognizing the existence of those marginally performing individuals who are now labeled as *learning disabled,* a common error was to group them under the same behavioral and programmatic labels as the retarded. Such an inclusion is simply not valid. As has now been clearly established, the learning disabled individual has, in general, greater potentiality, far more secure functional integrities, and is more positively responsive to relatively simple adjustments in teaching and instructional strategies than the retardate. Indeed, recent efforts to better legally define the field (Sontag, 1976) reaffirm the exclusion of these individuals "who have learning problems which are primarily the result of . . . mental retardation. . . ."

But, one should not "throw out the baby with the bath." Some of the deficit behaviors exhibited by retarded youngsters as they attempt to produce productive arithmetic behaviors are related more to poor approximation of criterion performances not yet acquired than to any causal or limiting dysfunction of retardation. Thus, one may in some instances carefully generalize from one area to the other in the definition of problem types. It is considerably less safe to generalize remedial programming steps since the residual integrities of the learning disabled individual may vary greatly from those of the retarded and instructional techniques and goals may differ significantly.

Problem areas such as those noted by Kaliski (1967) offer some helpful suggestions of where to focus remedial activities. She includes confused spatial relationships, visual perception difficulties, visual-motor association inadequacies, perseveration, difficulty with symbols, and cognitive disturbances. This list, however, was generated out of work with the brain-injured, and should not be quoted as parallel with or congruent to those of the learning disabled. The hypothesized relationship between brain injury and learning disability is far too tenuous to warrant such generalization. For example, *perseveration* is a problem behavior long recognized as a frequent concomitant of brain-injury. There is little indication that it warrants much attention as a major problem area or discriminating diagnostic behavior of the learning disabled. Care in generalization is needed.

However, it is possible to compile a fairly long list of descriptive arithmetic problem areas from the literature dealing with the brain-injured and/or retarded and to see in that list some of the same deficit behaviors readily observed in the learning disabled. Abstracting from the problem areas cited by some writers (Kaliski, 1967; Callahan and Robinson, 1973; Peterson, 1973; Burns, 1961; Cruickshank, 1948a, 1948b, 1946), attention is drawn to a number of different problem types as noted in Figure 2.3.

Any such list, obviously, could be extended as general behavior areas become further subdivided. To those used to working with elementary children in the arithmetic curriculum it becomes apparent that some highly general problem areas keep popping up among retardates, the learning disabled, and even in essentially "normal" children as they struggle with the day-by-day process of learning. The frequency with which these areas are noted causes one to suspect that the repeated mention of instructional adequacy as a meaningful variable in children's successful arithmetic learning may have considerable merit. A blanket criticism of teachers' ability or performance does not seem necessary. It appears more valid to assume that the problem may lie more in the lack of focus on the necessary interaction of two important variables: (1) the behavioral demands of the system at a particular level (i.e., course content requirements for the six months of grade three); and (2) the developmental and behavioral prerequisite readiness of an individual child. As Bartel (1975) so accurately writes:

1. Fluctuating attention due to poor attending strategy or decreased motivation stemming from unrewarding performance.
2. Perceptual disturbances such as inability to use principles of perceptual constancy and conservation.
3. Figure-ground confusion resulting in poor selection of critical details.
4. Spatial relationship confusions as often seen in body-image problems.
5. Visual-motor coordination difficulties.
6. Inability to understand or successfully use spatial, temporal, or sequential relationships.
7. Hyperactivity resulting in impulsive, careless, non-analytic performances.
8. Left-right confusion.
9. Verbal expression deficiencies.
10. Lack of adequate abstract conceptualization ability or strategy.
11. Specific arithmetic vocabulary acquisition and use deficits.
12. Problem solving technique problems.
13. Arithmetic operations difficulties.
14. Absence of prerequisite "readiness" behaviors.
15. Immature behaviors including non-operant strategies and perseveration.
16. Sequencing errors.
17. Specific reading difficulties.
18. Discriminating or recognizing essential stimulus characteristics.

Figure 2.3 *Problem areas cited in professional literature*

> . . .many children exhibit difficulties in arithmetic because their instruction has been directed at developmental levels for which they were not ready. A lack of readiness may characterize the performance of a child at any level of arithmetic functioning. Thus, a child may be unable to learn to count because he does not have a clear notion of one-to-one correspondence. A lack of readiness for long division may be demonstrated by a child who has not yet mastered the operation of multiplication.

Arithmetic readiness, as further outlined by Bartel, includes important clues to successful identification of specific behavioral deficits and the consequent need for specifically designed and planned remedial activities. She lists six readiness areas, which, though not exactly congruent with those listed or implied by others, are certainly helpful in such identification processes. She includes:

- Classification
- Discrimination (based upon relevant properties)
- One-to-one correspondence
- Seriation or ordering
- Spatial representation (including perceptual elements)
- Flexibility and reversibility
- Conservation

The process of more specifically defining readiness areas is dealt with later as part of the analysis of arithmetic curriculum content by level.

LEARNING DISABILITY DEFINITION AND ARITHMETIC

As was discussed in Chapter 1, despite the variety of theoretical approaches and orientations which lead to as many different definitions of learning disabilities as there are individual practitioners in the field, there are some major points which achieve substantial consensus. These points, agreed to by most theorists and practitioners, are indicative of current diagnostic and treatment emphases present in the field today. Therefore, they have relevance to any approach aimed at arithmetic learning abilities. In trying to carefully form the focus of attack on arithmetic difficulties, it is helpful to see how such delineation is shaped by these points.

The Principle of Disparity

Briefly stated, this principle notes that there is a meaningful difference between what an individual is capable of doing and what the individual can be observed doing in a specific academic area. This has significant ramifications for dealing with the learning disabled child in arithmetic. Most importantly, it indicates that one should not expect to find a total absence of all arithmetic skills, all abstract conceptualization, all symbolic performances, or whatever behaviors are involved. Instead, it would be more typical to find areas where lack of specific learning has led to a more generalized deficit. Analysis of the sequential behaviors which must be successfully undertaken in order to multiply, for example, should help the diagnostician arrive at some defined task which is not being adequately performed. The firm implication is that with removal of the specific problem, general performance should improve at least to a level commensurate with the individual's overall demonstrated level of ability. Thus, the most important tasks facing the practitioner are:

1 Know the sequential tasks prerequisite to the final criterion behavior.

2 Identify which of these tasks are being performed inadequately.

3 Establish a program or regimen which will provide the necessary learning experiences, remove the deficit, and build the missing prerequisite skills.

In arithmetic, which is so dependent upon an absolutely essential sequence and order, the relevance of the strategy called for in principle is obvious.

General Nervous System Involvement Not Assumed

The implications of this consensual point are important. There is no assumption, implied or stated, that the individual, due to some dysfunctional or substandard brain or neural structure, is incapable of, prevented from, or led away from the successful completion of ordinary behaviors expected of individuals of his or her age and experience. No particular shaping of basic organic functions, neural pathways, central nervous system structure or similar processes, or physiological attributes is assumed to be necessary. Again, the emphasis is upon determining a general level of expected performance, denoting specific discrepancies, and then providing the necessary experiences necessary for the individual to successfully apply the capabilities already present.

Primary Physiological Problems Are Excluded

The relevancy of this point is simple. If an individual is incapable of seeing, hearing, feeling, handling, moving, or any other purely physical function necessary for being involved in arithmetic learning, then these problems must be dealt with apart from, and in most cases, prior to any assault on a specific learning disability. This is certainly not to say the individual has no problem, or that such problems that exist should not be attacked through school related programs. Rather, it is to indicate that the problem is one of inability to receive or become involved in necessary learning experiences, and therefore is a matter of lack of physiological integrity which must be resolved. It is not a specific learning disability. As a matter of course, most school or clinic diagnostic programs examine this possibility early in the process before making learning disability assumptions. If a child cannot see, obviously such a child cannot visually discriminate. All learning disability programs which help teach visual discrimination are dependent upon the ability to receive visual stimuli. Some visual discrimination problems may be resolved quickly by obtaining correctly prescribed glasses.

Certain Categories Routinely Excluded

For a specific learning disability to be present it is assumed that the child has had the opportunity to receive typical educational experiences, and that despite the presence of sufficient ability to profit from such experiences, learning has not taken place. Atypical instructional activities are required in order to remove what is, or at least should be, a temporary deficit, a temporary inadequately performed behavior. Certain categories, including the retarded, economically deprived, and the emotionally disturbed, are excluded. This is because they involve either some inability of the child to ever profit from normal classroom arithmetic performance, such as the retarded individual who needs special goals as well as methods (Peterson, 1973); or they represent those who simply have never had the opportunity to experience learning in a typical situation. Both represent peculiar and significant problems, but neither are learning disabilities. A retarded child may need to recognize different coins for everyday living but might never, even under optimal conditions, be expected to master long division. A child who has never seen money may have trouble recognizing different coins, but given even average exposure to learning experiences with coins such a child can and will develop the necessary discrimination behaviors. In other words, the child does not have to be taught discrimination and is not suffering from a learning disability.

Relevance to the Educational Situation

The skills required of a child by an arithmetic curriculum are perhaps clearer and more succinct than almost any other basic academic activity. Correct answers are exactly right, and wrong answers are visibly in error. Problem solving has specific relevance to certain kinds of tasks and situations and lacks the sometimes confusing indefiniteness of less precise skills such as penmanship, creative writing, or even spelling (with its many alternatives and primary and secondary accepted forms). Thus, remedial activities in arithmetic are designed to help a child perform a specific task as clearly outlined at a well-defined level within an academic curriculum. There is no intent to make a child mathematically oriented, or arithmetically inclined. Specific tasks, operations, processes, skills, and integral parts of an academic curriculum, can all be denoted and defined. This is a major asset in both diagnosing problems and in planning remedial efforts.

This is a major reason for dealing with *arithmetic* rather than *mathematics* in this text. The former involves skills and behaviors more easily defined and observed than the latter.

There seems to be no reason why arithmetic should not be considered as an academic discipline where learning disabilities may be observed. Neither is there any demonstrable reason why those remedial strategies already proven successful in other academic areas where specific learning disabilities have been found might not equally successfully be applied to arithmetic. Each of the consensual definition points seems to apply to arithmetic as well as other academic areas.

Chapter 3

Identifying Specific Arithmetic-Learning Disability Problems

In order to pinpoint exactly how these two major considerations interact, a description of the nature of the problems encountered in such interaction must be given. Both the arithmetic curriculum content and the large variety of possible learning disabilities need to be defined and categorized in some schematic fashion.

The need for accurately identifying the content and demands of the arithmetic curriculum at different levels has been well established. As noted previously, identification of behavioral demands implicit in the curriculum is essential as an early step in getting at and helping remove learning disabilities which hinder arithmetic learning. Gagnè's (et al., 1962) approach to analyzing the hierarchial steps of learning can be applied to this problem. Any learning task can be analyzed into a hierarchy or sequence of subordinate tasks. Arithmetic with its fixed sequence of operations is easier to analyze in this fashion than some other learning tasks. If a student's behavior pattern of subtasks matches the established learning hierarchy, then learning is, as Gagnè states, not only better but easier.

A simplistic, but important step in outlining the contents of the arithmetic curriculum is to note as Freidus (1966) has that if the child (the brain-injured child in Freidus' reference, but true as well of other children) having problems with arithmetic is to improve, the teacher or the educational experiences available need to provide the child with help in four major ways. The child needs help in:

1 Receiving sensory information reliably.

2 Processing the received information for essential meaning.

3 Subsequently organizing and executing a response appropriate to the preceived meaning.

4 Finally, establishing and using some form of self-correcting monitoring habit to determine whether or not the executed behavior is right or wrong, appropriate or inappropriate, part of an algorithm worth storing for future use or an idiosyncratic event applicable the one time only.

If a learning disability worker were to confine diagnostic efforts towards identification of children's difficulty with these four broad areas alone as a basis, considerably effective remediation could be accomplished. But, finer and sharper analysis can help remedial efforts become even more effective within more economical time frames demanding less effort. Such analysis should consist not only of finer identification of subsets, but it should also include an examination of curriculum demands from several different orientations. Three such orientations are discussed, followed by a system for meaningful and practical integration of the contribution of each.

Analyzing the Curriculum in Terms of Academic Content

A most obvious way to view the arithmetic academic area is to look at what the curriculum demands of a student by virtue of formal content areas. Content areas might be more clearly recognized if one were to describe them as a teacher would in talking to a visiting parent. Content areas are those curriculum categories referred to when a teacher says, "Today the children are working on _____." Such categories will often correspond to the titles or subtitles of books, chapter headings in texts, or labels attached to certain work periods of the school day. Included would be such words or phrases as: numbers, adding, fractions, ordering, problem solving, money usage.

In order to establish a useful analysis of curriculum content areas, certain steps must be followed:

1 Identification of those areas most frequently mentioned or used by teachers.

2 Analysis of what the terms actually mean (particularly for various age levels). "Adding" may mean one thing for a second grader and have quite another, more complex meaning for a fourth grader.

3 Determining how content of one type interacts with content of another at the same level. And, identifying how content of one type interacts with content of the same type at both simpler and more difficult levels.

Such an analysis could be undertaken for any or all academic levels. In the application of the system outlined later in this book only three general levels are involved: (1) *Pre-School Readiness,* (2) the first year or two of exposure to arithmetic (called the *Introductory Level* in this text), and (3) the one- to two-year period of experience following the introductory period (called the *Post-Introductory* period in this text). Due to the diversity of grade-level tracks and plans and the meaningless designation of chronological age, these three broad categories are used instead of specific grade or level designations. Individual teachers should have no trouble applying them to a specific curriculum plan or school system.

There is no shortage of ideas about what material is or should be covered within these three periods.

Pre-school readiness level. The importance of this period in the preparation of a child for later learning experiences has been stressed by many. As Schroeder (1965) says, "If a teacher is to work with a child having trouble with arithmetic due to any one of a number of problems, the appraising of readiness is *the* initial step in any program plan and an essential skill." Hollister and Gunderson (1954) suggest an inventory of pre-school readiness essential for first grade arithmetic work. They would include the ability to count, ability to recognize number quantities, ability to select a correct number group, ability to match number symbols, and ability to recognize number symbols. Wallace and Kauffman (1973) add concepts of quantity and some concept of sets to the list. Mann and Suiter (1974) include the vocabulary of spatial and temporal relationships as an important readiness skill. The general importance of language as a necessary precursor of arithmetic performance is affirmed by Smith and Lovitt (1976) and also by Smith (1969). Smith and Lovitt further offer that arithmetic readiness can be behaviorally described as consisting of the ability to discriminate among and remember auditory and visual stimuli, to accurately perceive spatial orientations and to translate these into temporal sequences, to associate different stimuli, and finally to adequately express one's self in order to be able to communicate the results of covert or "internal" problem solving.

Form perception and some ability to deal with ordinals are added to the list by Peterson (1973). Smith (1974, 1968) has attempted to denote the major dimensions which all readiness behaviors represent. They are:

1 Fundamentals
2 Reasoning
3 Computation
4 Problem solving
5 Concepts and skills
6 Applications

Such a list, though lacking in any real behavioral descriptions, and thus demanding further definition by the user, has merit for establishing levels of progressive readiness as the learning child passes from one curriculum level to another.

Smith (1969) has outlined the basic skills requisite for satisfactory achievement in arithmetic. This list, further translated into immediate behaviors which can be observed and measured in the classroom, has proven to have practical application:

1 Ability to learn and use the language of arithmetic.
2 Relating elements in one group to elements in another (correspondence).
3 Conservation.
4 Reversibility.
5 Ordering.
6 Associating numbers and numerals.
7 Auditory memory.
8 Visual memory.
9 Perceptual-motor skills.

Apparently the problem is not one of finding lists or categories, but of making some useful consensual sense out of them. Without some precise technique such as factor analysis, any ordering is quite arbitrary and may be judged only in a pragmatic way rather than on the basis of whether or not some absolute areas have been firmly identified. At present, the most workable selection criterion seems to be on the basis of frequency of use by teachers.

The introductory level. In looking for useful delineation of content areas at this level we depend in part upon some of the same sources which listed readiness areas. Bartel (1975), Freidus (1966), and Smith (1969) have made contributions which offer assistance in such definition. Freidus identifies some areas which are largely elaboration of readiness areas. These include using sequential values, comparing relationships, measuring, and some self-correction skills in working with parts-to-wholes and parts-to-parts problems.

These initial, introductory months also see the child exposed to beginning operations of addition and then subtraction. Usually such operations content is initiated with a horizontal adding operation, which closely resembles and probably benefits from some transfer from reading $1 + 1 = 2$. After the horizontal operation is grasped and some conceptual understanding is achieved, the operation is shifted to a vertical format. This format more closely approximates those higher order operations demanded later in multiplication and division, for example,

$$\frac{\begin{array}{r} 1 \\ +1 \end{array}}{2}.$$

Content at this level most frequently deals with single integer problems and numbering, and ordering only from 1 to 10 (Resnick et al., 1973). The concept of "zero" or "nothing" may or may not be included.

As Smith (1974, 1968) points out, the whole idea of computation and problem solving is introduced here. During this period the child is initially exposed to abstractions in the sense of solving "hands-off," vicarious problems rather than simply manipulating concrete examples of arithmetical concepts (for example, being asked how many wheels most cars have rather than counting the wheels on a car). The child experiencing the introductory arithmetic curriculum is first exposed to simple algorithms and laws, though their presence may only be noted and emphasis about usage and the necessity of correct application may be underplayed. Some simple application may be seen in easy sentence solving problems (Wilson, 1967). Conservation application becomes an important part of the child's functional skills and forms the basis for later identification of the presence and function of more abstract and complicated laws.

Post-introductory level. Readiness, broadly interpreted, becomes increasingly more important as the student progresses upward through succeedingly more difficult levels. The post-introductory level to a large extent is an elaboration of the introductory level, hence, satisfactory learning of introductory skills first is vital. Despite this overlap, as the child moves out of the introductory level the content of the curriculum does show some noticeable change. Increasing demands are found for abstract thinking and what Piaget calls *generalizing assimilation*, and what others (Meeker, 1969) describe as *divergent thinking*. Problem solving begins to require more transfer to and from verbal and symbolic situations. Shape and form use become more than discrimination problems, and begin instead to take on properties and involve applications which are precursors for simple geometry concepts (Johnson and Myklebust, 1967).

Sentence solving (Wilson, 1967), wherein a child must not only demonstrate reading proficiency, but also the capability to abstract from reading materials those relevant stimuli essential for problem solving, becomes an important addition to the curriculum. Applications take on farther reaching and more meaningful implications. The child begins to learn applications which have direct and immediate use in problems of everyday life outside the classroom. Therefore, reinforcement or frustration, depending upon the level of accomplishment, is immediate and strong. Symbol abstractions and their use become more complex. New operations including multiplication and division must be faced and total mastery of the basic addition and subtraction skills is essential. As Strauss and Lehtinen (1947) observed some years ago,

> Delaying veridical functions while skills are taught with some degree of thoroughness may involve a delay in arriving at a functional use of learning which the child who is already experiencing difficulty in solving his day-to-day problems cannot tolerate.

In such cases, knowing the sequence of content of the curriculum is of absolute necessity since it is the sequencing aspect which may have to be temporarily altered.

At this level, as with the other two, there are plenty of ideas about what is or should be involved. Again, the task is one of selection and focus so that those areas most crucial to the largest number of children in many situations can be discriminated.

ANALYZING THE CURRICULUM IN TERMS OF SPECIFIC TASK ANALYSIS

Trying to pinpoint frequently encountered and perhaps even crucial learning experiences in the arithmetic curriculum has some aspects which overlap with content analysis but actually involves a quite different approach. This assault on the problem represents an attempt to describe what the child is doing as he or she progresses through the curriculum and the varied content areas. Commonly, this approach is behaviorally oriented in the *Skinnerian* sense of the word, but this is not always or necessarily so. Within this general framework there seems to be at least four major *task analysis* approaches with slightly different emphasis or focus.

Task-analysis of identified content areas.   In this approach the problem is to define common specific progressive behaviors which are encountered at more than one level and to analyze the behavioral demands present at each level. Thus, the content area of arithmetic vocabulary would be analyzed for the demands actually involved in *word* or *symbol recognition, usage,* and *application* for each level (three in this case). Once such different final task behaviors are established, then instructional sequences relative to a particular criterion level or subcriterion level may be constructed and applied. Aukerman (1972) offers a good example of this approach in attacking the problem of reading in mathematics in the classroom. Under this strategy, reading (in relationship to the arithmetic curriculum) is subdivided into identifiable and sequential levels. Aukerman includes:

1 Ability to identify important ideas when read.
2 Development of a specialized arithmetic vocabulary.
3 Development of an awareness of the importance of specialized reading cues-such as punctuation (*5-gal. cans* is considerably different from *5 gal. cans,* for example).
4 Following of written arithmetic directions including translating words into arithmetic symbols (four becomes *4,* or *less* becomes − for example).
5 Chart, graph, and table reading.
6 Verbal problem solving including searching for answers as well as reading forclues or directions.

Resnick (et al., 1973) identifies six content processes which cross over successive level lines and, though having much in common, need to be separately analyzed for each different level. They identify decision making, classifying, divergent thinking, synthesizing, conservation, and hypothesizing. To a large extent, much of the work of Piaget (1952, for example) follows this general strategy.

An advantage of this approach is that it helps identify crucial behaviors which may be hidden under broader, less operational terms found in any general content listing. To the extent that this analysis can be categorized in observable and measurable behavioral terms it is helpful in planning both assessment and remedial activities.

Task-analysis of processes in the general curriculum flow. Those seeking to apply this strategy share much in common with the preceding orientation. The major difference lies in the assumption that the behavior generalized is much more basic and perhaps less readily apparent in curriculum content descriptions or such broad categories as reading, problem solving, or arithmetic operations. If one were to adopt Gagnè's (1970) eight types of learning (see Figure 3.1) as important indications of what and how an individual learns, this approach might fit very well in any attempt to analyze a child's behavior. One could look for the exact demands of the curriculum relevant to such a basic task as acquiring the skill or strategies of concept learning, or chaining, or any one of the eight listed. The specific learning skill would then be taught with the assumption that such learning is involved in arithmetic performance at a certain level. A great deal of time is spent under such a plan in trying to analyze exactly where and to what degree a certain basic learning process is involved in the curriculum activities. Dunlap and House (1976) outline a comprehensive diagnostic plan which is perfectly congruent with this approach. The steps they suggest taking are:

1 Determination of a terminal task.

2 Application of task analysis to identify prerequisite skills to the terminal task.

3 Placement of skills into a hierarchy showing the relationship of each skill to other prerequisite skills and to the terminal task.

4 Construction of test items to measure each skill in the hierarchy on 3 levels: enactive, iconic, symbolic.

5 Administration of the test.

6 Analysis of the child's performance on the test items.

Johnson and Morasky (1977) have written in detail about the building of remedial programs for learning disabilities following such a procedure. Others following such an orientation include Mann and Suiter (1974), Aukerman (1972), and Schroeder (1965).

---

1. Signal learning
2. Stimulus-response learning
3. Chaining
4. Verbal association learning
5. Multiple discrimination learning
6. Concept learning
7. Principle learning
8. Problem solving

Figure 3.1 *Gagnè's eight levels of learning*

Simple or purely operational task-analysis. The third approach noted under this aegis is really only an elaboration of the principles mentioned under task-analysis of processes with the inclusion of some special limitations on where to start identifying behaviors. Under this more limited and precise strategy, the preceding steps outlined by Dunlap and those of Johnson and Morasky would be followed except that analyzers would not start with any curriculum outline or preconception about processes. Instead, initial steps would seek to analyze the content of those specific behaviors desired. Next, the behaviors being produced by the child under observation would be studied and analyzed. Finally, some identification and means for acquiring the sub-criterion tasks lying between what the child does (obtained from a behavior analysis) and what the child is supposed to be doing (obtained from a task-analysis) would be sought. The emphasis is almost completely upon performance behaviors which can be readily observed, measured, and described. Walbesser and Carter (1972) note how such performance classes can be used as operational guides in setting up instructional guides. They point out that final task behaviors or criterion objective behaviors ought to be in such terms as the child being able to identify, distinguish, construct, name, order, describe, state a rule, apply a rule, demonstrate, etc. Such firmly behavioral classes have direct and easy application to arithmetic performance where criterion behaviors are fairly easily described and delineated.

Analyzing the curriculum in terms of commonly identified learning disability behaviors. This last approach to identifying those curriculum demands which seem to be causing a child difficulties comes from a direct concern for children whose learning disability causes poor performance in arithmetic. This can be contrasted with an approach which is directed at general clinical teaching in arithmetic (Reisman, 1972), which is used to help children with all levels of ability and all kinds of arithmetic problems stemming from a variety of causes.

It is assumed in this text that there are children having difficulty with arithmetic whose sole difficulty can be due to the effect of some learning disability. Certainly this seems to receive cross validation in other areas, such as reading. There are children who are not just poor readers but who cannot move ahead in the learning of reading due to the blocking effect of a specific learning disability, such as inadequate form discrimination. Such an orientation seeks to establish those already identified learning disability areas which seem to have the closest relationship to arithmetic performance. For a pool of learning disability areas from which one might select, it would be possible to list almost every subtest area on the major diagnostic instruments used in learning disability work. Each of these instruments such as the *Illinois Test of Psycholinguistic Abilities* (Kirk, McCarthy and Kirk, 1968), the *Purdue Perceptual Motor Survey* (Roach and Kephart, 1966), the *Meeting Street School*

Screening Test (Hainsworth and Siqueland, 1969), many reading invento-ries, and a number of compilations of diagnostic and remedial-tool areas such as those prepared by Mann and Suiter (1974) and Valett (1967), contain separate subtests or parts relevant to areas identified with varying degrees of cross-validation.

At the present time, selection of many of these available sub-areas has been primarily based upon either an observed or inferred relationship to those areas better defined in task-analysis, or according to individual whim, personal preference, or various expediencies related to time, skill, and inter-est of the user.

This approach has proven to be helpful in the author's firsthand experi-ence with children. There do seem to be children whose arithmetic perform-ance suffers due to the presence of a learning disability. When such a disability is correctly identified and attacked under this approach, improve-ment often follows. It is the assumption of this text that such an approach could be infinitely more useful to the general practitioner in both the classroom and clinic, if the possible interactions between curriculum content demands, results of task and behavior analyses, and the identifiable learning disabilities could be made more readily available. The last section of this chapter outlines a procedure for accomplishing such an objective, and the following chapters provide specific guidance for using and applying such a system.

A STRATEGY FOR RELATING ARITHMETIC DIFFICULTIES TO LEARNING DISABILITIES

The rationale for such a system is quite simple. The practitioner should be able to assemble certain baseline information about a particular child experiencing arithmetic difficulties. This information should include a descrip-tion of the areas of curriculum content at which the child is having difficulty. It should also include the general level of performance-demand that the child is facing. Following this, it should then be possible to check diagnostically for indications of the presence or likely presence of behaviors characteristic of an identifiable specific learning disability. This assumed relationship could then be reaffirmed by use of informal techniques and, if necessary, by formal diag-nostic activities. If the hypothesis is confirmed it should be possible to draw upon an established bank of sample appropriate instructional sequences or activities designed to improve or provide missing deficit behaviors.

Mechanics for such a procedure are simple. A series of materials are provided to help the practitioner identify any one of the several factors rele-vant to the interaction of curriculum content and specific learning disabilities. These factors should include:

1 Behavioral examples a child with no problems should be able to perform.

2 Behavioral examples of typical deficit behaviors frequently observed when a child is performing at subcriterion levels.

3 Ideas and sources for informal diagnosis in as many interacting situations as possible.

4 Examples of instructional ideas, worksheets, and activities helpful in incrementing deficit behaviors.

An example may help demonstrate the strategy in action. Figure 3.2 suggests a 2 × 2 cross-referencing chart for that portion of a curriculum dealing with distinguishing a printed "3" from a printed "8." Applying each of the preceding four points, one should be able to find pertinent and important information for each of the four cells.

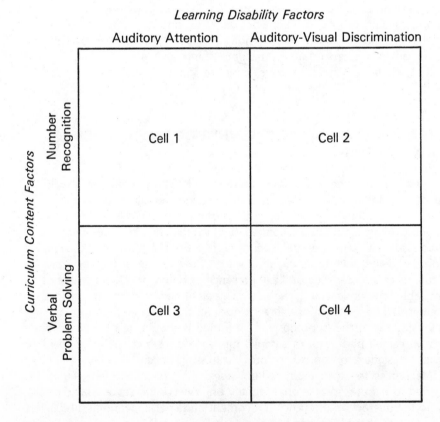

Figure 3.2 Cross-referencing chart for printed "3"-"8" discrimination

Cell 1, for example, would either cite or direct the reader to sources which note criterion-level performances, signs warning of deficits, screening and diagnostic procedures, and guidelines for remedial activities. These activities would be relevant to the interacting of the curriculum demands for number recognition as affected by the learning disability area of auditory attention. Each of the other three cells would provide similar information for each of the possible interactions which the chart encompasses.

By carefully matching observed behavior to criterion and deficit models cited in the source material, and by validating assumptions drawn from such matching by applying the outlined screening and diagnostic activities, the teacher should be able to clearly define the type of difficulty present in many children having trouble discriminating "3" from "8." In some cases, further, more sophisticated diagnostic work might be necessary. Appropriate remedial activities could then be initiated, again following the outlined directions in the resource material.

Such careful determination of the exact nature of the difficulty is very important. Relieving an auditory attention problem related to number recognition involves far different procedures than does remediation of an auditory-visual discrimination problem related to verbal problem solving.

This system, described in brief, provides a means for quickly and accurately pinpointing the problem requiring attention.

The strategy, described in more detail hereafter, applies such a system to the interaction of learning disabilities and arithmetic performance of children at each of the three levels mentioned earlier. The learning disability areas selected remain constant for all three levels as there seem to be ample evidence strongly suggesting their relevant presence at each of these stages of arithmetic performance. Figure 3.3 lists the learning disability areas selected along with operational-behavioral definitions for each area. No ordering or hierarchy within the list is intended.

Content areas have been varied from level to level, but represent a fair sampling of current textbooks, literature in the field, and opinions of teachers and others concerned with teaching elementary arithmetic. These content areas are listed in Figure 3.4. Again, no ordering or hierarchy should be assumed in the lists except that where a common content area appears for two levels it is safe to assume that some sequencing of behaviors and incrementing difficulty is involved.

Cross-referencing charts for each level will be found in the appendix. The charts will provide reference to information for each of these categories:

1 Problem-free behavior.

2 Sample task when deficit child may display difficulty.

3 Do-it-yourself diagnostic activities.

1. Memory disabilities—problems in recalling on demand bits of information perceived or learned a few moments before.
2. Visual and auditory discrimination disabilities—problems in recognizing that two separate auditory or visual stimuli or patterns of stimuli are the same or different.
3. Visual and auditory association disabilities—problems in relating separately perceived visual or auditorial stimuli or sets of stimuli to each other.
4. Perceptual-motor disabilities—problems in recognizing the need for or in performing specific eye-motor behaviors or relating visual stimuli to motor responses or motor cues to visual stimuli.
5. Spatial awareness and orientation disabilities—problems in recognizing or adequately using temporal or spatial relationships between objects.
6. Verbal expression disabilities—problems in communicating information to others (either by speaking or writing).
7. Closure and generalization (convergence-divergence) disabilities—problems in interpolating parts from wholes or extrapolating to wholes from parts.
8. Attending disabilities—problems in keeping sustained focus of attention on a problem solving task over a space of several minutes.

Figure 3.3 *Specific learning disabilities types included on all cross referencing charts*

Pre-School Readiness Level
1. Number recognition
2. Counting
3. Grouping
4. Relationships vocabulary
5. Verbal expression

Introductory Level
1. Vocabulary
2. Relationships, sets
3. Operations (addition and subtraction)
4. Grouping
5. Problem solving
6. Verbal expression

Post-Introductory Level
1. Operations (multiplication and division)
2. Rule application
3. Written problem solving and expression
4. Nonwritten problem solving and expression

Figure 3.4 *Curriculum content areas included on cross-referencing charts*

4 Non-arithmetic situations where similar behaviors are required.

5 Remedial objective if problem is confirmed.

6 Sample remedial activity.

Each chart will have curriculum content areas on one axis and learning disability areas on the other so that every possible combination is listed. It is assumed that these charts will provide a ready-referencing handbook for the practitioner by referring the reader to those pages in this book which provide the information pertinent to each particular cell.

Chapter 4

The Prescriptive-Diagnosis Process

While it may seem superfluous in a book such as this to devote special attention to the need for clearly identifying the learning disabled child, it is not. Many people assume that such identification is virtually automatically done or already adequately handled through existing school testing programs. Unfortunately, this is often not so.

It is true that learning problems caused or magnified by deficits in the basic learning processes, commonly referred to as specific learning disabilities, become highly visible as they blossom into major academic difficulties. Recognition only at that late point in the child's academic career, however, is a genuine tragedy. It is a tremendous waste of an individual's potential in the most important formative years, which necessitates expenditures of time and money far beyond the levels required if earlier prescriptive diagnosis had been successfully accomplished.

Since the interaction of learning disabilities and arithmetic can be so subtle in the early school years, it is even more true that careful, precise, well-planned, and effective screening-diagnosis-recognition techniques should be easily available to the classroom teacher.

Johnson and Morasky (1977) have listed some reasons for schools and school personnel becoming involved in early identification procedures. They note that early identification of learning problems allow some semi-preventive activities to be initiated since in the earlier stages problem behaviors may be only loosely formed and not yet habitual or automatic. An early start on problems allows new directions of learning to be established for the individual child without having to undo, unlearn, or extinguish inadequate or incorrect behaviors—processes which are difficult and expensive in terms of time and drain on the motivational reserves of both pupil and instructor. They also point out that early screening procedures allow school personnel to identify not only those children with problem behaviors, but also those with special talents, individual abilities which are unusual in type as well as quality, and others who may have atypical approaches to subject matter or learning behaviors. They note the importance of having early baseline data for a child against which later performances in different situations or within the context of special remedial procedures may be measured. Finally, they stress the importance of involvement of many different school and home personnel in the school's program. Early identification procedures often facilitate this either through direct use of many of these people or through their involvement in follow-up activities in response to data gathered in the identification process. All of these reasons are equally valid in reference to early identification of learning disability-arithmetic problems.

In answer to the general question of why work so hard on early identification of these children, three specific answers seem to stand out.

The need for individual remedial prescriptions. These are children who are going to need special help in order to successfully perform in the arithmetic sector of the curriculum. Individualized instructional programs for such children cannot be planned until their problems are defined.

The need for special supportive attention. Arithmetic is a vital part of the curriculum. Without arithmetic skills an individual simply cannot be a normally functioning member of society. The importance of these skills is not lost on even the very young child who must use them in many different aspects of every day life. As my four-year-old nursery school daughter recently said, "Daddy, I need a dime for milk. What's a dime?" Inability to perform in this area offers a very real threat to the pupil's overall ego strength and self-concept. Helping the arithmetically deficit child consists of more than teaching activities focused on the arithmetic curriculum. It requires constant attention to maintaining the child's overall academic motivation, aspirational level, and self-concept as a potentially capable person. Many children, when faced with failure in such an important area as arithmetic, reflect their frustration and fear across a wide segment of the curriculum ranging far from arithmetic skills alone. Early identification helps schools alert personnel and family to the need for special emotional as well as educational support.

The need for effective integration with curriculum and peers. A wide variance of performance is expected in the young pupil. Smith and Neisworth (1969) point out that the usual classroom may contain students who:

1 Do well in all school subjects by performing at a level that is consistent with their "predicted" ability.
2 Exhibit unequal achievement in certain subject areas which require similar skills for an effective performance.
3 Have developed the basic technical skills for a subject, but are deficient in applying these skills efficiently.
4 Have not developed basic precursive or technical skills for a subject, or apply the processes involved in the subject inconsistently.
5 Are intellectually superior and do well in all subjects, or are intellectually superior and underachieve in all subjects.
6 Are mentally retarded and do not understand regular classroom instruction.
7 Have emotional problems which impede adequate performance in academic areas, or restrict effective interaction with classmates or authority figures.
8 Have other specific problems such as perceptual-motor difficulties, communication disorders, social difficulties, or physical disabilities that reduce their ability to perform effectively at a minimum level in all areas.

Still, there are some aspects of the curriculum where developing skills are so obviously sequential and progressive that any regular negative deviation begins to cause an individual student "out-of-phase" problems which are highly visible and difficult to handle. Most classroom days revolve around an integration of specific learning steps and peripheral enrichment activities which allow the child to practice and entrench those facts and behaviors acquired. Thus, children learning to count will be given opportunity, outside of the time specifically assigned to arithmetic, to count goldfish in the aquarium, ladder rungs on the fire truck during a field trip, and perhaps even peas on the plate in the cafeteria.

Such added experiences make the classroom a living place and very important to the young child. There is no way a child who is excluded from sharing such activities alongside peers can experience the same richness, appreciation, and joy of learning as children who receive them. Therefore, if a classroom contains children with special problems who, by the nature of their problems, may be prevented from sharing such activities, the teacher needs to know so alternative experiences may be developed. Planning time is required for such alternatives. Though it may appear that enrichment activities are spontaneous in the efficient classroom, everyone who has taught knows that long hours of searching, organizing, planning, and creating are necessary. Early identification helps provide this lead time.

LEVELS OF IDENTIFICATION

Identification is not a simple, one-level procedure. Most really good identification programs are set up with three separate levels or processes of identification involved.

Screening

The first level, and the one most often overlooked or shortchanged is screening. The reasons for screening include all those cited earlier from Johnson and Morasky (1977). It is a procedure to help schools in the early identification of children with potential problems. This screening will prevent development of more severe problems, call attention to varying ability levels, provide economic savings, gather data, and increase personnel involvement. Specifically, screening seeks to *broadly* classify students' abilities in academic area(s) according to some classification procedure which matches the school's capabilities for handling individual differences. This latter qualification may need some explanation. Screening programs should be established for the purpose of identifying those major groups of children which the school is prepared to help or direct to other help-providing sources. Thus, the parameters of a screening program should be drawn from those already established by virtue of the nature of the available program itself. Unless this is true, data gathered about children will have no particular use except to underline the absence of suitable responses by the school.

Grouping, categorization, or classification is necessarily broad and general in screening, with no attempt to label or measure narrow, specific, individual problems. Grouping usually takes the form of roughly categorizing students' ability or performance level on a continuum divided into very broad segments. Thus, a screening procedure may describe a child as having advanced abilities, or as having no apparent problems, or displaying signs of some potential problem development, or perhaps as needing more individualized diagnostic effort.

In other words, the screening procedure is not a specific, focused diagnostic effort as much as it is an attempt to roughly categorize or "screen" a group of pupils to see what large identifiable segments matching the school's program are present.

This general attempt to roughly categorize students so that those with special abilities and those with special diagnostic needs may be better identified represents the first level of identification.

To summarize the points which characterize this level and discriminate it from the next two levels:

1 The purpose of screening is to roughly group students according to the capabilities of the school's or classroom's program, not to identify specific behavioral deficits.

2 Screening ususally does not involve any detailed or specific remediation procedure or prescriptive activity. It often does cause some students to be placed in categories for further observation so that prescriptive remediation procedures may follow.

3 Screening is usually less formal, less standardized in a technical sense, and may involve fewer professionally trained psychometric or diagnostic personnel.

Group Diagnosis

This second level of identification is used with groups already established as needing specific diagnostic work through some type of screening process. It usually uses more standardized instruments, and more specifically trained personnel. Group diagnosis is looking for specific problem areas through a division of a major academic task into more detailed subtasks. Diagnostic testing does not necessarily assume that the resulting classification of pupils will match existing programs or facilities. Quite the opposite is often true. It is frequently found that special programs must be developed, now materials found or created, referrals made to outside sources, etc. The purpose is to definitely specify children with specific problems as a preparatory step to remedial prescription—whatever that may involve.

Group diagnostic work is more economical of time than individual diagnosis and is preferred whenever possible by many school personnel for that reason. It usually uses standardized instruments, or parts of them, and more finely groups or classifies the problems of students than does screening. However, even when group diagnostic procedures are possible it is almost always true that some individual diagnostic work with the problem pupil is necessary. In the best of circumstances this may consist only of rechecking and cross-validating findings obtained through group procedures. Seldom can one move directly from group obtained diagnoses to specific remedial programs without at least some confirmation of findings in individual cases. It is more often true that group procedures represent only a step closer to final diagnostic data gathering and that sometimes extensive further diagnostic observation is required in individual cases.

Individual Diagnosis

This most intense and highly focused level of diagnosis involves obtaining data regarding a given individual in specific situations relevant to definite skills, abilities, and performance behaviors. It requires good staff observational skills, a full awareness of the demands of the curriculum and school situation, and thorough knowledge of the potential range of learning difficulties a child may encounter. Thus, fewer paraprofessionals or lay assistants may be used.

A GENERAL STRATEGY

While there are a number of different approaches to this process, the method explained in this book is largely that of task analysis interwoven with a clinical teaching emphasis. The steps are quite plainly outlined in much of the professional literature devoted to this approach.

1 A child is noted as presenting behaviors which at least hint of deficit or sub-criterion behaviors, that is, a learning problem (perhaps observed in screening).

2 With an analysis of the required learning task at hand (the inexperienced worker may have to initially spend time studying the curriculum demands in order to prepare such a task analysis), the child's behavior is carefully observed and analyzed against the criteria of the analyzed task. How well does the child do that which is required?

3 Deficits, mismatches, and incongruencies are noted and analyzed for common behavioral denominators. The focus here deals with looking for common productive remedial directions, not for common etiologies. Attention is centered on means to the goal, not causes.

4 Remedial prescriptions are established which are designed to increment deficit behaviors, revector misdirected behaviors, decrease too hyperac-

tive behaviors, practice undeveloped but necessary behaviors, or whatever is necessary to cause the observed behavior to better match the criterion obtained in the task analysis.

5 The remedial program is activated and steps two through four are repeated as often as necessary with the program being consistently remodeled and updated until definite pupil progress is noted and the goal of individual behavior-criterion congruency is obtained.

Perhaps the most important point to note in this process is that it is virtually impossible to isolate the diagnostic procedure from the prescriptive remediation process. Diagnosis which serves only a labeling purpose is largely a waste of time. Instead, it needs to be part of a creative process which directs teacher and learner behavior along a designated productive path toward a specifically defined goal. It is ongoing, not encapsulated in the early stages of a case alone. Good diagnosis functions as a self-correcting process, a servo-mechanism, and a conceptual gyroscope to keep teacher and learner steadily on a demonstrably efficient learning path.

The material in this book is primarily concerned with steps for carrying out this third level of diagnostic-remediation. Some of the material has relevance for informal screening and some examples might not be used for group diagnosis. However, the intent is to provide the practicing teacher with the design and materials for observing and measuring the behavior analysis task and responding with appropriate remedial prescriptions in those instances where more intensive individualized diagnosis does not seem necessary.

Chapter 5

Implementing the Strategy

As was noted earlier, it is assumed that most of those who proceed to use this material will bring some basic knowledge with them, seeking to complement their own developed expertness and skill with information from another area of knowledge. Such a search should be initiated with the idea that acquisition of additional information will make the application of already possessed skills more effective, more efficient, or both.

The material included in this book deals with two major areas: (1) the arithmetic aspects of the elementary school mathematics curriculum, and (2) certain common aspects of specific learning disabilities. It is assumed that the involvement and knowledge most apt to be already in hand by users will be either one of these two areas. Thus, it is presumed that those most often in a position to apply the following material will be at least basically conversant with either the relevant curriculum materials and content or with some aspect of specific learning disabilities. With this in mind, the format and content included in subsequent chapters offers a basic outline of important aspects of each area, and concentrates on the behavioral factors which ensue when the two areas interact.

The mathematics instructor is pictured primarily as using the material to better understand how learning disability aspects affect learning behaviors in the arithmetic curriculum. This type person is expected to be able to interpolate within and add to the basic curriculum outline materials presented, drawing upon personal experience and knowledge.

On the other hand, the user already conversant with general aspects of the specific learning disability should similarly be able to personally enrich the learning disability outline while seeking for basic direction and help from the arithmetic vector.

For those individuals familiar with neither of the two aspects, further preparation in both curriculum matters and the nature and characteristics of specific learning disabilities will probably be a necessary prerequisite step to maximum effective use. Once these background areas have been explored, this material should prove helpful in applying the more general, theoretical, and esoteric aspects covered in less application-oriented texts.

The advanced practitioner with experience in both areas will find that the materials contained here can prove helpful and time-saving in setting up remedial programs and outlining some informal diagnostic steps and remedial objectives to the less informed professional, aide, or even the layman.

FORMAT AND LAYOUT OF RESOURCE MATERIALS

Chapters 7, 8, and 9 contain the resource materials for the three curriculum levels, Pre-School Readiness, Introductory, and Post-Introductory. The material is assembled by grouping according to each of the categories of curriculum and learning disabilities. For example:

Readiness Level

Number Recognition Interacting With:

- Memory disabilities
- Visual and auditory discrimination disabilities
- Visual and auditory association disabilities
- Perceptual-motor disabilities
- Spatial awareness and orientation disabilities
- Verbal expression disabilities
- Closure and generalization disabilities
- Attending disabilities

The same format is then repeated for the next curriculum content area at the readiness level and so on through all content areas. The headings are set to one side to facilitate finding and using them. Within each separate interaction area identical subclassifications are to be found. These are:

- Problem-free behavior
- Sample task where deficit child may display difficulty
- Do-it-yourself diagnostic activities
- Non-arithmetic situations where similar behaviors are required
- Remedial objective for confirmed problems
- Sample remedial activity

Pages are numbered in the usual fashion, but in addition, a letter-number code will be given for each curriculum area-learning disability type interaction. For instance, in the example A-4, the letter refers to a designated curriculum area and the number to a learning disability type. The letter and number designations are listed in Figure 5-1 and also will be found at the beginning of each of the three resource chapters and in the appendices.

In addition, there are locater charts for each of the three levels which list page location and code number for each of the three levels. These charts, a reduced sample of which is to be seen in Figure 5-2, are found at the beginning of each of the three resource chapters and in the appendix as well.

SOME GENERAL PROCEDURES FOR PRESCRIPTIVE DIAGNOSIS

Implicit in the source material which follows are some definite procedures for obtaining data needed to make the behavior-criterion match measurement and the remedial steps which should then be followed.

CURRICULUM CONTENT AREAS	LEARNING DISABILITY TYPES

Pre-school Readiness Level

A. Number recognition

B. Counting

C. Grouping

D. Relationships vocabulary

E. Verbal expression

Introductory Level

F. Vocabulary

G. Relationship—Sets

H. Operations (addition and subtraction)

I. Grouping

J. Problem solving

K. Verbal expression

Post-Introductory Level

L. Operations (multiplication and division)

M. Rule application

N. Written problem solving

O. Nonwritten problem solving

LEARNING DISABILITY TYPES

1 Memory

2 Visual-auditory discrimination

3 Visual-auditory association

4 Perceptual-motor

5 Spatial orientation

6 Verbal expression

7 Closure-generalization

8 Attending

Figure 5.1 *Letter and number codes for curriculum content areas and learning disability types*

Looking for signs of problems in regular classroom work. The first of these is pure observation. Initial identification of a child who may have learning problems comes about through noting examples of behavior or "warning signs" which warrant more intense analytical procedures. It simply is not feasible to put every child through a diagnostic process, though more and more schools are requiring all entering children to participate in a screening program. Whether the initial observation takes place in the structured context of a screening program or within the more flexible context of an individual classroom, the observer learns to look for two types of "signs."

The first sign is the presence of those behaviors which indicate the successful performance of the child with no problems—literally criterion-level behavior. These are indications that the child is capable of and presents those behaviors necessary to satisfactorily perform required tasks under certain specifications. In the following sections, problem-free behaviors are noted for each area where a curriculum content area and a learning disability behavior interact for each of the three levels. These are intended to communicate to

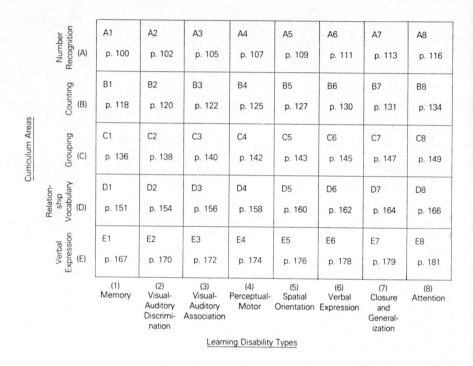

Figure 5.2 *A reduced copy of the locater chart for the Pre-School Readiness Level*

the reader the type of positive cues the observer seeks in the preliminary stages of screening or diagnosis.

The second type of sign is the presence of observed behaviors which are typically seen in children who cannot or do not perform at criterion levels. Such negative cues are of two types. The most obvious is where a designated behavior is simply not up to standard. A child who spells *street* as *streat* has some type of spelling problem. This is an obvious cue that the required performance is deficit. However, for the convenience of those using the material in this book, samples are included of some classroom tasks in arithmetic where a child having difficulty may display such problems to an alerted observer. While only a single example is presented for each interacting curriculum area and learning disability problem type for each of the three levels, it is not difficult to generalize and find other such high visibility tasks where one may look for hints of problems.

Using material designed to elicit behavior for diagnostic analysis. In this second step, the teacher may wish to introduce special demands into the classroom situation (called "embedding" a measure) so that a child's response behavior to specific stimuli may be observed. Or, informal screening and "testing" measures may be utilized for the same purpose. Examples of such "do-it-yourself" diagnostic activities are also included for each interaction point on the three levels. The collection of self-built "homemade" informal diagnostic and remedial materials is a process familiar to every classroom teacher. The creative initiative of teachers in providing such materials is one of the major strengths of today's schools. The sample procedures provided in this text attempt to direct these activities along a line which will maximize their focus on designated arithmetic curriculum content as it interacts with some learning processes where learning disabilities frequently develop.

Searching for non-arithmetic examples of deficit behavior in areas to which the problem may have generalized. School personnel may be concerned with obtaining some confirmation of hypothesized deficit behaviors or determining the possible broadening effect of noted problems. Many times, the learning problems of children which center in a specific curriculum area will also begin to spread and surface in other areas. This ripple effect, like the spreading waves from a stone dropped in a pond, may become increasingly subtle as other situations become removed from the major problem area. However, it is useful to note these effects both in terms of preventing the spread of effect and also because such observations may serve to confirm tentative problem diagnoses. Included here are examples of non-arithmetic situations where spreading problem behavior may be observed. These are instances of behavior perhaps not resembling at face value simple deficit behaviors, but found to be frequently present when certain learning problems exist. Thus, school absence may not appear to be related to multiplication problems, but it may be a behavioral reaction typical of second grade children having such difficulties. Problems of this type, gathered from personal observation, teacher reports, and research data are included. The experienced teacher will quickly see the application of these examples and the new teacher can easily learn to use such signs to help with the initial identification stage. In a similar vein, Figure 5.3 lists some of these commonly seen general behavioral indices as reported by Meier (1971).

Deciding on whether or not to seek outside help. Obviously after going through these preliminary prescriptive diagnostic steps, the teacher or other practitioner comes to a point where he or she must decide whether enough information, feasible activities, and professional skills are available to successfully carry remediation through to a successful conclusion. The major motivation for writing this book has risen out of practical experience that indicates that in many cases the practitioner on the firing-line can quite adequately carry out all these steps. However, there are instances where these less sophisticated and less formal activities simply do not provide the necessary definitive information to move on toward effective remediation. At this point, more sophisticated prescriptive information should be sought. It may come from the same personnel applying more formal and sophisticated methods and instrumentation, for instance using a formal diagnostic instrument such as Key-Math (Connolly, Nachtman, and Pritchett, 1971). Or, it may consist of referring to other personnel for help. School psychologists, arithmetic specialists, remedial reading teachers, school nurses, and other special pupil personnel workers may all be sources of additional helpful information.

In any event, it is necessary to have enough diagnostic information to be able to pinpoint a deficit behavior area and to establish meaningful remedial objectives. Such information may come solely from the use of those informal materials included here, jointly from these sources coupled with additional information from other sources, or in the instance of more complex and difficult cases, from other sources alone. Once such information is in hand, the practitioner is ready for the next step.

Establishing a remedial objective. It is simple to state what should be done; it is often more difficult to actually do it. The remedial objective should clearly define the specific goal of the remedial steps in such a manner that those involved with applying remedial activities can judge the appropriateness of their efforts. And, to those who are merely observing (such as parents), it should clearly define the purpose of what is being done. The objective should not be a simple restatement of criterion behaviors, but instead should relate to the type of activity being provided or the demands being placed upon the pupil using the activities. For each sample remedial activity presented here, a remedial objective is provided. Naturally, as activities vary, remedial objective statements may, too.

Preparing and using remedial materials. The final step is the preparation and use of remedial materials and activities. There are many arguments for using homemade materials. Johnson and Morasky (1977) note three important ones: immediacy, flexibility and adaptability, and economy. The importance of these is obvious. Once a problem is discovered, the quick availability of remedial materials is a valuable resource. Being able to make materials fit individual needs of pupils and the nature of the situation is equally valuable. The last point needs little emphasis—it makes little sense to spend valuable school budget money for expensive remedial materials when they can be produced as well and infinitely more cheaply at home.

Revising and reworking the prescriptive diagnostic process. Although the detailed steps involved in implementing and revising this process are beyond the scope of this text, they are a vital part of the process

BEHAVIORAL INDICE	PROPORTION OF ILD** CHECKED BY TEACHERS		
	1/3	1/2	2/3
Avoids work requiring concentrated visual attention	X		
Unable to learn the sounds of letters (can't associate proper phoneme with its grapheme)	X		
Doesn't seem to listen to daily classroom instructions or directions (often asks to have them repeated whereas rest of class goes ahead)		X	
Can't correctly recall oral directions when asked to repeat them		X	
Can't pronounce the sounds of certain letters	X		
Unable to correctly repeat a 7 to 10 word statement by the teacher (omits or transposes words)	X		
Is slow to finish work (doesn't apply self, daydreams a lot, falls asleep in school)		X	
Overactive (can't sit still in class—shakes or swings legs, fidgety).	X		
Tense or disturbed (bites lip, needs to go to the bathroom often, twists hair, high strung)	X		
Unusually short attention span for daily school work			X
Easily distracted from school work (can't concentrate even with the slightest disturbances from other students' moving around or talking quietly)			X
Mistakes own left from right (confuses left-hand with right-hand side of paper)	X		
Poor drawing of diamond compared with peers' drawing	X		
Poor drawing of crossing, wavy lines compared with peers' drawings	X		
Poor drawing of a man compared with peers' drawing		X	
Poor handwriting compared with peers' writing		X	
Reverses or rotates letters, numbers, and words (writes "p" for "q," "saw" for "was," "2" for "7,"			

Figure 5.3 *Behavioral indices identifying different proportions of learning disability second graders**

*From Meier, J. H. "Prevalence and Characteristics of Learning Disabilities Found in Second Grade Children." *Journal of Learning Disabilities* 4 (1971): 1–16.
**Identified learning disabled.

BEHAVIORAL INDICE	PROPORTION OF ILD CHECKED BY TEACHERS		
	1/3	1/2	2/3
"16" for "91") far more frequently than peers	X		
Reverses and/or rotates letters and numbers (reads "b" for "d," "u" for "n," "6" for "9") far more frequently than peers	X		
Loses place more than once while reading aloud for one minute	X		
Omits words while reading grade-level material aloud (omits more than one out of every ten)	X		
Reads silently or aloud far more slowly than peers (word by word while reading aloud)			X
Points at words while reading silently or aloud		X	
Substitutes words which distort meaning ("when" for "where")			X
Can't sound out or "unlock" words		X	
Can read orally, but does not comprehend the meaning of written grade-level words (word-callers)	X		
Reading ability at least 3/4 of a year below most peers		X	
Has trouble telling time		X	
Can't follow written directions, which most peers can follow, when read orally or silently		X	
Difficulty with arithmetic (e.g., can't determine what number follows 8 or 16; may begin to add in the middle of a subtraction problem)	X		
Cannot apply the classroom or school regulations to own behavior whereas peers can	X		
Excessive inconsistency in quality of performance from day to day or even hour to hour	X		
Has trouble organizing written work (seems scatterbrained, confused)		X	
Seems bright in many ways, but still does poorly in school	X		
Repeats the same behavior over and over		X	
Demands unusual amount of attention during regular classroom activities	X		
Seems quite immature (doesn't act his/her age)	X		

Figure 5.3 *Continued*

itself. In most cases, some redefinition of the problem area and subsequent redefining (often only a refining in more detail) of remedial activities is involved. Prescriptive diagnosis is an ongoing activity and even the highly experienced and specially trained professional must continue to work out "bugs" which develop. Backtracking to review possible sources of problems which hinder the remediation process is an important part of the process which must be included.

APPLYING THE GENERAL PROCEDURES

To summarize, there are seven general procedural steps involved in diagnosis:

1 Looking for signs of problems in regular classroom work.
2 Using material designed to elicit behavior for diagnostic analysis.
3 Searching for non-arithmetic examples of deficit behavior in areas to which the problem may have generalized.
4 Deciding on whether or not to seek outside help.
5 Establishing a remedial objective.
6 Preparing and using remedial materials.
7 Revising and reworking the prescriptive diagnostic process.

Successful prescriptive diagnosis and remediation requires adequate understanding and application of each step. Figure 5.4 flowcharts the actual strategy process. Following are some guidelines for actually applying the general procedural steps.

Looking for signs in regular classroom work. The materials included in subsequent chapters are those which the practitioner will actually use while working with deficit children. They are based upon the premise that, in many cases, the effects of specific learning disabilities impinge upon the arithmetic performance of afflicted children, resulting in disparate behaviors which can be noted by the alert observer. Such an observer must be sensitive to both the curriculum content areas covered in this material and the types of specific learning disability used to pinpoint such interaction behaviors.

Each of the three curriculum levels has been subdivided into more discrete arithmetic performance areas based upon input from those well-versed in curriculum content. Though total agreement is impossible to obtain, there is strong consensus that these are at least major areas of concern. The learning disability types have been similarly gathered from firsthand experience with many learning disabled children. Neither the curriculum content areas

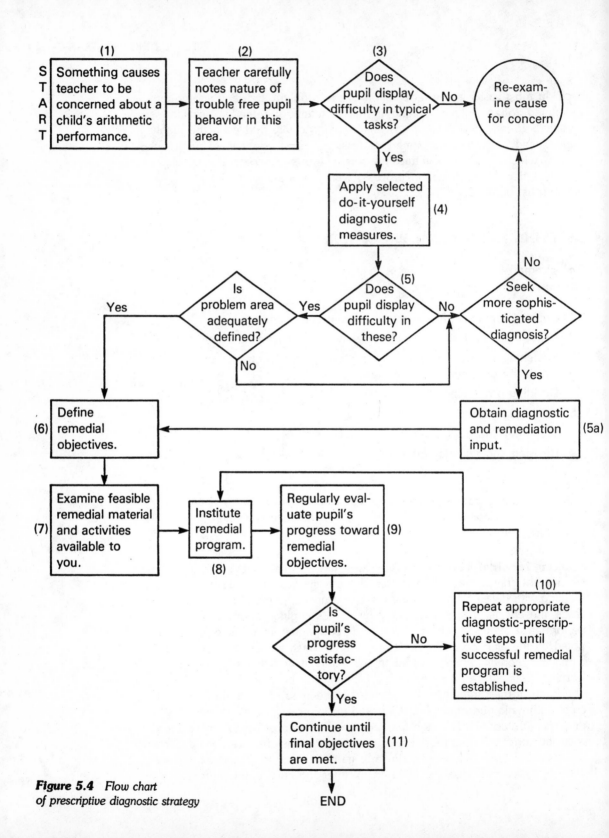

Figure 5.4 *Flow chart of prescriptive diagnostic strategy*

nor the learning disability types should be considered as exhaustive or exclusive. They are representative, and allowing for great variance of opinion, they reflect some consensus of importance among those representing both factors.

As an initial step in application of the strategy, the practitioner should become thoroughly familiar with the descriptions and explanations of both these categorizations. Chapter 6 contains a general explanation of what is included in the curriculum content areas for each of the three levels—Pre-School Readiness, Introductory, and Post-Introductory. Also in Chapter 6 is an explanation of the specific learning disability types used.

Once familiarity with these categorizations is gained, the practitioner begins to focus observation, based upon personal knowledge of either curriculum or learning disabilities, as it parallels these descriptive categorizations. The starting point of analysis should be in the factor most familiar to the user. Thus, the curriculum expert will find it easier to first categorically define the curriculum area involved; while the learning disability specialist will most likely initiate the search from the opposite approach.

Once a fairly clearcut definition of area or type is formed, the observer seeks to establish the presence of behavioral data matching the other categorization scheme. The selection process first must deal with informal observation until areas are sufficiently pinpointed to warrant introduction of embedded measures, informal, or perhaps formal diagnostic procedures. Some trial and error is to be expected. But, the child should not be subjected to a routine detailed diagnostic workup of all areas or types until the area of trouble is confirmed. If such unwarranted procedures seem necessary, insufficient general observation has been involved.

At this step, as in others, the practitioner may often have to supplement personal observation with new or confirming data from others. The designated examples of trouble-free behavior and typical task examples where difficulties may be observed will help guide such selective observation. Once the focus of behavioral observation has been narrowed (not always to a single interaction point, but almost always to a relatively few), the practitioner is ready for step two.

Using materials designed to elicit behavior for diagnostic analysis. The second step consists of attempting to check out hypotheses about potentially deficit behavior which have been formed as a result of the observations in step one. Trial and error again may be necessary to some extent since hypotheses are exactly that, and, many times are not confirmed, necessitating further search. However, step two should be even more highly focused than step one in terms of being careful not to demand too many individualized, attention-getting, personal diagnostic performances from the child. In other words, no child should be required to move methodically through each and every possible diagnostic task.

Smith and Neisworth (1969) express some precautions about collecting behavioral data from informal measures and these should be carefully noted. They warn that:

1 Every activity selected for the purpose of evaluation should be part of an ongoing program . . . (and) should reflect all the many nuances of the real classroom situation.

2 Activities should be interesting to the student being evaluated.

3 Activities for diagnosis should be selected to measure specific educational dimensions.

4 Activities should be developed to measure directly a child's performance in each of these (specific dimensions) specific skills.

5 Every diagnostic activity should be chosen for objectivity.

6 Activities should be varied enough that the youngsters do not become too familiar with the tasks.

7 Activities selected to diagnose areas of educational relevance should provide valid measurement of the behavioral dimension.

8 Children should be tested on more than one occasion to gain a reliable evaluation.

The do-it-yourself diagnostic activities included in subsequent sections are limited in the same fashion as are the potential problem areas samples. That is, they are examples only and the individual practitioner will need to supplement them with additional or perhaps different tasks. Almost all classroom personnel have the ability to do this if given some guidelines to follow. The examples are designed to provide the guidelines and direction rather than definition.

If one enters step two with a strong feeling that observations have been accurate and correctly focused and yet fails to find behavioral confirmation in the informal diagnostic activities, it is probably wise to seek more structured and perhaps more formal diagnostic instruments gathered by the same personnel, or seek help from other professionals. Such additional input may either confirm or fail to confirm hypotheses based upon preliminary observations. If no confirmation is obtained, the entire problem area may need to be reexamined. If the more detailed or formal diagnostic analysis confirms the observation generated hypotheses, such additional information may be used in moving on to subsequent steps.

Searching for non-arithmetic examples of deficit behavior in areas to which the problem may have generalized. Although listed as a third sequential step, this will often be merged with step two. There are aspects of remedial planning which require the planner to know the extent to which problems have generalized and the areas affected. The child's general motivation as influenced by concern, guilt, loss of self-esteem, and similar matters, is frequently affected as much by areas outside the immediate academic area as by the problem-related tasks themselves. Obtaining information in these other areas will give the planner additional insight into the range of the problem and other aspects of the child's general functioning may be of prescriptive value.

A specific word of warning should be introjected here. While such areas may serve to partially confirm more specific diagnostic work, the practitioner should be constantly aware that the process does not work very satisfactorily in reverse. That is, one should not assume from problem behavior observed in some area only distantly related to arithmetic that arithmetic problems exist. The "ripples" do not flow back to their source with that much clarity and may indeed arise from any one of many sources. In actuality, this whole use of subtle indices, useful as it can be when applied with caution, should be used with a great deal of care and only in a generally supportive fashion rather than as specific diagnostic data. General problem behaviors can come from many different sources.

Once general observational input, and informal (and in some instances formal) diagnostic information has been gathered, coupled with whatever information may be forthcoming from areas outside of arithmetic, the practitioner is again faced with a decision. If the collected data is sufficiently definitive and if the individual's familiarity with remedial materials and activities is adequate, then it is appropriate to proceed to the next step, that of defining remedial objectives. Often, however, the practitioner will find it helpful to involve others in re-analyzing the problem preparatory to defining remedial objectives.

Establishing a remedial objective. For such definition to proceed smoothly and effectively it is necessary to establish two sets of information. First, an analysis of the behavior required of the normal child must be precise, clearly understood, and expressible in relevant behavioral terms. Thus, those involved with establishing remedial objectives must be able to say, "The child needs to be able to do *this*." And the *"this"* must be precise. Such a statement is clearly the end-product of a task analysis of some sort. Second, the behavior of the child at its present level and nature must be equally well defined, that is, "He is presently doing or not doing *this*."

The remedial objective(s) rises out of the relationship existing between these two sets of data and the steps necessary to proceed meaningfully from one to the other—from what the child is doing to what he is required to do. These steps (and therefore the remedial objectives) must be stated so precisely that no room exists for misunderstanding or misinterpretation. This will prevent future tasks of evaluation of outcomes and the possible need for re-prescribing, both of which are extremely difficult and sometimes impossible.

Preparing and using remedial materials. A number of fine commercially prepared and attractive remedial program kits and plans are available. Every teacher and educational clinician's desk is full of catalogues and brochures promoting these materials. A wide variation in validity and effectiveness is present. Many are expensive, overpriced, and lacking in quality. Not infrequently, homemade materials will suffice equally as well as commercially prepared materials.

Perhaps the two major issues confronting those who would prepare homemade remedial activities are: (1) Are these materials valid in that they help the child achieve the stated remedial objective and thus remove deficit behaviors, and (2) are the materials and activities in a format that makes them easily applicable by each type of person who might have need to apply them? Johnson and Morasky (1977) point out some basic questions which those preparing homemade materials should ask themselves to assure that materials are adequately oriented to remedial goals. These are:

1 Ask, "What am I trying to do with this material?" not "What is the material meant to accomplish?" As effective as it may be in meeting an advertised goal, if that goal is not congruent with the user's goal then efficiency is forfeited.

2 Ask, "How do I intend to apply the materials?" It is the application dimensions including the general context, the immediate situation, the assets, and limitations in users which are all important. A ship is useful only where there is water.

In the material which follows there are sample presentations of the type of remedial materials and activities which may be used to help the child achieve the stated remedial objective. Again, it is expected that the individual practitioner will generate more and different ideas relevant to different remedial objectives and pertinent to individual children and situations.

In many of the examples presented, some specific advice on how to use the material is offered. It may be helpful to think of almost all such remedial activities as involving two main steps. Using the remedial example presented later for the interaction of number recognition with memory at the pre-school readiness level, the two steps can be outlined.

The *remedial objective* is to provide the child with progressively demanding practice in recalling numbers recently encountered or learned. The *remedial activity* is undertaken by using number presentations included in normal classroom activities, for example, the teacher noting on the blackboard the number of tulips brought to class by a pupil that morning, or the number of pupils wishing to buy milk that day.

Two main steps are involved:

1 Shaping

Stage 1: Immediately after the number has been presented, the pupil is asked to recall that number. Reinforcement for correct responses is important. Errors should be followed by, "No, the number was_____." Then the entire procedure should be repeated. Errors may be initially reduced by using single numbers and obviously emphasized presentations.

Stage 2: As criterion level recall is produced, the length of time between presentations and recall is progressively increased in small incremental steps. It will be helpful at this stage to alert the child that subsequent recall will be called for, thus helping the pupil to develop memory intent in noting numbers.

Stage 3: Recall demands should shift to an irregular schedule with such demands being presented at varying time lengths, sometimes even running into the following day(s).

2 Performance Practice

Once criterion levels have been obtained in the shaping procedure, the child should regularly be given practice through requiring performance of the newly acquired ability to further strengthen the learned behavior. This can also be done by occasionally asking informal questions such as, "What is the number on the door of our classroom?" or "What number did I write on the blackboard when I was talking about triangles?"

Revising and reworking the prescriptive diagnosis process. It is frequently necessary to revise and reshape remedial programs, in much the same fashion as the physician determining the exact appropriate dosage to prescribe for different patients sharing the same complaint. Individual factors demand individualization and it is frequently impossible or at best extremely difficult to forsee all the individual factors prior to undertaking remediation steps. Those using this approach should not be discouraged by the need for revision. Indeed, being sensitive to such developing revision needs and being able to respond effectively to them is the prime characteristic distinguishing the top-notch remedial specialist from the journeyman.

SUMMARY

While the strategy sets up a specific sequence of activities and outlined procedures to be followed, the real intent is to provide a handbook of material, arranged for quick and easy use, which will facilitate what should become a highly personalized approach characterized by individual differences in skills, knowledge, interests, and needs. The practitioner should feel free to deviate from specific content outlines or sequences when practical considerations and effectiveness seem to warrant it.

PART II

SOURCE MATERIAL

Chapter 6

Curriculum Content Areas and Learning Disability Types

As noted previously, it is virtually impossible to arrive at any breakdown or categorization of curriculum content which will meet with universal approval. Curricula and content variations by grade level are much too diverse across the nation's school systems. Those selected here do not represent purely arbitrary selections, however. They do have considerable consensual validation in that each represents an important area found in virtually every curriculum model. Each represents areas of performance where children frequently have problems. And finally, resident within each area are tasks and demands for certain performance behaviors found to be susceptible to the negative influence of a variety of specific learning disabilities. The content areas are divided by level. No particular hierarchy or sequential flow of content areas is intended within a level.

It should be specially noted that the author's intent and therefore the purpose of this work is to help children learn effectively rather than to label or categorize problems. All children learn in some way; learning disabled children frequently learn in atypical or unusual ways. Sometimes the problem is what is so loosely called "readiness." Sometimes it is lack of developed skills. Sometimes, techniques or materials are at fault. The categories used here, admittedly arbitrary and necessarily flexible, are useful only in helping to pinpoint areas of behavior where non-effective learning is evidenced. They should not be given more credence in terms of some absolute schema than they are worth.

PRE-SCHOOL READINESS LEVEL CURRICULUM CONTENT AREAS

It should be emphasized that the Readiness Level is, above all, a "get ready for," "prepare for" period during which necessary, vital, prerequisite behaviors are acquired. If deliberate care is not taken, it is easy to slip into too many of the actual beginning operations and tasks of arithmetic itself, thus causing confusion and nonproductive overlap with the Introductory Level where more initial manipulations are covered.

This becomes quite obvious when various formal curricula are examined. In the sub-area of grouping, for example, these curricula rather quickly and smoothly move from the readiness steps of becoming aware of the concept involved in developing "sets," to the formulation of arithmetic sets themselves, such as learning to recognize shapes based upon mathematical properties held in common—literally geometric sets.

Such a smooth transition in the classroom is, of course, desirable for student and teacher alike as developing complexity is gradually incremented and more demanding encounters proceed in small easy and seemingly natural steps. At the same time, it offers pitfalls for those seeking to accurately identify problem areas or to denote missing essential behaviors. In such tasks, the differentiation between preparation for and actually performing arithmetic tasks must be clearly made. The less-than-satisfactory final performance, the "he simply can't add" diagnosis, does not supply the data needed for planning and programming adequate remediation activities.

This segment deliberately assumes a narrow view of the child's progressively developing arithmetic skill, experience, and knowledge by focusing largely on the "getting ready" tasks. One cannot exclude all actual exposure to arithmetic tasks since perusal of almost any elementary curriculum syllabus would confirm the presence of such activities prior to grade one. Still, the emphasis remains on "preparing for" rather than "doing" arithmetic. In some cases, the point at which the continuum is severed into a *readiness* versus *introductory* dichotomy is necessarily arbitrary. Others might wish to make the separation either earlier or later along the continuum. This can easily be done by the user without doing injustice to the outline and materials presented here as long as progressive individual steps are clearly outlined along the format of a broad task analysis.

The five readiness-level curriculum content areas covered here are: number recognition, counting, grouping, relationship vocabulary, and verbal expression.

This selection is a summation of much feedback from workers in the field. Even so, one simply cannot say that the areas are independent or share nothing conceptually or in practice. The opposite is often true. For example, counting almost always involves verbal expression. But since it is necessary to find out which of these two interacting skills the child is using, or not using, the areas are considered separately here as outlined steps for diagnosing problems are presented. A child may fail to ride a bicycle due to lack of balance or failure to make the pedals go round. The two must work together but represent separate potential problem areas. Remedial activities are categorized in a parallel fashion to facilitate taking corrective steps once diagnosis is obtained.

Number Recognition

Curriculum content for readiness development in number recognition at this level consists primarily of learning to identify by sound and sight the names and arabic symbols for 1 to 10. Such a process involves, as a basic preliminary skill, the discrimination of a symbol as distinct from a meaningless figure and specific differentiation between number and letter symbols.

If the range of numbers is increased beyond 10, general approaches and principles remain the same. Though the teacher may get into the numerical values associated with these symbols (for example, four of something), this is a secondary process more associated with counting and grouping. Essentially, it is a skill most often developed subsequent to number recognition.

Counting

There are four discriminating steps to developing counting skills which are a necessary readiness prerequisite to later arithmetic processes and operations. These are:

1 Counting as a rote, memorization process where the numbers are recited in order because they are learned that way. This does not involve a conceptual awareness or understanding of any ordering.

2 Counting with an awareness of the importance of order. This task involves some sequencing skills, the ability to start and stop at arbitrarily selected positions in the counting chain, and some reversibility skills (a procedure greatly enhanced by the current youngster's exposure to rocket countdowns!).

3 Counting of things. This represents a step beyond the mere use of verbal or written symbols. It involves a matching of the counting symbols (one, two, three) to things being counted (one, two, three, as ascribed to separate objects such as three drinking cups). This requires the development of conceptual correspondence between those words first learned by rote, later endowed with counting properties, and a parallel property of numberness, countability, etc., in objects or things apart from the counting symbols themselves.

4 Matching the consummate number reached in counting (for example, "one, two, three" with "three" being the consummate number) with a sense of quantity existing in some set of objects. This is, of course, merely a conceptual extension of step three, but it represents a higher order of conceptualization which may not be present in the previous step.

Grouping

Since arithmetic basically involves a process for expressing certain properties of objects or groups, grouping is an important segment of the readiness curriculum. Once basic discrimination strategies are acquired, this curriculum area is concerned with sorting and classification procedures. For the readiness level child, these procedures consist primarily of learning to perform these activities upon command using such already learned discriminable cues as color, simple shapes, gross differences in size, and to some extent the use of objects, for example, grouping of things to wear. The child may or may not be required to verbalize the grouping or sorting classifications used in such decisions. When such expression is required, it is usually so well integrated in the overall process as to not represent an easily recognizable separate content area. It may be, however, that a given child can group, but not verbalize the reasons used even though the child has selected and used correct ones. Because of this possibility, the need for verbal expression represents a distinct area considered separately later in this chapter.

Once sorting and classification skills are at criterion levels, the readiness curriculum works with sets and matching activities. The steps are fairly straightforward. They are:

1 Developing an awareness of the concept of "set."
2 Learning to match equivalent or "same" sets (usually by drawing lines from elements of one set to corresponding elements of another).
3 Learning to match subparts or elements of two sets in order to determine or make judgments relevant to equivalency of the two. When 1:1 equivalence is not established, the child is taught to use appropriate relationship vocabulary to describe differences or nonequivalencies, for example, "The two piles of books are not the same because this one has more books."

The entire grouping curriculum is preparation for translating the relationship vocabulary into quantitative terms. "More books" may be more precisely stated as "two more books" and even later as "20 percent more books."

Relationships Vocabulary

A significant portion of the readiness curriculum is involved in providing the child with the elemental terms necessary to verbally comprehend and express actions in the preceding three general areas. Primarily, at this level, these terms are of a relational nature including such terms as *nearer* and *farther*, *taller* and *shorter*, *more* and *less*, *greater than* and *less than*, and some superlatives such as *tallest, most, least*, etc. Other terms, somewhat less often used but important nevertheless, are those labeling fractional relationships such as *some, every, part, one-half*, and *all*. In addition, some positional relationship terms are taught, including *top, bottom, middle, above, below, beside, first, last, outside*, etc.

The vocabulary is built essentially through curriculum activities using familiar objects, and taking advantage of everyday situations, activities, and common sets. These activities consist of sorting, classifying, and positioning common objects and then verbally identifying very simple relationship words describing the result or noted condition of objects involved.

Verbal Expression

Teaching arithmetic and mathematics is so integrated with verbal and sometimes abstract conceptualizations, that it is necessary for a child to have developed the strategy of verbally expressing the components in various arithmetic operations. Such verbalization will later provide self-generated corrective feedback as well as providing the basis for the teacher to judge the adequacy of strategy and performance of the student acquiring specific arithmetic skills. Readiness curriculum content consists primarily of integrating verbal behaviors within the parameters of the other areas previously discussed. Thus, the child is consistently required to provide verbal descriptions of what he or she may be doing. The teacher always provides a verbal redundancy for motor acts and covert problem solving. This includes such informative dialogue as, "When I am looking at the two piles of books to see if they are the same, I am counting them this way: 'One, two, three . . .' to see if the number in each is the same." Children are required to do the same and are encouraged in their efforts. Verbal expression in arithmetic activities is more a strategy than an entity of its own. Fortunately, children of pre-school years tend developmentally to accompany even spontaneous play with verbal descriptive expression. This curriculum content area simply expands upon a typically present developmental trait and assures that it is well-established and therefore present for necessary later use in arithmetic activities.

It should be specially noted that verbal expression, although sufficiently important to be listed as a separate curriculum component, obviously overlaps a great deal with the Verbal Expression sub-area included in the Specific Learning Disabilities list. Most of the criterion and deficit behavior examples are conceivably common to both. As verbal behavior required of the child becomes more complex, it might be helpful to think of this portion of the arithmetic curriculum slowly changing from simply teaching the child to talk about arithmetic objects, events, and ideas to teaching the child to use verbal problem solving skills in seeking arithmetic solutions. The major discriminating factor should be that as far as learning disabilities are concerned, problems in this area are related to all aspects of verbal communication including production, response, reporting, and explanation. As a defined portion of the Readiness curriculum, verbal activity is concerned with arithmetically relevant behavior of problem solving. The worker using these materials should find it easy to generalize across both aspects or to use only the specific orientation of one function or the other as the situation warrants.

INTRODUCTORY LEVEL CURRICULUM CONTENT AREAS

In many schools this level most closely coincides with the first and second grades. The dividing lines between this level and the ones preceding and following it do not necessarily directly match grade division, however. In some areas, introductory level material may well be introduced late in the kindergarten year or may be delayed until several months into the first grade. At the upper end of the level, the dividing point between introductory and post-introductory material may vary even more as individualized pacing of different classrooms result in an accelerated or slowed pace.

The most viable argument for including the six content areas considered here is that they have some approaches, materials, and concept-levels in common. The six areas are *vocabulary, relationships-sets, operations, grouping, simple problem solving,* and *verbal expression.*

Five of the areas, excluding operations (which is, in most schools, almost totally new at this level), start out early in the year with an extensive review and some relearning or overlearning of areas covered in the readiness level. Characteristic of all the areas is an increased range and an accelerated pace. It is also noticeable in this level that the child is actually encountering arithmetic content, not merely items and activities related to or in preparation for arithmetic.

Involvement typically moves through a concrete to abstract form, though abstractions remain quite simple and uninvolved. When old areas are reencountered, it is typical at this level for alternative methods or uses to be introduced. Inverting operations and renaming exercises are typical of this.

The pupil more and more experiences learning by actively *doing,* as in measurement, manipulation of number lines, and using words to explore arithmetic problems. Rules and algorithms are introduced and the importance of doing arithmetic "things" in certain, specified, lawful, and repeatable ways is subtly incorporated in the child's learning experiences.

At this level, the child is now actually working with arithmetic. His or her successful learning experiences become vital since basic concepts, methods, and even attitudes, each vital to the more complex operations and problem solving to follow, are being shaped as virtually automatic habits.

Vocabulary

Vocabulary curriculum content at the Introductory level consists initially of some review of basic terms learned at the Readiness level. These terms, primarily relational in nature, include: *bigger* and *smaller, before* and *after, more than* and *less than,* etc. Initial vocabulary teaching at this second level stresses reinforcement of these previously learned terms. Then, as the child evidences regaining or maintaining a firm grasp of these, the extent of the new vocabulary becomes widely increased. The pace of learning is accelerated and terms rather highly specific to areas under direct study are introduced. These include such concept terms as: *hour-hand, minute-hand, names of coins, arrow* and *point, number-line, addition-boxes,* etc. Specific attention is paid to relating terms to abstract ideas and newly introduced arithmetic processes. Children are faced with a more difficult learning situation since such terms are not as easily visualized, demonstrated, or seen in concrete examples. Such terms include: *difference, value, fraction, equation, sum, times,* etc.

Relationship-Sets

As with vocabulary, initial Introductory curriculum content in Relationships-Sets is heavily involved with review, primarily with such things as 1:1 correspondence and cardinal numbers of sets. Empty sets (zero values) will usually be reviewed or introduced early if they have not been part of the Readiness curriculum.

With almost every part of the Introductory curriculum a standard sequence of presentation is used. Ideas, concepts, and operations are each first introduced with demonstration and pupil manipulation of concrete objects. This is followed by pictorialization, then through pictorialization accompanied by numerical notation, and finally, through numerical notation alone. Pupils are often looped back through this sequence. This is usually caused by a stage seeming to be beyond easy grasp, or other difficulties or confusion being encountered.

Specific content at this level typically includes the combining and separating of sets of ten or less; ordering and grouping properties of sets (used with addition here in preparation for reintroduction in multiplying operations later); place values in the 1's, 10's and sometimes 100's; addition and subtraction (from a doing and undoing orientation); additive multiplication of a simple nature; relationships (for example, greater than and less than) accompanied by symbols and used in number sentences; some standard units of measurement; and fractions (1/2, 1/3, 1/4) in a sectional and concrete demonstrative fashion rather than an operational manner. Some operational fractions may be encountered in time and money concepts.

Operations (Addition-Subtraction)

Only the operations of addition and subtraction are included in the Introductory level. In every instance the same four sequential steps as mentioned previously (manipulation, pictorialization, pictorialization with numerical notation, and numerical notation alone) are used as the child proceeds through increasingly complex subtasks of the addition and subtraction processes. The basic idea of addition and subtraction as "doing and undoing" is maintained throughout. The child is consistently encouraged to use renaming, check on the reasonableness of obtained answers, and to verify correctness through use of inverse operations as taught.

Number facts are taught to the sums of 10 at first and later to the sums of 18. Number sentences, both open and closed, are introduced and then used extensively, although only those number sentences which are *direct* are typically used at this level. Simple algorithms with pictorial representation and then alone are taught at this level.

Ordering and grouping properties are stressed in addition work. When progressing from single-digit, to two-digit, to column addition, the pupil encounters first renaming without carrying, then renaming with carrying. In subtraction, the initial phase involves no borrowing (regrouping) or renaming, with these becoming introduced later in this level.

Grouping

Grouping at the Introductory level is used most directly with measurement activities. Groups are compared for equality (as in size) and for similarity of characteristics (as in pattern, design, or other individual characteristics). Comparisons deal mostly with "more than-less than" and "same-different" decisions.

Measurement itself is introduced first with pupil-created nonstandard units followed by the gradual and progressive involvement of standard measurement units such as the primary ruler. Activities include comparisons (equal-unequal, bigger-smaller), then simple measurements involving daily encountered manifestations of such continua as time, linear distance, liquids, weight, and money.

Problem Solving

Problem solving at the Introductory level introduces little reading of words, though reading of numbers is involved. When introducing problem solving steps the same four-step sequence is used—moving from manipulation, to pictorialization alone, to pictorialization with numerical notation, and to pure numerical notation. The operations are, of course, limited to those explored at this level, namely, addition and subtraction.

In the early stages, simple word problems are introduced. These are invariably involved with concrete objects and primarily call for comparative relationship solutions. Direct number sentences are then presented. Following this, the pupil is taught to create simple word problems often using pictorial representation of problems as a stimulus. Then, direct number sentences are created from simple word problems which involve only a single step or operation.

Number lines as an aid to problem solving computation are introduced. The child is encouraged to make summation estimations based upon developing understanding of place values and then to check the reasonableness of the estimated answer. Mental, that is nonwritten, computation is urged as part of the shaping process preparing the child for future handling of more abstract data.

Verbal Expression

The most commonly adopted educational approach to teaching arithmetic is that of "guided discovery." Every child needs verbal and written expression to participate in such joint experiences.

At this level of the curriculum, number usage has evolved past the simple recognition and manipulation stage. Numbers become tools of exploration, the means whereby discoveries and solutions are communicated. Simple motor responses or equally simple "yes-no" verbalizations no longer suffice. Therefore, the teacher early in this level begins to model the use of language as a viable part of arithmetic function.

Operations and processes written on the board are verbalized at the same instant, thus providing parallel sensory input for the listening child. The child is then encouraged and directly led to perform the same functions in the parallel modes of doing and verbalizing. Talking problems through and discussing problem solving approaches are introduced as a preliminary step to creating word problems and later number sentences derived from such word problems. Corrective feedback through verbal trial and error problem solving is introduced. Explaining of complex operations and verbalization of abstract ideas becomes an integral part of the curriculum. The child who cannot or will not verbally communicate at this level is faced with almost certain deficit performance evaluation.

POST-INTRODUCTORY LEVEL CURRICULUM CONTENT AREAS

To a large extent, arithmetic at this level represents a simple extension and progression of areas already learned. This is coupled with considerable review, repetition of previously learned algorithms and operations, and reworking of previously solved problem areas.

Yet, despite all the review and relearning, the post-introductory child becomes involved with an arithmetic which is new in form, far more complex in operation, and deliberately more precise in its functions. Two-step problems are solved, and operations are expanded to include multiplication and division, stressing their relationship to the earlier learned operations of addition and subtraction. While earlier experiences were usually oriented around concrete manipulations, work at this level begins to move more toward the abstract, primarily through involving mental problem solving. It is important though that the child is constantly reminded of the everyday applied usefulness of new skills and concepts.

There is a demand for greater precision, application of immutable "laws," and accuracy in the recall and use of number facts. Application of learned rules and algorithms is far less casual at this level as the child is being readied for the more complex concepts and problems to be met in subsequent grades.

Children at this level must begin to use other academic skills such as reading and writing in connection with arithmetic. They are encouraged to accept more responsibility for data collection and fast selection in arithmetic problem solving, and thus develop more independence in their arithmetic work. In this way, arithmetic becomes more an individual skill and less of a group activity than it was earlier when all worked on common problems using teacher-presented data. Yet, in other ways, more group interaction is fostered through developing arithmetic communication skills, learning to give and accept feedback, and cooperate in verbal, nonwritten problem solving.

In summary, this level can be thought of as comprising interrelated yet separate phases. One phase strengthens and reaffirms previously acquired skills and concepts. Another phase opens up almost entirely new vistas relevant to abstract problem solving and far more sophisticated involvement than previously encountered.

The curriculum is divided into four major aspects: operations, algorithm and rule application, written problem-solving and expression, and finally, nonwritten problem solving and expression.

Operations (Multiplication-Division)

As is true with the actual arithmetic steps involved, the operations encountered at this third level are the logical and sequential extensions of those learned previously at earlier levels. Multiplication and then short-division sometime later, are introduced as extensions of different ways to view addition and subtraction.

Multiplication is introduced first by skip-counting, next by the joining of equal sets, then as repeated addition, and finally through use of number lines. Number facts are usually learned in two major groups, most often up to and including the 5X9 facts in the first group, and once these are mastered, going on to 9X9 facts. The commutativity of multiplication is stressed through example and practical activities. Horizontal multiplication is learned first and then vertical algorithms are explored and used. By the end of the level, children are usually multiplying single-factors by some two and three digit numbers (for example, 6X12) with regrouping.

Division follows a similar development. Its relationship to multiplication is first stressed through partitioning and then reforming of sets. Division's relationship to subtraction is stressed as a parallel of multiplication's relationship to addition. The "horizontal-then-vertical" algorithm sequence is also followed in learning to do division problems. Problems first present the child with sample quotients, and then later introduce quotients with remainders.

The same four-step presentation sequence noted in the Introductory level (concrete manipulation, pictorialization, pictorialization with numerical notation, and notation alone) is also used consistently with operations at this level. Throughout the process the naming and labeling of different parts of the operations is emphasized.

The number facts are heavily stressed since progressive involvement with increasingly complex operations assumes the automatic, habitual recall of number facts. To assure this necessary basis for successful use of operations, children encounter frequent review and repetition requiring number facts both with and without subsequent operations.

Rule Application

Although the child is introduced to algorithms and rules early in his school experience, certainly prior to this level, such initial exposure is more casual. Primarily, rote memorization was covered, with little emphasis on exact preciseness regarding how these are used in problem solving. A child may have earlier learned through workbook activities that a penny is smaller in size and value than a nickel, for example. But at this level, the rule must be mastered absolutely and extended through understanding of the simpler meanings of $\frac{1}{5}$, $\frac{2}{5}$, etc., as they relate to use of coins and in solving problems about money.

It is at this stage that such rules and immutable facts of arithmetic thinking must be applied. Sometimes this is only incidentally encountered as a child learns to divide dollars by cents. At other times, it is most central to the problem being solved as the rule denotes the correctness of answers, for example; "How many 1¢ pieces of candy can be bought with a nickel?"

The major areas covered up to and through this level are those related to the four operations (rules of regrouping, the structure of short division, for example); measurement (inches in a foot, centimeters in a meter, minutes in an hour, pints in a quart, ounces in a pound); and geometry (shape, sides and angles, diameter and radius, shape or size congruence, symmetry). Some introduction to area and solid figures may be encountered, but only on a simple level.

Written Problem Solving

Materials, operations, and processes encountered in both Written Problem Solving and Nonwritten Problem-Solving are quite similar. There are, however, some important discriminable behavioral differences. In most classroom learning situations, both teacher and pupil will be using the two modes almost literally at the same time, or at least closely intermeshed. The advantage of dividing the content into two separate areas lies in it being helpful to know whether the child's verbal (auditory input and verbal output) or written (reading and writing) arithmetic behavior is involved. Individual examples as noted in the following two sections should help in that process.

The pupil is taught to code into proper algorithm form material collected through any type of sensory input and to analyze and interpret simple graphs and tables. Labels must be produced and recorded as well as recognized and used.

On the simpler levels, problem solving involved very little reading and almost no written expression outside of plain numerical notation, such as writing down a number as an answer or simple number sentences. At this level, the pupil is increasingly involved with using and producing written material relevant to problem solving. Things must be recorded as a result of what is read, as well as from what is seen or heard. Data for computational use are drawn or collected from written and oral material. The child must be able to read and write word problems and number sentences and to move from one to the other in both reading and writing modes.

In addition to these new forms of problem-solving and expression, the child is required to extend them to the additional operations being learned at this level, to use them in two-step problem solving, and apply them to a variety of practical data areas where they will be encountered. These include such formats as money, time, weight, and linear measurement. Independence in problem solving is introduced since the reading and writing processes are more individual and private. Data or operational steps are increasingly drawn from written material at a more individualized pace than was true of the more common oral inputs of the previous level.

Nonwritten problem solving

In one way, the material encountered in this area at the Post-Introductory level is a simple extension of verbal expression at the Introductory level. The child is encouraged to verbalize his or her arithmetic actions, to elicit and give feedback, and to explain operations and ideas. The differences are primarily in the number and complexity of the operations involved, in the interaction of this area with other areas, and in the less frequent use of redundant input through parallel systems. For example, problems will be encountered and discussed without simultaneous visualization.

The operations are increased from two to four (including division and multiplication now) with considerable emphasis on being able to orally relate the relationship between simpler operations and the newer more complex ones (addition and multiplication, for example). The child must be able to verbally interpret that which is heard or read and must be able to verbally supply missing data, operations, or other relevant information.

Logical thinking, sensible estimation, and nonwritten problem solving become more prominent in arithmetic problem solving and the child is required to develop the necessary vocabulary and expressional skills to communicate information about these things.

More and more experience is presented with data collection in areas of money, time, measurement, weight, etc., preparing the child for using arithmetic as a tool in problems of everyday living. Therefore, an additional list of labels and names are encountered and the use of these new symbols in arithmetic problem solving is explored extensively in a verbal as well as written format.

Because of the increased emphasis on reading and writing skills, the child is faced with the need for a more ranging and more precisely meaningful verbal expression ability. Then, privately encountered data and information can be transmitted rapidly to others for both problem solving and feedback purposes. These skills are practiced extensively at this level.

LEARNING DISABILITY TYPES

As listed in Figure 3-3, eight separate specific learning disability types have been selected for inclusion here. These do not actually portray or represent in any definitive manner a specific demonstrable categorization of learning disabilities similar to what one might find in a listing of types of well-defined medical problems with proven etiologies or well-established aberrant behavior syndromes. Stringent, fixed labeling and categorization type have never proven to be very meaningful in treating learning disabilities and have been quite legitimately subject to attack when used. The "types" mentioned or used here only represent broad observable groups of deficit behaviors included in some form or another in almost every published list of LD diagnostic classifications, problem lists, or areas of major concern.

Different theorists would establish different hierarchies of importance for the areas included. Certain types might be excluded by some, while it is certainly conceivable that additional types might be included by others.

The eight types offered in this strategy are used because of the general consensus that they are problem behaviors observable in many learning disabled children. They represent the most commonly reported concerns of elementary level educators as observed in the firsthand clinical experience of the author. They can be seen to be interacting with the arithmetic curriculum areas of the elementary school, and they lend themselves to on-the-scene diagnostic and remedial activities. Briefly described, the eight types are:

Memory Disabilities

These are personified by those children who find it difficult to recall on demand or adequately remember bits of recently acquired information which may be necessary for immediate problem solving of a variety of types. Teachers frequently anecdotally describe children experiencing this type of difficulty by saying, "He's smart enough, and can do lots of things, but when you tell him something new or when he hears or reads something new, it just seems to go in one ear and out the other."

Visual-Auditory Discrimination Disabilities

This type problem consists primarily of difficulty in performing useful comparisons to establish like or unlike judgments. Almost all basic pedagogical tasks involve some aspect of discrimination as a primary component of successful performance. As can be seen in later materials in this book, disabilities of this type are a near-fatal threat to adequate arithmetic performance.

Visual-Auditory Association Disabilities

When a teacher describes a child by saying, "She just can't seem to put two and two together unless it is staring her in the face!" it is likely that association difficulties are being noted. Associations of visual and auditory stimuli function in almost every aspect of arithmetic and mathematics apart from the simplest of the elementary readiness steps. Association behavior represents an ability to deal in abstractions and usually some form of symbolization—both fundamental components of arithmetic.

Perceptual-Motor Disabilities

While the exact nature and importance of the perceptual motor skills in the total learning disability field is currently being debated, there is no argument that much of the performance behaviors necessary in arithmetic (everything from writing numbers to moving decimal points) demands activity of this type. Problems affecting this segment of learning behavior present major hurdles to the developing arithmetic pupil.

Spatial Awareness and Orientation Disabilities

Some theoretical approaches place this type of problem behavior as a subset of the perceptual motor area, and indeed it may well be. In arithmetic behavior, however, there are sufficient temporal, spatial, and orientational factors in the many conceptualizations and operations included in the curriculum to warrant a separate categorization for prescriptive diagnostic purposes. Telling time, simple geometry, and the whole prepositional vocabulary of position interact with this type.

Verbal Expression Disabilities

Inability to express ideas is of concern when viewed in any part of the elementary school curriculum. Of particular concern to the arithmetic teacher is the inability to communicate information or request information necessary for successful choice of appropriate operations and arithmetic problem solving. Inability to adequately speak or write arithmetic information is a severe handicap to the young elementary school child.

Closure and Generalization

Much of arithmetic, and subsequently mathematical conceptualization, involves as a basic ingredient the ability to extrapolate upon or interpolate within an established set of data or information. Closure or generalization problems (called convergence and divergence in some approaches) prevents the child from moving beyond a 1:1 use of arithmetic information and ideas. The child is confined to the "here and now," demonstrably present, information. Therefore, the child experiences difficulty with virtually all the refined analytical processes of arithmetic and mathematics. Such a simple concept as the relationship of two halves to a whole involves both of these aspects.

Attending Disabilities

Practical clinical experience has led the author to believe that a significant proportion of learning disabilities involve a failure to apply or a misapplication of the basic strategies of selective attention on the part of the learner. Many failures to learn seem to occur at least partly because the child is deficient in attending behaviors. Selective attending with its concomitant role in filtering out extraneous information and focusing on pertinent facts, is a vital prerequisite to arithmetic adequacy. Deficit behaviors in this type of disability can easily be seen interacting destructively with defined portions of the elementary arithmetic curriculum.

It should be noted that problems in attending have not been subcategorized on the Introductory and Post-Introductory levels for two reasons:

1 If attending disabilities still exist at these two levels, they tend to be so generalized as to be observable throughout each separate aspect of the curriculum.

2 If the teacher is uncertain as to whether or not the problem is one of deficit attention, the diagnostic steps outlined at the Readiness level may be either applied directly or easily expanded to evaluate children at the two subsequent levels.

Chapter 7

Pre-School Readiness Level Materials

Curriculum Areas	(1) Memory	(2) Visual-Auditory Discrimination	(3) Visual-Auditory Association	(4) Perceptual-Motor	(5) Spatial Orientation	(6) Verbal Expression	(7) Closure and Generalization	(8) Attention
(A) Number Recognition	A1 p. 100	A2 p. 102	A3 p. 105	A4 p. 107	A5 p. 109	A6 p. 111	A7 p. 113	A8 p. 116
(B) Counting	B1 p. 118	B2 p. 120	B3 p. 122	B4 p. 125	B5 p. 127	B6 p. 130	B7 p. 131	B8 p. 134
(C) Grouping	C1 p. 136	C2 p. 138	C3 p. 140	C4 p. 142	C5 p. 143	C6 p. 145	C7 p. 147	C8 p. 149
(D) Relationship Vocabulary	D1 p. 151	D2 p. 154	D3 p. 156	D4 p. 158	D5 p. 160	D6 p. 162	D7 p. 164	D8 p. 166
(E) Verbal Expression	E1 p. 167	E2 p. 170	E3 p. 172	E4 p. 174	E5 p. 176	E6 p. 178	E7 p. 179	E8 p. 181

Learning Disability Types

Figure 7.1 *Pre-school readiness locator chart*

CURRICULUM AREA:
Number Recognition

LEARNING DISABILITY TYPE:
Memory

Pre-School **A–1**

Problem-free behavior

The child can, on request, accurately recall number recognition concepts (names or labels) recently learned or encountered.

Sample task where deficit child may display difficulty

In a classroom activity the child has practiced matching spoken number names to arabic symbols, for example, "Four means the same as 4." Following the exercise the child is required to answer the question, "What is the name of the number I have written on the blackboard?"

Do-it-yourself diagnostic activities

Choose one child to be the "dog trainer." Call on several children to play the "dogs" in this game. Whisper a number between one and ten to each child and instruct him* to be sure to remember his number. The "dogs" walk around in a circle until the trainer calls on, points to, or taps a child. The child who is chosen must step out of the circle and either say his number or point to it among an array of numbers written on blackboard or on posted flashcards. The trainer may also be called upon to display a flashcard number at which point the child given that number steps out of line and says, "I am number _____."

---

*Throughout this section the masculine pronouns are used purely for convenience. Obviously there is no logic for assuming that the activities covered or the problems defined are relegated to one sex or the other.

Non-arithmetic situations where similar behaviors are required

Children having problems may find it difficult to apply a labeling or naming skill apparently learned to criterion previously. For example, a child may have apparently learned that four is the same as 4, or that drawing tools are in blue boxes, but when, at a later time, the same child is directed to go to drawer four or to the blue drawer, he may show confusion. The observer should be sure that the difficulty rises out of memory of recognized objects or symbols and not from misunderstood directions or similar problems.

Remedial objective for confirmed problems

The child will be provided with progressively demanding practice in recalling number names and labels recently encountered or learned.

Sample remedial activity

Specific memory demands are placed upon the pupil by regularly requiring him to recall numbers encountered in the classroom. The activity may be informally carried out by using number presentations included in normal classroom activities, e.g., by the teacher noting on the blackboard the number of tulips brought to class by a pupil that morning, or the number of pupils wishing to buy milk that day.

Two main steps are involved:

1 Shaping

Stage 1: Immediately after the number has been presented, the pupil is asked to recall that number. Reinforcement for correct responses is important. Errors should be followed by, "No, the number was _____." (Use no emphasis on the error response.) Then the entire procedure should be repeated. Errors may be initially reduced by using single numbers and obviously emphasized presentations.

Stage 2: As criterion level recall is produced, the length of time between presentation and recall is progressively increased in small incremental time steps. It will be helpful at this stage to alert the child that subsequent recall will be called for, thus helping the pupil to develop memory intent in noting numbers.

Stage 3: Recall demands should shift to an irregular schedule with such demands being presented at varying time lengths, sometimes even running into the following day(s).

2 Performance Practice

Once criterion levels have been obtained in the shaping procedure the child should regularly be given practice through requiring performance of the newly acquired ability to further strengthen the learned behavior. This can also be done by occasionally asking informal questions such as, "What is the number on the door of our classroom?" or "What number did I write on the blackboard when I was talking about triangles?"

CURRICULUM AREA:
Number Recognition

LEARNING DISABILITY TYPE:
Visual-Auditory Discrimination

Pre-School **A–2**

Problem-free behavior

The child can select from a group of numbers those which match or fail to match a model.

Sample task where deficit child may display difficulty

Given a deck of number flashcards, the child can either place those which are alike together, or correctly match each card to a displayed array of numbers.

Do-it-yourself diagnostic activities

Tell the children that they are going to play "Postman." Prepare ten picture houses numbered one to ten, with pockets beneath each house. Hang the pictures on a bulletin board or lay them on a table in random order. Also prepare ten envelopes numbered one to ten. Be sure that the numbers on the envelopes are the same size, shape, and color as those on the houses so that the task is a matching, not an association, one. Place the envelopes in a small bag which will be used as the mailbag. Pick out an envelope or have the child pick out one and "deliver" it (point to or otherwise identify to which house it should go).

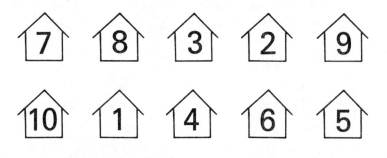

Non-arithmetic situations where similar behaviors are required

Though a child may be quite able to rotely recite his home phone number, he may have difficulty finding or selecting the correct numbers on the phone dial. Similarly, the child may experience difficulty in correctly identifying his own numbered coat hook, clothes basket, or schoolroom number—even though he may be able to recite the correct numbers when asked. If the problem is in the auditory area, the child may be confused by such questions as, "Do you live on Maple Street?" or "Is your telephone number 555-1234?"

Remedial objective for confirmed problems

The child will be provided with practice in selecting from an array of numbers presented visually or orally those which match or fail to match a designated model.

Sample remedial activity

The teacher should be concerned primarily with the child's retention of previously learned material in order for discrimination to take place. One way to focus on this is to present increasingly complex discrimination tasks. Do not expect the child with a deficit in this area to remember a large amount of detail or complexity. Start with what the child can remember and add increasingly complex problems (or figures). The following worksheet examples demonstrate such a process.

Direct the child to put a circle around the line which is the same as the number in the box. (If eye-hand coordination necessary for using the pencil is not adequate, flashcards or flannelgraph numbers may be used.)

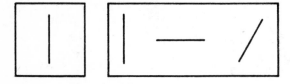

The next phase will be telling the child to put a circle around the number which is the same as the number in the box. This should be repeated for each number 1 through 9. The task may start with 2 numerals most easily discriminated (1, 8) and then proceed to more difficult discriminations (3, 8).

| 4 | | 3 | 3 | 3 | 3 | 4 | 3 |

Increasing difficulty in discrimination decisions is introduced next. Tell the child to put a circle around the number which is the same as the number in the box. (If additional worksheets are needed, the entire series may be repeated with the child being asked to circle those which are *not* like the model.)

| 4 | | 1 | 2 | 3 | 4 | 5 | 6 | 7 | 8 | 9 |

CURRICULUM AREA:
Number Recognition

LEARNING DISABILITY TYPE:
Visual-Auditory Association

Pre-School **A–3**

Problem-free behavior

The child is capable of number usage (identification, matching, naming, etc.) even though the presented numerical symbols may be of different size, texture, intensity, or be displayed in a different number of dimensions (for example, two dimensional vs. three).

Sample task where deficit child may display difficulty

The child is required to match flashcard numbers with spoken numbers or three-dimensional block numbers.

Do-it-yourself diagnostic activities

Using a plywood sheet with at least five rows of five nails each (use finishing nails which have no sharp, flat heads) and some yarn, make a number on the board. Give the child two flashcards with numbers on them, one of which matches the number on the board. Ask the child to show or tell you the number on the card which is the same as that made on the board. Vary the size and color of the yarn numbers and their position on the board.

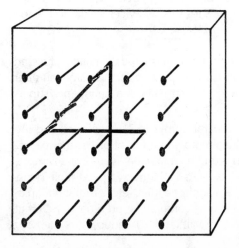

Non-arithmetic situations where similar behaviors are required

Children suffering from a deficit in this area may display remarkably different levels of number recognition performance in different contexts, such as home and school environments, or when different media (printed worksheets as opposed to blackboard presentations) are used. This is because matching has not been learned except on a direct 1:1 basis when all properties are identical, rather than through recognition of the number itself. The problem frequently generalizes to labels and names of all types. Thus, a child may be able to point out various athletic equipment, such as a kickball, but have trouble choosing the correct ball to use for that purpose once on the gym floor.

Remedial objective for confirmed problems

The child will be provided with practice in associating numerical similarity even though the context and form in which the numbers appear may vary greatly.

Sample remedial activity

The child must first be shown by example and demonstration that numbers may be formed in different sizes and styles. It must also be demonstrated that numbers appear in many different contexts without changing themselves. Magazine and newspaper ads offer many opportunities for this. Activities similar to the following may be used:

1 Using number flashcards, a child is directed to circle with a crayon the same number wherever it appears in a newspaper supermarket ad.

2 A numeral from 1 to 10 is selected and the child attempts to think of places that particular number might be seen. For example, "5" is seen in highway speed limit signs, on a telephone dial, etc. "Situation" pictures or photographs presenting a target context will tend to reduce the memory factor.

CURRICULUM AREA:
Number Recognition

LEARNING DISABILITY TYPE:
Perceptual-Motor Use

Pre-School **A–4**

Problem-free behavior

The child can demonstrate ability in working with number recognition through use of perceptual-motor skills.

Sample task where deficit child may display difficulty

The child is asked to correctly identify or choose a number by crossing it out on a worksheet; or, if the number is a wood or cardboard cutout, selecting and picking it up.

Do-it-yourself diagnostic activities

Direct the child to join in group "airwriting" of numbers. Stand alongside the pupils or in front of them, facing the same direction, and demonstrate airwriting by drawing large sweeping figures in the air. A 4, for example, should be written with the finger and arm so it is almost two feet high. Random numbers are selected and individuals should be observed. Ordinary paper and pencil or blackboard writing of numbers may also be used, but may be somewhat more threatening to the deficit child, resulting in more inhibited behavior examples.

Non-arithmetic situations where similar behaviors are required

Sometimes a breakdown will occur in what appears to be a perceptual-motor application of number information the child apparently knows. Such a child, for example, knows the correct TV channel for a favorite program but always asks someone else to turn the channel selector.

Remedial objective for confirmed problems

The child will be provided with practice using perceptual-motor skills in the process of recognizing numbers. Care must be taken to assure that both the perceptual-motor and number recognition behaviors are a part of any remedial activity.

Sample remedial activity

A child should be encouraged to participate in as many movement exercises as possible. The development of the muscles will help the child move easily into many activities. For example, write a number on the chalkboard. Ask the child to imagine that he has a large board in front of him. Using a beanbag as chalk, he is to "write" the number. Encourage the child to "write" as large as possible at first. Then direct him to do the same exercise on the floor. Next, the child can be asked to write with hands, elbows, feet, etc.

Other activities might include finger writing in the sand, or tracing large numbers drawn on the sidewalk, blackboard, or large sheets of newsprint.

CURRICULUM AREA:
Number Recognition

LEARNING DISABILITY TYPE:
Spatial Orientation

Pre-School **A–5**

Problem-free behavior

The child can consistently produce (select from samples, write, point to, etc.) numbers in their correct spatial orientation.

Sample task where deficit child may display difficulty

Ask the child, "Which of these numbers is standing up straight?" He should correctly identify the arrowed "4."

Do-it-yourself diagnostic activities

Using cutout cardboard numbers or a worksheet, present numbers in various rotated positions and ask the child to identify the number which is correctly positioned. For example, ask the child to circle the 6 which is standing up straight in Line A, or to circle the 5 which is standing on its head in Line B.

A.

B.

Non-arithmetic situations where similar behaviors are required

Any type of inversion error may be indicative of this problem. These may occur in the typical academic areas such as numbers (confusing 9 for 6) or letters (confusing b for d). Errors may also be seen in confused handedness, positional directions (such as placing an object "behind" something as opposed to in "front," or pasting a picture on "front" of a book instead of on the "back"), or even sometimes in dressing habits such as getting shoes on the wrong feet or coats on upside down.

Remedial objective for confirmed problems

The child will be provided with practice recognizing or creating the correct spatial orientation in number recognition. Substrategies may involve shaping either the recognition of different spatial or positional orientations in numbers or in developing an awareness of the importance of such orientations to number recognition.

Sample remedial activity

The activities should focus on the child's understanding of spatial concepts. Only with full awareness of what each spatial concept means in terms of real-life situations will the child ever be able to efficiently use the concepts when needed. These opportunities to demonstrate acquired conceptual understanding of spatial concepts must be presented so that the amount of understanding present does not have to be inferred. Exercises may need to be repeated several times to provide the child with sufficient time to thoroughly learn the spatial concepts involved.

The sample remedial activity requires the teacher to direct the child to circle or indicate all the numbers which are standing up.

4 ო ㄥ 3 2 ை 5 ∞ 9 ᴎ 1

The next phase is to tell the child to circle or indicate all the numbers which are upside down.

Finally, direct the child to circle or indicate all the numbers which are backwards. (This activity should vary from circling not only the correct numbers, but also circling the incorrectly-oriented numbers.)

CURRICULUM AREA:
Number Recognition

LEARNING DISABILITY TYPE:
Verbal Expression

Pre-School A–6

Problem-free behavior

The child can verbally express answers to number recognition problems.

Sample task where deficit child may display difficulty

Presented with a flashcard showing a single number, ask the child to respond aloud with the correct nominal label. For example, show the child a 3, and ask, "What number is this?" The child should then respond, "That is a three."

Do-it-yourself diagnostic activities

Almost any number game requiring only verbal responses can be used. The "Postman" game previously cited can be used by having the child verbally announce the house to which a letter should go. Identification of the house and verbal involvement is increased if each house has both a number and an animal's picture on it.

Non-arithmetic situations where similar behaviors are required

When a child's verbal expression is underdeveloped or presenting problems, he or she may commonly resort to a substituted motor response. This might include pointing to answers or writing answers when solving problems dealing with numbers. The child will avoid, whenever possible, the use of the verbal response mode.

Remedial objective for confirmed problems

The child will be provided with practice and experience in using the verbal expression mode in number recognition, that is, in learning and using the verbal labels by which numbers are recognized.

Sample remedial activity

These activities are used to develop the child's verbal expression of recognized numbers. In the classroom, the child should be occasionally given the opportunity for leadership to increase his use of verbal commands. Classroom situations should be structured so that the child exhibiting deficit behaviors must voice answers as often as possible. The child's use of written or nonverbal communication should not be reinforced.

One activity includes having the children make construction paper balloons of different colors. Each child is assigned a number to write on his balloon. The child with deficit behavior should be called on to identify the numbers on each child's balloon. This activity may first be used in a small group to give the child practice.

For an individual exercise, tell a child to assign numbers to figures in a story picture. Then ask him to describe the activity of each figure, using the characteristic number instead of name.

CURRICULUM AREA:
Number Recognition

LEARNING DISABILITY TYPE:
Closure and Generalization   Pre-School **A–7**

Problem-free behavior

The child can recognize a number when only part of the number is seen, or can subdivide a number into its parts.

Sample task where deficit child may display difficulty

When visually presented a dotted-line number, ask the child to correctly identify it or point out subparts peculiar to a certain number. For example, ask the child to add the missing part to a vertical line to transform a 1 into a 4. Also ask the child to point out subparts—such as the two circles which comprise an 8.

Do-it-yourself diagnostic activities

A number of activities are possible, each involving the use of incomplete numbers which the child identifies. Activity A includes presenting cards to the child which have dotted numbers on them. Instruct the child to complete the numbers. In activity B, the child is also told to complete a number made on a pegboard. Activity C consists of asking the child to finish an incomplete number on the blackboard or in a sandbox. At a more difficult level, ask the child to construct numbers from straight lines and arcs, as shown in activity D.

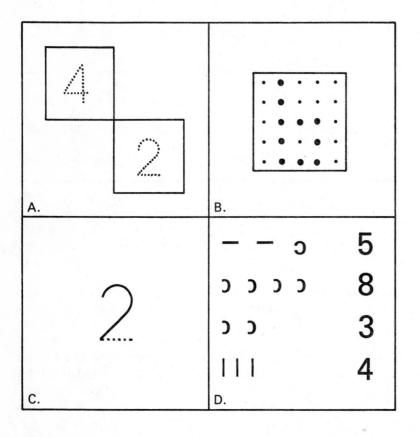

Non-arithmetic situations where similar behaviors are required

The child having problems in this area may take an unusually long period of time and may exhibit air writing, finger tracing, or physical reconstruction of missing parts when trying to identify numbers, symbols, or a labeling cue.

Remedial objective for confirmed problems

The child will be provided with practice in becoming familiar with the parts of numerals which assist in his identification and then in actually using these parts to acquire recognition skills.

Sample remedial activity

When given only part of a number or geometric shape the deficit child has difficulty recognizing what the whole number is. Remediation exercises consist of gradually reducing the portion of a number needed to be seen for recognition. Be sure to start the child with shapes or numbers he consistently recognizes before removing any portion. The following activity is an example of such a gradual reduction of the whole. (Jigsaw puzzles involving numbers are also useful.)

Give the child a sheet of paper with dotted numbers on it. The numbers should progressively have fewer dots. Tell the child, "These numbers have part of their lines gone. Trace over the number until it is all there and then tell me what the number is."

CURRICULUM AREA:
Number Recognition

LEARNING DISABILITY TYPE:
Attention

Problem-free behavior

The child's attention to number recognition problem solving procedures and details maintains a consistent quality throughout an exercise.

Sample task where deficit child may display difficulty

Direct the child to respond when it is his turn to name a number presented on a flashcard. Establish some order to the presentation, then randomly call on children. When the objective of the exercise is shifted to pointing out the discriminating aspects of numbers (names, angles, arcs, etc.), the child should attend to appropriate details.

Do-it-yourself diagnostic activities

During a flashcard exercise, start out by calling on children in some set order to name the number presented. This might be done by calling on all the boys first, all the girls first, or the order in which they are sitting. Then deviate from this pattern to test the child being screened to see if he can respond even though he didn't expect to be called on. The focus is not on remembering the number, but rather on his attention behaviors. In other exercises, strategies or clues to recognition may be given (for example, "Say 'yes' if this number has a circle in it."). Ability to follow the shift in focus and demand precludes attention difficulties in number recognition.

Non-arithmetic situations where similar behaviors are required

Highly inconsistent number recognition behavior is a clue to this type of problem, particularly if performance levels out when attention is forced by the teacher playing an authoritarian role or by giving focused individual supervision. "Silly" mistakes in confusing numbers differing in almost every property (for example, mistaking 1 with 8) may also indicate attention problems if other deficits are absent.

Remedial objective for confirmed problems

The child will be provided with practice in maintaining or shifting attention as it is characteristically relevant to number recognition.

Sample remedial activity

A child will miss much usable information in the classroom if he is not attending to what the teacher is saying or if he is not focusing where being directed. A child who has this problem needs additional help in knowing when and where to pay attention. The use of cues before a teacher calls on the child form the basis of the following activity.

Engage in any questioning activity typical to the classroom. Before directly querying the deficit child, give that child a cue that you are going to call on him for an answer. The cue could be a piano chord, a bell ring, a knock on the blackboard, pointing, etc. Pair the cue with the child's name and ask him a question. If he responds, give him verbal praise like, "I'm glad you were paying attention." If the child does not respond, try the cue and his name again, tap him on the shoulder, or backtrack one step and start again.

After a fair amount of questions (so that the child is responding regularly), reduce the use of the cue, using it every fourth time the child is called on, for example. Continue to use the child's name and an attention-getting tone of voice.

Once the child demonstrates general attending behaviors, repeat the procedure with statements, directions, and questions involving numbers. Typical explanations may include, "I'm going to point to several shapes on this page. Some of them are numbers. When I point to a number I'm going to ask someone to name it."

CURRICULUM AREA:
Counting

LEARNING DISABILITY TYPE:
Memory

Pre-School **B–1**

Problem-free behavior

The child is able to recall an amount of objects recently counted.

Sample task where deficit child may display difficulty

Tell the child to count certain objects at the back of the classroom (bottles of glue, scissors, boxes of straws, etc.), and ask him to remember the number counted. Another method might be asking the child to correctly report to the office the number of absences counted in class.

Do-it-yourself diagnostic activities

Place three or more objects on a table in front of the child and have him or her count them. Cover the objects, wait five seconds, and with the objects still covered, ask the child how many objects there were.

Non-arithmetic situations where similar behaviors are required

Inability to accurately recall recent past experiences which have numbered properties (such as not remembering how many fire engines were seen on a field trip) may indicate a deficit in this interaction area if similar memory problems are not encountered when numbers are uninvolved and if there is no question of number recognition ability.

Remedial objective for confirmed problems

The child will be provided with practice in remembering information gained through counting.

Sample remedial activity

For more complex arithmetic skills to develop, the foundations of counting must be strong. The child who cannot remember how many objects he just counted cannot be expected to do well in addition or subtraction, for example. This fundamental skill must be developed to the degree where the child no longer is concerned about remembering recently counted objects. In the following activity, the increasing length of time between the counting of items and recall should be carefully noted so as not to be too quickly paced for the child.

Tell the child to listen carefully while you bounce a ball any number of times. Immediately ask the child to count how many times the ball was bounced. The amount of time between bouncing the ball and asking the child for the count should be slowly increased, a little at a time.

The activity can be expanded into a group game. One child bounces a ball X times and calls on another child for the count. If the second child answers correctly, that child can bounce the ball again and call on another player. Delay of response can be introduced very naturally by having the choosing child look at every other child at least once before making a choice.

CURRICULUM AREA:
Counting

LEARNING DISABILITY TYPE:
Auditory-Visual Discrimination

Problem-free behavior

A child can discriminate between or match sets of objects on the basis of different or same amounts.

Sample task where deficit child may display difficulty

Place five beads on a string and direct the child to match it. The child should be capable of doing so.

Do-it-yourself diagnostic activities

Tell the children that they are going to play "Milkman." Prepare outline pictures of several houses with cutout faces pasted inside the house. The number of faces should vary from house to house. The children are given small boxes containing pictures or cutouts of milk bottles, boxes of eggs, and packages of butter. The purpose of the game is to deliver the correct number of milk bottles, eggs, or pounds of butter, to match the people living in a house.

Non-arithmetic situations where similar behaviors are required

A subtle indication of problems may be seen in confusion in following ordered sequential directions, such as "First shut the door, then take off your coat," or "Put the block with the one on it on the bottom of the pile, the block with a two next, etc." The child can remember the separate parts but the ordering of directions, a subset of counting, proves difficult. The child is unaware that the order of his behavior does not match the order of directions given.

Remedial objective for confirmed problems

The child will be provided with practice in visual or auditory matching activities where counting behavior is a necessary prerequisite to successful performance.

Sample remedial activity

Activities similar to the diagnostic activity will help the deficit child. Additionally, any game which requires the players to have a given number of pieces to start (such as checkers) is helpful. Although most regular games of this type are too advanced for the typical readiness child, made-up games are simple to construct. A practical game with eventual far-reaching useful generalization is "Store." The child purchases grocery products (cutout cardboard pictures will do) with a specified number of tokens. The products should have the "price" marked by a label carrying the appropriate number of marks. For example, mark a loaf of bread xxx, not 3.

CURRICULUM AREA:
Counting

LEARNING DISABILITY TYPE:
Visual-Auditory Association

Pre-School **B-3**

Problem-free behavior

The child can relate common quantities in different sets of objects though the context or nature of the two sets may share no other logical relationships.

Sample task where deficit child may display difficulty

Ask the child to correctly identify a matching set in worksheet problems.

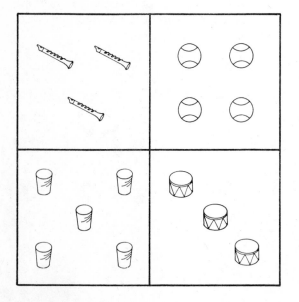

Do-it-yourself diagnostic activities

Any activity may be used where a child is visually or orally presented with a number and then asked to count out an equal number of objects. Many common opportunities of this type can be found in the typical classroom day.

For a more formal approach, present a worksheet with at least four sections. In the top of each section draw a number of objects with the numbers one through ten below them. Ask the child to circle the number which is the same as the number of objects presented.

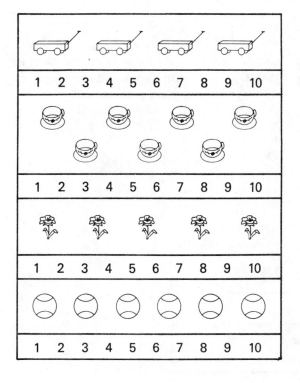

Non-arithmetic situations where similar behaviors are required

This problem may surface in a child's failure to perceive errors in matching to a quantity model. An example of this may be the child not obtaining the right number of napkins to match the number of children drinking juice. Similar situations may occur where number is the only or main quantity held in common by different sets of objects.

Remedial objective for confirmed problems

The child will be provided with activities involving grouping and categorizing where counting provides the necessary decision making information.

Sample remedial activity

Give the child practice in recognizing that subsets can be grouped together on the basis of quantity. The ability to count the items in each set is a necessary prerequisite.

Question and answer sessions involving questions such as, "Which of these pictures have two animals in them?" will be helpful. Or, more motor-directed responses may be used as in telling the child to draw a line connecting the two sets that have the same number of items.

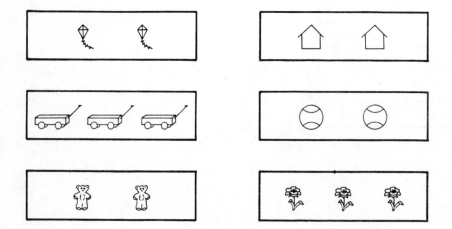

CURRICULUM AREA:
Counting

LEARNING DISABILITY TYPE:
Perceptual-Motor Use

Pre-School **B–4**

Problem-free behavior	The child can demonstrate counting activities by using motor responses.
Sample task where deficit child may display difficulty	On request, direct the child to hold up the proper number of fingers to match a number on the blackboard, or cut and paste on paper the correct number of circles or squares in response to oral directions.
Do-it-yourself diagnostic activities	Oral directions for this activity may be used or a set of prepared cards with two columns may be used. On one side, list or picture some activities such as tapping, jumping, or clapping. On the other side, place a number which indicates the number of times each activity should be done. Name an activity or have the children draw a card and have the children perform the activity the required number of times.
Non-arithmetic situations where similar behaviors are required	The major observed difference between this and the association-counting interaction area is that this deficit child can and may count and identify common "countable" properties, but he may not be able to match them with motor performance. Thus, the child may be able to tell you how many scissors to lay out to be sure every child has a pair, but he will fall down in the actual process of counting out the correct number from the drawer.

Remedial objective for confirmed problems

The child will be provided with practice and experience in counting where perceptual-motor activities are used to enumerate the objects counted.

Sample remedial activity

These exercises should be at a simple level so the child may easily obtain competency in them. This will help keep the child's motivation high for the rest of the remedial activities in an area which is not itself necessarily exciting.

Using bean bags and a wastebasket, children can be allowed to play "basketball" with a given number of turns or shots providing the necessary experience.

Another activity might include having two or more children roll a ball back and forth between themselves. Instruct them to keep track of the number of times they can do so without missing and to then mark that number on a printed sheet of numbers.

Though the game of jacks is too physically advanced for most children of this age, a similar game is a useful remedial activity. Ask the children to see how many blocks they can count and pick up and put in a box within some defined time period.

CURRICULUM AREA:
Counting

LEARNING DISABILITY TYPE:
Spatial Orientation

Problem-free behavior

The child is able to place or direct the arrangement of tangible examples of integers into their proper order or position.

Sample task where deficit child may display difficulty

Pose the following problems either using flannel board forms, flashcards, or worksheets. The child should provide the correct number(s).

Tell the child to fill in the missing numbers:

A ___, 6, ___
B 7, ___, 9

Ask the child how many of the numbers are standing up.

A. 3 3 ω 3 ω ω

B. 4 4 4 4 4 4

Do-it-yourself diagnostic activities

For this activity, make dot-to-dot drawings by tracing a simple drawing using dots instead of lines. Number the dots in the correct sequence. (Commercially-prepared dot-to-dot pictures may be used also.) Ask the child to connect the dots. Any discrepancies should be noted.

Non-arithmetic situations where similar behaviors are required

Difficulty in correctly following dot-to-dot drawing patterns is a simple but good clue to difficulties. Unusual inability to recognize differentiation of separate parts of a picture to be colored (failing to see that a tree is separate from a roof and therefore should be a different color) is another.

Remedial objective for confirmed problems

The child will be provided with practice recognizing or giving the correct serial position or order in counting.

Sample remedial activity

It may be necessary to first present a few two- or three-item sequences before attempting the following remediation activities. The use of comic strips as examples of a sequence of events might also be a helpful first step. The following activities start on a simple dot sequence and gradually develop into the more complex sequence of numbers. Worksheet exercises provide practice in sequencing by number, first with objects all alike, then with different shapes, then with numbers, etc.

Direct the child to start with the box containing one circle and then draw a line to the box with two circles, then three circles, and so on. As the exercise progresses, move to an unordered sequence.

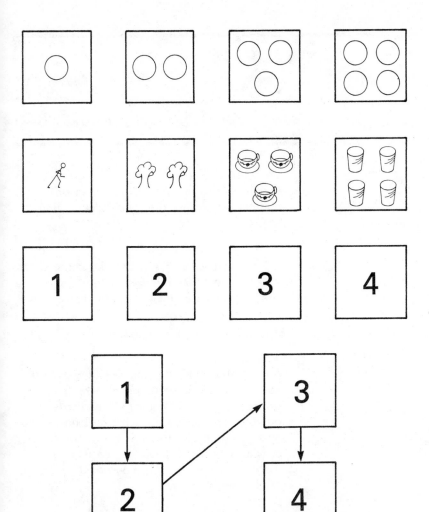

CURRICULUM AREA:
Counting

LEARNING DISABILITY TYPE:
Verbal Expression

Pre-School **B–6**

Problem-free behavior	The child is able to count aloud from 1 to 10 and is able to demonstrate aloud how a total number was obtained through silent counting.
Sample task where deficit child may display difficulty	When the child is asked how he counted ten erasers, he should be able to demonstrate orally how the total of ten erasers was achieved.
Do-it-yourself diagnostic activities	Almost any number game requiring only verbal response can be used. For example, hold up a flashcard and call on a child to say the number. Then have that child call on a classmate and tell him to clap (or do some other activity) that many times. The focus here is on the child giving the directions rather than the child receiving them.
Non-arithmetic situations where similar behaviors are required	A child encountering difficulties in this area may too often depend on a motor or written response to a question which asks for counting information. If asked, "How old are you?" the child will respond only by holding up fingers or by writing the answer.
Remedial objective for confirmed problems	The child will be provided with experience in counting aloud or in reporting totals reached by silent counting.

Sample remedial activity

The child with this deficit must be regularly urged to verbalize. Even if the activity does not include arithmetic concepts, the child should be encouraged to orally explain as he performs. Discourage motor demonstration unless accompanied with a verbal explanation. Give the child obvious attention and verbal praise for his first few attempts at verbalization and continue to intermittently reinforce these efforts.

Activities that incorporate counting and verbal skills include songs and chants such as "One potato, two potato, three potato, four . . ." or "One little, two little, three little Indians . . .", and many of the rhythmic chants used with jumping rope.

CURRICULUM AREA:
Counting

LEARNING DISABILITY TYPE:
Closure and Generalization

Pre-School **B–7**

Problem-free behavior

The child is able to pick up and complete a counting sequence already in process.

Sample task where deficit child may display difficulty

Ask the child to "count off" or complete the 1 to 10 process when a preceding child has already counted part of the sequence.

Do-it-yourself diagnostic activities

Seat ten or fewer children in a circle. Direct a randomly chosen child to begin a count off around the circle. Tell the other children to orally call out the next number in sequence when it is their turn. This exercise can be repeated several times, with a different child each time starting the count off.

Number blocks may be presented in a left-to-right sequence which have the first few numbers and the last number in a series. The child should be told to fill in the missing numbers.

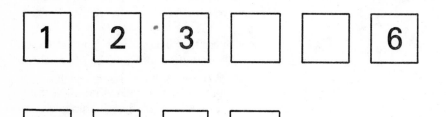

Non-arithmetic situations where similar behaviors are required

Responding out of turn even if the activity involves no counting per se may be the result of a deficit in this area. Inability to explain or figure out "what comes next" in a sequence of events is also a warning sign.

Remedial objective for confirmed problems

The child will be provided with practice in completing number sequences or in filling in missing parts of a counting sequence.

Sample remedial activity

Remedial activities for this deficit behavior should focus on the correct completion of a series or sequence. It may be necessary to start off at a very simple level, for instance, "What comes after 1, 2, _____?" Sequences should also be included that are not necessarily arithmetically oriented, but which the child encounters frequently, such as: getting dressed, tying shoes, and eating lunch. Discuss with the child what motions he uses to complete the activity and the order in which they are done.

Activities may include opportunities in picking up a counting sequence when a group counts off. Or, using cards representing consecutive sets of increasing quantity, ask the child to continue a sequence or fill in the missing card. For example:

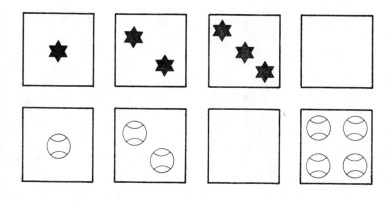

Another activity might include having the children sit in a circle. Give one child a card to hold to clearly mark him as number one. The other children have no identifying cards. After the children have all assumed a sequential number identity, ask one of them to step into the middle of the circle. The children, by counting off, are to try to determine which "bird" has flown away.

CURRICULUM AREA:
Counting

LEARNING DISABILITY TYPE:
Attention

Problem-free behavior	The child pays attention to an entire sequence of enumeration.
Sample task where deficit child may display difficulty	When the class or teacher is counting off and it's the child's turn he must respond promptly and appropriately.
Do-it-yourself diagnostic activities	Have the children sit in a circle. Ask one child to begin counting off and ask another child to continue or pick up the counting as in the previous exercise. As a second step, assign each child his own number. The children are then directed to say this number at the appropriate time in an oral count off. The child with attending difficulties will not be able to respond as well as others during subsequent count offs with a new number.
Non-arithmetic situations where similar behaviors are required	If a child frequently stops and starts over again in any sequential activity, makes false starts when trying to imitate modeled sequential behavior, or "draws a blank" when asked to make a simple response of which he is easily capable, problems in this area may be suspected.
Remedial objective for confirmed problems	The child will be provided with practice in attending to the sequencing aspects of numerical labeling which allows one to count correctly.

Sample remedial activity

Getting a child who exhibits deficit behavior in attending to focus on the activity presents a real problem. Pairing the activity with a reward (some obvious reinforcement) will help the child start activities with full attention focused on the task at hand. This initial focusing behavior itself deserves verbal praise, such as, "I'm glad you're paying attention so you can get this one right!" The following activity can be presented as a game between you and the child, and can be expanded to include other children as necessary.

Bounce a ball any number of times. The child may count silently or aloud. When you stop, ask the child how many times the ball was bounced. Gradually add children to the group. Have one child start bouncing the ball from one to ten times. This child calls on another child to tell how many times the ball was bounced. If the right answer is given, the answerer may take a turn bouncing the ball. This exercise can also be used with jump ropes, clapping, or jumping.

Even more enthusiasm may be gained by having a chosen child shout, "Stop" when a certain number is reached.

For another activity, form the children into two circles, one inside the other. Each pair of children is given a number. The teacher, or some child counts aloud. When the count stops those children are "it." The child from the outside circle runs around the circle in an attempt to get back "home" before being caught by the inside-circle child.

CURRICULUM AREA:
Grouping

LEARNING DISABILITY TYPE:
Memory

Problem-free behavior

The child can group objects or events according to some classification scheme recently learned.

Sample task where deficit child may display difficulty

Ask the child to remember what materials are stored in certain places, or who is his assigned partner in "buddy" activities. Difficulty may also be seen in atypical procedures followed in special circumstances such as those used to evacuate the schoolroom during a fire drill, or in assembling materials according to a grouping scheme (such as color).

Do-it-yourself diagnostic activities

Place a series of objects in a straight line or circle on a table in front of the child and name them. Either real items or pictures of objects such as a train, car, cat, and dog may be used. After the child has been told the name of each object, the objects are kept exposed for an additional few seconds. The child is cautioned to look carefully at the objects and to remember them. Then the child is directed to close his eyes while the order of the objects is rearranged. The child is then told to open his eyes and to put the objects back in their original order.

Non-arithmetic situations where similar behaviors are required

The deficit child will frequently make errors in routine tasks such as not assembling all the materials needed for a certain activity or failing to perform all the activities in a clean-up procedure (like the routine established for disposing trash, trays, and dirty dishes in the school cafeteria).

Remedial objective for confirmed problems

Practice will be provided in exercising memory as it relates to the properties of groups.

Sample remedial activity

The memory demands placed on the child require him to be able to recall sets, groups of activities, instructions, and numbers or properties which allow grouping. Many activities provide children opportunities to practice recalling groups. For example, tell the child that he is going to play a game and he must remember all the items the person before him said, plus add one of his own. Say, "If we were going on a trip we would take a suitcase. In the suitcase we would put a _____."

Many common childhood games lend themselves to working on this interaction. Children like to play grouping games based on color ("Find something blue."); number ("What parts of our body come in two's?"); function ("Name things we eat with."); and sound ("What animals make loud sounds?"). Constant reminders to recall the criterion for a grouping exercise will help tie in the importance of memory to the process.

CURRICULUM AREA:
Grouping

LEARNING DISABILITY TYPE:
Visual-Auditory Discrimination

Pre-School **C–2**

Problem-free behavior

The child can discriminate whether or not an entity fits with a model group on the basis of some presented criterion characteristic and whether or not two groups are identical.

Sample task where deficit child may display difficulty

Worksheets requiring the child to match or group objects present difficulty for this child. He may have trouble selecting the proper group to connect with the item in the left column.

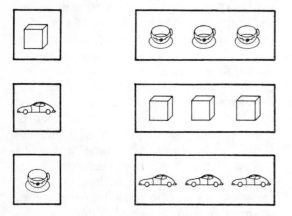

Do-it-yourself diagnostic activities

Worksheets requiring the child to determine whether or not two groups of objects are alike or different can be used. Other worksheets may require the child to determine whether or not two separate groups of objects are the same. Varying levels of difficulty can be

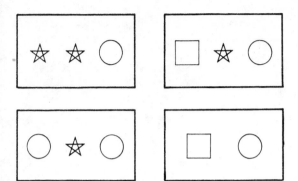

included. For example, tell the child, "There are four groups of objects. Put an X through the group that does not belong with the others."

Non-arithmetic situations where similar behaviors are required

Indiscriminant sorting activities such as putting away a pair of scissors with the crayons can be the result of problems in this area. Worksheet activities which require practice in the form of repetitive reproduction of a model symbol or shape may be unusually difficult.

Remedial objective for confirmed problems

The child will be provided with practice making decisions about whether the properties of a single item are the same as a group of items and whether or not two groups of items are the same or different.

Sample remedial activity

Activities that provide the pupil with practice in sorting, matching, or repetitive productions of groupings are helpful. For example, direct the child to draw a line from each shape to the group where it belongs.

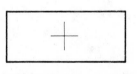

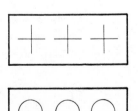

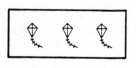

Another activity may include telling the child to circle the groups that are the same.

CURRICULUM AREA:
Grouping

LEARNING DISABILITY TYPE:
Visual-Auditory Association

Pre-School **C–3**

Problem-free behavior

The child can discriminate similarity of certain common attributes of two or more elements of a set, even though the separate elements may differ in all other respects. Thus, sets may be examined for same/different decisions on the basis of the individual elements having only one characteristic in common.

Sample task where deficit child may display difficulty

In using three sets of triangles, squares, and circles, each set a different color, ask the child to sort according to shape or color.

Do-it-yourself diagnostic activities

Use worksheets that require the child to group objects holding some single characteristic in

common. For example, direct the child to put a circle around those items in the box that go together.

Non-arithmetic situations where similar behaviors are required

The child not performing at criterion level often shows such obvious problems as finding it difficult to understand that both coins and currency are money. He may also be unable to identify the common use of such unalike objects as a crayon, a pen, and a typewriter.

Remedial objective for confirmed problems

The child will be provided with practice in grouping where objects have only a single property in common.

Sample remedial activity

These activities deal with the child's ability to perceive similarities among the elements of a set. Worksheets which require that grouping be based on some relatively abstract characteristic will be helpful. Direct the child to draw a line from each shape in the box on the left to the group where it belongs.

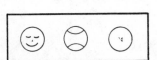

CURRICULUM AREA:
Grouping

LEARNING DISABILITY TYPE:
Perceptual Motor Use

Pre-School **C–4**

Problem-free behavior

The child can perform grouping activities which require the physical manipulation of separate objects to demonstrate the presence of a set.

Sample task where deficit child may display difficulty

Ask the child to group alphabet blocks so that all the letters, or all the animals, or all the same color are face up.

Do-it-yourself diagnostic activities

Place several beads of different colors and shapes on a table along with an empty egg carton. Ask the child to sort the beads according to either their color or their shape. On a somewhat more difficult level, direct the child to string the beads, keeping all beads of like color or shape together. Observe how the child handles the beads during both the sorting and the stringing processes.

Non-arithmetic situations where similar behaviors are required

Putting jigsaw puzzles together or inserting and turning a key in a lock may elicit problems for the deficit child.

Remedial objective for confirmed problems

The child will be provided with practice in applying perceptual-motor skills to the process of grouping sets by actually doing, rather than by simply perceiving grouping cues.

Sample remedial activity

A good remedial exercise can be provided by having a child perform physical sorting activities. A box of mixed nails and screws of various sizes can be sorted by shape, size, or function, for example.

Group games may also be used where children literally sort or group themselves. Prepare cards by drawing a circle, square, or triangle in one of three colors on each. Give each child a card. Tell the children to form a circle and march to music. When the music stops, hold up a black and white card showing a shape, or a three-colored card with no shapes on it. According to the cue given, the children should sort themselves into groups of shapes or colors.

CURRICULUM AREA:
Grouping

LEARNING DISABILITY TYPE:
Spatial Orientation

Pre-School **C–5**

Problem-free behavior

The child can group entities when the distinguishing common characteristic is temporal, spatial, or orientational.

Sample task where deficit child may display difficulty

Worksheets requiring the child to group all animals whose tails are "up," or to identify the color of the object "first" or "last" in a line, or to separate larger objects from small ones cannot be readily handled by the deficit child.

Do-it-yourself diagnostic activities

Prepare a worksheet on which there are pictures of objects, some of which are upright and some of which are upside down. Tell the child to circle all the objects which are standing upright.

Non-arithmetic situations where similar behaviors are required

Hints of a possible problem come from a child having difficulty finding his place in line, or ordering objects in relationship to each other, such as putting chairs away neatly under a table.

Remedial objective for confirmed problems

The child will be provided with practice in recognizing and grouping objects which, despite other differences, possess similar temporal, spatial, or orientational properties.

Sample remedial activity

The development of spatial and temporal awareness is an important skill for a child. Worksheets and activities should provide exercises in recognizing spatial orientation in grouping activity.

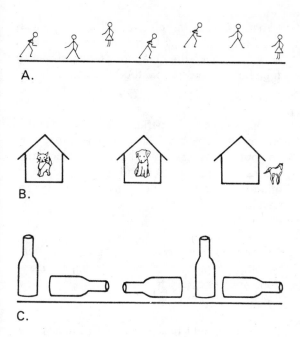

A.

B.

C.

In activity A, direct the child to draw a circle around the children who are jumping up. Activity B is performed by telling the child to draw a circle around those animals which are hiding inside their house. In activity C, tell the child to circle those bottles which are lying down.

CURRICULUM AREA:
Grouping

LEARNING DISABILITY TYPE:
Verbal Expression

Pre-School **C–6**

Problem-free behavior

The child can explain or give directions for grouping using only verbal explanations and cues.

Sample task where deficit child may display difficulty

Ask the child to explain to a visitor the rationale for storage of activity materials.

Do-it-yourself diagnostic activities

After any playtime activity during which many materials were used, such as crayons, scissors, paper, etc., ask the child to tell the other children how to put away their materials—making sure that all the crayons are put away together, all the scissors together, etc.

Non-arithmetic situations where similar behaviors are required

A child can correctly perform tasks such as putting away paints and chalk or getting ready to go out to recess, but cannot explain the process. Reluctance to be a leader or helper to other children in such tasks may be a warning.

Remedial objective for confirmed problems

The child will be provided with practice in verbalizing the process of making grouping decisions and creating sets.

Sample remedial activity

The child should be encouraged to explain or help demonstrate in a verbal manner activities or games relating to groupings.

Pictures of groupings can be used with blanks for descriptive words. The blanks to be filled in can be called for orally and supplied verbally.

Everyday endeavors may be accompanied by question and answer activities. For example, you may say, "We put crayons and pencils and pens all together in this drawer because they are all things we do what with?"

CURRICULUM AREA:
Grouping

LEARNING DISABILITY TYPE:
Closure and Generalization

Pre-School **C–7**

Problem-free behavior

The child can shift from one grouping characteristic to another on demand or can find less than obvious discriminating attributes for decision making once a model process has been demonstrated.

Sample task where deficit child may display difficulty

Ask the child to sort objects according to one characteristic (such as shape). Then request that he sort the same object on the basis of another characteristic (such as color).

Do-it-yourself diagnostic activities

Place several beads of different colors and shapes on a table along with an empty egg carton. Ask the child to sort the beads according to their color. After this sorting is completed, ask the child to sort the beads according to their shape. Observe how easily the child can switch to the new sorting process. Children with closure-generalization disabilities will become confused when asked to make this shift. The task may be made more demanding by requiring a shift in the characteristic used to sort and demanding that the child determine the new characteristic without help.

Non-arithmetic situations where similar behaviors are required

When a familiar object takes on a new meaning, the child will be unable to shift to a new criterion for fitting that object into a set. As an example, the child will have difficulty learning that an arrow can denote direction as well as be shot from a bow. This child may also have trouble finding hidden figures embedded in a picture.

Remedial objective for confirmed problems

The child will be provided with practice shifting from one grouping characteristic to another and determining what single characteristic allows objects to be grouped together as a set.

Sample remedial activity

All remedial activities should emphasize the concept that a familiar object can have more than one grouping characteristic. An informal remediation activity could consist of sorting beads of different color, shape, or size. Have the child sort first according to one characteristic such as color, then another, such as shape, etc.

Worksheets may also call for such shifting of grouping characteristics. For example, tell the child to put a red circle around everything that makes noise, and a blue X through everything that is alive.

CURRICULUM AREA:
Grouping

LEARNING DISABILITY TYPE:
Attention

Problem-free behavior

The child will seek out and maintain focus on known important discriminating cues until a grouping problem is solved or activity finished.

Sample task where deficit child may display difficulty

Behavior can be most easily seen in a stable level of grouping performance over a series of problems where characteristics competing with the defined common factor become increasingly competitive. A task demonstrating this might be instructing the child to draw a line to the item where each separate object in the rectangle belongs.

Do-it-yourself diagnostic activities

Collect a series of pictures (old Christmas catalogues are a good source) where a common grouping characteristic can be seen in a variety of contexts. They should range from simple and uninteresting to highly interesting stimuli, such as round objects in a table setting picture ranging to round balls on a colored page of toys. The grouping characteristic difficulty should remain constant. The child's lack of attention is measured by the degree to which more interesting pictures draw his focus away from the common grouping problem.

Non-arithmetic situations where similar behaviors are required

Unexpected shifts in choice of attribute used in a grouping activity may be apparent. This may be seen in the child who shifts from writing 5's with various colored crayons to using one color to write many different numbers or letters. Deficits in this area may in fact resemble unwanted or uncalled for divergent production.

Remedial objective for confirmed problems

The child will be provided with practice in focusing and maintaining attention while working on grouping tasks.

Sample remedial activity

The guiding principle for any remedial activity is to require sustained attention over a sequence of grouping activities. The child can be given any number of tasks which require close attention to increasingly complex cues for sorting. For example, prepare a set of small cardboard figures representing three shapes (circle, triangle, and square). In the set there should be three sizes (small, medium, and large) for each shape. Each shape and size should come in three colors (red, yellow, and blue). There should be twenty-seven figures in all, three small yellow triangles, etc. Ask the child to group according to any one characteristic, then any two, then using all three, etc.

Colored pictures of objects cut from magazines and pasted on 3″ × 5″ cards provide similar exercises of this skill. Catalogues are especially useful since they combine more than one example of the same type object yet vary in some dimension, such as color.

CURRICULUM AREA:
Relationship Vocabulary

LEARNING DISABILITY TYPE:
Memory

Pre-School **D–1**

Problem-free behavior

The child can remember or recall recently-encountered words used to describe simple relationships.

Sample task where deficit child may display difficulty

Using a small toy and a box, demonstrate what *inside* and *outside* means. Later ask the child to correctly verbalize the positions when they are redemonstrated.

Do-it-yourself diagnostic activities

Show the child two pictures, one of a man and one of a little boy. Point to the picture of the man and explain that he is taller than the boy. Shortly later, show the pictures to the child and tell him that they are different in some way. Point to the man and say, "He is different from the boy because he is _____." The same type of procedure can be used with any relationship term.

Non-arithmetic situations where similar behaviors are required

Although some children will alert you to their inadequacy by retreating from verbal explanations to purely motor responses, a more common sign is a child trying to explain something and obviously groping for the correct word or using an inappropriate one. For instance, while trying to explain how people get larger as they get older the child may say, "He's tall because he's daddy." The intent to express relationship is present, but the accurate vocabulary is missing.

Remedial objective for confirmed problems

The child will be provided with practice remembering the terms, words, and labels used to describe the relationship of one object to another.

Sample remedial activity

Remembering the appropriate vocabulary for expressing relationships is important in many classroom activities. Involving both verbal and motor activities will help increase the child's confidence in remembering and using learned vocabulary.

This activity requires two sets of two boxes; one set for you, one set for the child. The larger box should be approximately 5″ × 8″ × 2½″. The other box should be small enough to fit in the first box. You and the child should paint each box as shown, making the corresponding outside and inside walls of both the same color. Paint the bottoms gray or black.

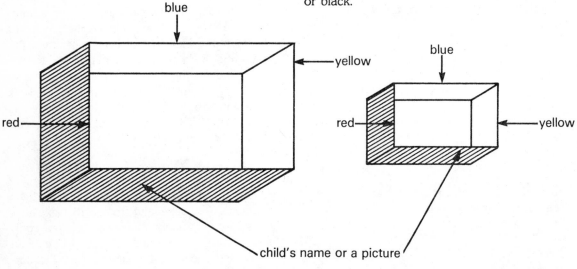

Start the activity by giving the child one pair of boxes. Hold up your boxes and talk about the size and color. Include such statements as, "This is the red end of the box.

This is the blue side of the box. This is the large box. It is larger than the small box. This is the small box." After each descriptive statement ask the child what was said.

Ask the child to then describe his boxes, using vocabulary similar to yours. Whenever he is correct, give praise by saying, "Yes, this is the blue side of the box." Correct the child's errors and have him repeat the correct description. For example, say, "No, this is the blue side. What side is this?" When the child replies, "This is the blue side," praise him and repeat, "That's right, this is the blue side."

During the rest of the day, attempt to engage the child in short conversations about other objects in the room that can be described in the same terms as those used in the lesson.

The next step in this activity involves using the boxes in some of the following relationships:

1 "Put the *small* box *in* the *large* box with the red ends together."

2 "Touch the red *end* of the *large* box."

3 "Put the *small* box *inside* the *large* box."

4 "Put the *large* box *over* the *small* box."

Always encourage the child to verbalize what he is doing. Use praise liberally. Follow up the lesson during the rest of the day with questions concerning similar relationships.

Another phase of this activity is to introduce an object to put inside the box, using the terms *outside* and *inside*.

Subsequent repetition of relationship words will help, for example, "The clock is *above* the floor. Where is the clock?" "The book is *above* the desk. Where is the book?" "The second floor is *above* the first. Where is the second floor?"

CURRICULUM AREA:
Relationship Vocabulary

LEARNING DISABILITY TYPE:
Visual and Auditory Discrimination

Pre-School **D–2**

Problem-free behavior

The child can correctly discriminate whether two successive seen or heard situations are alike or different on the basis of the relationship vocabulary used. (Visual vocabulary is functional only with the reading child.)

Sample task where deficit child may display difficulty

The child may have problems with presentation and question-answer sessions, such as, "The rabbit ran *under* the bush. The fox ran *beside* the bush. Did the rabbit and the fox go the same way?"

Do-it-yourself diagnostic activities

Presentations such as the following may be used to examine potential problem areas: "I am going to tell you where two toys are. You listen carefully and tell me whether they are in the same place or not. 'The doll is *in* the house. The wagon is *outside* the house.' Are the doll and the wagon in the same place or different places?"

Diagnostic exploration can range from simple relationship vocabulary to the more abstract. It can also determine whether or not the problem lies just with certain specific terms or in the whole general area of relationship vocabulary.

Non-arithmetic situations where similar behaviors are required

Children may show related difficulties in following directions or performing tasks which require matching vocabulary of any sort—not just relationship terms. For example, the child sent for a tool which "looks like a _____" may return empty-handed or show confusion about the directions. Problems may be seen in relating action directions to relationship motions, such as saying to the child, "Start when I lift my hand."

Remedial objective for confirmed problems

The child will be provided with experience in discriminating whether relationship vocabulary terms heard in descriptive phrases are alike or different.

Sample remedial activity

A simple remedial activity is to read or tell stories which have relationship vocabulary embedded within them, such as, "The cow jumped over the moon." Each time a relationship term is used, stop and query the child with a like or unlike repetition of the word. Then ask whether or not the same word was used. For example, say, "The cow jumped *over* the moon. Was the cow *over* (or *under*) the moon?"

CURRICULUM AREA:
Relationship Vocabulary

LEARNING DISABILITY TYPE:
Visual-Auditory Association   Pre-School **D–3**

Problem-free behavior

The child can supply spoken verbal phrases or words to visually perceived, nonverbal relationships.

Sample task where deficit child may display difficulty

The child operating at a deficit level in a typical workbook exercise cannot correctly match the label to the drawing when asked, "Which child, A or B, is inside the hula-hoop?"

Do-it-yourself diagnostic activities

Construct three piles of blocks of varying heights explaining that one pile is tall, one is taller than one other, and one is tallest. Ask the child to tell you, point to, or indicate in some way which pile is tall, which one is taller than one other, and which one is the tallest. The process may be repeated for other relationship terms.

Non-arithmetic situations where similar behaviors are required

Trouble with labeling used either formally (such as labels on drawers) or informally in routine speech is a commonly encountered warning. The child often can and will follow explicit directions, step-by-step (such as, "Open the box marked 'long pencils.' "). But on his own, he does not perceive that the label on the box has relevance to the physical attributes of the objects within.

Remedial objective for confirmed problems

The child will be provided with practice in matching correct relationship labels to perceived physical object relationships.

Sample remedial activity

To associate labels with perceived relationships, it is necessary for the child to practice actually making such associations. The remedial activities should require the child to associate the relationship expressed by the label with actual relationships.

One way to practice this is to give the child a label, such as *above* or *inside*, and require him to search for examples in a magazine or in the classroom. Differential association can be helped through the use of progressive worksheets. Ask children to solve such problems as, "Circle the horses that are outside their pens."

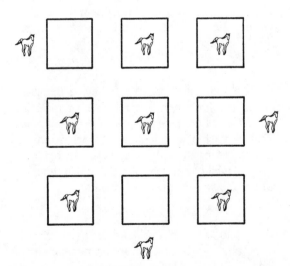

CURRICULUM AREA:
Relationship Vocabulary

LEARNING DISABILITY TYPE:
Perceptual Motor Use

Pre-School **D-4**

Problem-free behavior

The child can physically demonstrate relationships which have been received auditorially or observed in others.

Sample task where deficit child may display difficulty

The common "Hokey Pokey" game (Put your right foot in, put your right foot out . . ." and so on) is a good example of the type of where problems may appear.

Do-it-yourself diagnostic activities

One activity may be to simply ask the children to line up so that the shortest are the first ones in line. Another possibility is to play a game of "Follow the Leader." In this instance, require the children to physically respond to directions containing relationship words such as *inside* and *outside*, *up* and *down,* and so on.

Non-arithmetic situations where similar behaviors are required

A child may have trouble following directions which are limited to verbal cues or modeling behaviors. For example, a child may show total confusion or reluctance to act when told to line up next to the child closest to him in height, while otherwise being totally tractable when told to line up next to Betty.

Remedial objective for confirmed problems

The child will be provided with practice in physically demonstrating and experiencing the meaning of relationship terms.

Sample remedial activity

Requiring the child to actually perform manipulations relevant to relationship terms is an extension of the process of association which takes the activity beyond the purely textbook, school-room level. The following activities are typical of those which give a child practice in this area.

Ask the child to perform individual physical movements such as:

1 Lie flat and push forward.
2 Lie flat and push backward.
3 Walk sideward with a step-close action.
4 Walk sideward with a step-crossover action.
5 Walk forward.
6 Walk backward.

Once these basic body movements have been mastered, a game may be played with more than one child. Give each child a hoop and call out the following instructions:

1 "Put the hoop at the *side* of your body."
2 "Push the hoop *forward*."
3 "Push the hoop *backward*."
4 "Swing the hoop in *front* of your body."
5 "Swing the hoop at the *side* of your body."

The children who make no mistakes are the winners and can be rewarded with being allowed to be the leader. Other games, such as "Hokey Pokey," develop the same areas.

CURRICULUM AREA:
Relationship Vocabulary

LEARNING DISABILITY TYPE:
Spatial Orientation

Pre-School **D–5**

Problem-free behavior

The child can respond to vocabulary specifically relevant to temporal, spatial, and orientational relationships.

Sample task where deficit child may display difficulty

This can be easily observed in the child's response to prepositional phrases in speech *(in front of, next to, over by the)* and in use of time-related vocabulary such as *later, tomorrow, a little while ago.*

Do-it-yourself diagnostic activities

Make a map of the classroom which includes a seating chart with each child's name on it. Have each child find his or her seat on the chart. Then ask questions about who sits next to him, whose seat is farthest away from his, whose is nearest, and so on.

Non-arithmetic situations where similar behaviors are required

Although difficulties may be sometimes seen in areas such as telling time, such are not uncommon at this age. Difficulty with physical relationships such as *taller, beside,* or *in front of* as they relate to everyday activities in the gym, the dining hall, the home, or on the playground may indicate generalization of the problem.

Remedial objective for confirmed problems

The student will be provided with practice in recognizing and responding to spatial, positional and orientational relationship vocabulary.

Sample remedial activity

A.

B.

C.

The example activities involve two types of relationships: (1) physical relationships that consist of an object in spatial relationship to another object, and (2) temporal relationships which, because of their nature, cannot be as easily demonstrated in all respects.

Questions concerning physical relationships can be asked in terms of, *how many* or *which ones,* depending on the child's level of achievement. In activity A, you may ask questions such as:

1 "Which ones are below the line?"
2 "Which ones are above the line?"

Questions for activity B may include:

1 "Which ones are inside?"
2 "Which ones are outside?"

Activity C questions may include:

1 "Which ones are inside the ▢ ?"
2 "Which ones are outside the ▢ ?"
3 "Which ones are inside the △ ?"
4 "Which ones are only inside the △ ?"
5 "Which ones are inside both the ▢ and the △ ?"
6 "Which ones are outside both ▢ and △ ?"

In the area of temporal awareness, discuss with the child things he did *yesterday.* Have him name at least four things. Then have him name four things he will probably do *tomorrow.* Keep a list of these things and discuss it two days later, stressing the idea of the items he planned *tomorrow* he did *yesterday.* This can also be done with the concepts *before* and *later.*

Another activity in temporal awareness is practicing *first, last, before* and *after* with a series of two or three cards depicting sequential acts. For example, include pictures of (1) a bare foot, (2) a foot with a sock on it, and (3) a foot with a sock and a shoe on it. Encourage the child to sequence and label the steps or respond to an ordered sequence question, such as, "Which picture comes last?" or "Which picture shows what we put on our foot first when we get dressed?"

CURRICULUM AREA:
Relationship Vocabulary

LEARNING DISABILITY TYPE:
Verbal Expression

Pre-School **D–6**

Problem-free behavior

The child can demonstrate adequate relationship vocabulary by producing and using the correct words rather than by merely responding to them.

Sample task where deficit child may display difficulty

While working with a ring tower where each succeeding ring is smaller than the one before, ask the child to explain the task verbally and describe the size-position relationships involved.

Do-it-yourself diagnostic activities

Ask one child to be the leader and as such to tell the other children how to line up before they go to gym, art, lunch, etc.

Another suggestion is after hearing a story, tell the children they will play "Movie Set." Choose one child to play the movie director. He or she will be in charge of telling the "players" where each of them should stand on the "stage." You might give the movie director a list of words which would aid him in this role, such as *next to, near to, far away from, farther from,* etc. Note how well the child uses the relationships vocabulary that he has learned.

Non-arithmetic situations where similar behaviors are required

Inability or reluctance to "show and tell" or explain events or personal activities involving relationships is a common warning sign. Children usually know when they have trouble expressing themselves and an "Oh, forget it!" attitude is a quite common avoidant response.

Remedial objective for confirmed problems

The student will be provided with practice in producing and using correct relationship vocabulary.

Sample remedial activity

This activity concentrates on giving the child the opportunity to use physical performance to increase the use of verbal expression. The best activities seem to follow a game format and an informal approach to providing the child with practice in verbalizing relationships outside the lesson structure.

The "Bean Bag" game consists of two to four players using bean bags. Mark on the floor or on the ground large squares in rows and columns. In each square write one word to be practiced. For example: *big, tall, short, later,* etc. Each player has three throws with the bean bag. He must use, define, or demonstrate the meaning of the word where his bag was tossed in order to score a point.

CURRICULUM AREA:
Relationship Vocabulary

LEARNING DISABILITY TYPE:
Closure and Generalization

Pre-School **D–7**

Problem-free behavior

The child is able to demonstrate more than a rote memorization of phrases by correctly applying relationship vocabulary to a range of examples in a variety of settings.

Sample task where deficit child may display difficulty

Ask the child to complete sentences like, "If Henry is the tallest, then George must be _____ then Henry," or "If this piece is too big to fit in the puzzle then I must look for a _____ piece."

Do-it-yourself diagnostic activities

Exercises such as the following which apply the relationship vocabulary to other situations can be used:

1 A car is long, a bus is __(longer)__.

2 A pencil is long, a baseball bat is __(longer)__.

3 This ribbon is too short to tie my hair with so I must find a __(longer)__ one.

This can be used in any number of activities including playing "Dress-Up" when the sleeves are too short or the pants too long, etc. The specific vocabulary involved can be varied to help pinpoint deficits.

Non-arithmetic situations where similar behaviors are required

Indicative of problems in this area may be unusual amounts of difficulty with first exposure to a new type of worksheet where directions or format are changed. For example, the child may have trouble with a worksheet where successive problems move from top to bottom rather than left to right.

Remedial objective for confirmed problems

The child will be provided with practice in expanding his relationship vocabulary to a broad list of terms correctly applied to relationships perceived in a variety of settings.

Sample remedial activity

Remediation should begin in a one-on-one situation, using only a few relational terms. A game such as "Follow the Leader" where directions are given orally and not demonstrated can be used. Until the concept is secure, only the same specific response is required. For example, when working with the terms *inside* and *outside*, the child should demonstrate this with the same block and box each time the direction is given. Gradually the child is asked to perform in other similar and then not so similar situations. New terms are introduced gradually in much the same manner, always added to and included with the earlier terms so the child begins to relate the vocabulary terms to each other. Once a moderate amount of success is met, reinforcement and maintenance of these skills can be carried out in a small group or class games such as "Treasure Hunt" which can be played on the playground. Read the directions of the "Treasure Map," such as: "Walk *under* the swings, *around* the big tree, and *behind* home plate on the baseball diamond."

CURRICULUM AREA:
Relationship Vocabulary

LEARNING DISABILITY TYPE:
Attention

Pre-School **D-8**

Problem-free behavior	The child sufficiently attends to relationship vocabulary cues so as to be able to adequately perform classroom tasks requiring that type of information.
Sample task where deficit child may display difficulty	When given a series of directions such as, "Put the paper *on* the shelf, your crayons *inside* your desk, and the scissors *behind* the paper cutter *on* the counter," ask the child to carry out all aspects of the directions equally well.
Do-it-yourself diagnostic activities	Tell the child to pick up a long pencil, give it to you, get a large piece of paper, and come sit near you. Emphasis is not on the motor behavior itself, but rather on how well the child attends to you and the instructions. Since memory is also involved, make sure the child's problem is not just one of memory by first administering the informal diagnostic activity for Relationship Vocabulary with Memory.
Non-arithmetic situations where similar behaviors are required	The most common sign of a problem is the child not following directions (such as putting his name on the wrong part of the worksheet). The child, to perform successfully, must attend to all verbalized relationship cues, not just those carefully pointed out or delineated.

Remedial objective for confirmed problems	The child will be provided with practice in focusing attention on relationship words as they appear in speech.
Sample remedial activity	Using a puppet stage, a small doll, and a box, demonstrate a relationship (doll inside, under and above box). Close the curtains and then ask the children to tell where the doll was. Viewing time can be shortened as children gain facility. Using a film strip or a storybook, depicted relationships may be emphasized. Then, when the projector is turned off or the book closed, the children then tell you if the rabbit was behind or in front of the rock, etc.

CURRICULUM AREA:
Verbal Expression

LEARNING DISABILITY TYPE:
Memory

Pre-School **E–1**

Problem-free behavior	The child can recall what word cues, recently encountered, are (were) important in solving a problem.
Sample task where deficit child may display difficulty	This difficulty can easily be observed in the child's ability to discuss recent activities which may have dealt with such arithmetically-related problem solving such as one-to-one correspondence decisions, sets, or grouping.

Do-it-yourself diagnostic activities

Refer to the Do-it-yourself diagnostic activities for Grouping with Memory. As noted there, place three objects on the table, then remove one and ask the child which object is missing. Then ask the child to explain how he remembered which ones there were and how he recalled the missing one. (This could be done with any of the three other memory activities at the readiness level if the child had difficulty with this activity initially.)

Read a story to the children, preferably a story which involves numbers. Afterward, ask them to tell you about the story, especially the main characters and what they did, how the story ended, and so on. Answers to questions dealing with arithmetic ideas and concepts should be particularly revealing.

Non-arithmetic situations where similar behaviors are required

The deficit child has difficulty remembering what verbal cues (words read or heard in a story, for example) led to a stated conclusion. The child may be able to state a correct conclusion, for example, "The ant was smarter than the grasshopper," but not be able to explain how or what words led to such a conclusion.

Remedial objective for confirmed problems

The child will be provided with practice in recalling verbal descriptions, explanations, and accounts of arithmetically-related events or facts.

Sample remedial activity

The remedial activity focuses on the child's ability to recall verbal activities. It is necessary to progressively increase the length of time between the initial verbal presentation and subsequent discussions which focus on what the child remembers as well as his verbal ability to communicate it.

This area is one of the most natural in which to develop good remedial exercising. The simplest format is one of storytelling in which some arithmetic facts are encountered. "The Three Bears," with its numerical, size, and other relationship variables, is an excellent example. Remediation steps are simple.

1 The child is presented with verbal material.

2 The child is asked to recall the verbal material.

3 Reiteration of the presentation-recall sequence is repeated with increasing timespread as often as necessary.

"Show and Tell" offers opportunities for similar activities. Parents can be encouraged to go through the sequence in everyday household activities. For instance, the mother might say, "I'm going to toast three slices of bread this morning." Later she may ask the child, "How many slices did I toast?"

CURRICULUM AREA:
Verbal Expression

LEARNING DISABILITY TYPE:
Visual-Auditory Discrimination

Problem-free behavior

The child can explain how or why separate stimuli or patterns of stimuli are the same or different.

Sample task where deficit child may display difficulty

In a matching exercise where the child is to circle the item that matches the one in the box, ask the child to give his reason for the choice.

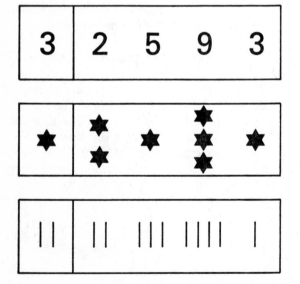

Do-it-yourself diagnostic activities

Ask a child who already knows how to discriminate or match numbers by counting or grouping to explain to someone else (perhaps another child) how such discriminations are done. Note especially how the "teaching child" explains why stimuli are similar or different and the quality of his verbal expression of these concepts.

Non-arithmetic situations where similar behaviors are required

The most common hint of verbal problem solving deficits in any area is a general reluctance to attempt such activity. A warning in this area typically consists of a drastically different level of interest in a matching/discriminating activity and conversations about such activity. Nondeficit children are usually as eager to tell *how* and *why* as they are to *do*. Verbally deficit children would far rather *do*.

Remedial objective for confirmed problems

The child will be provided with practice in matching verbal expression behaviors to other auditory-visual discrimination activities.

Sample remedial activity

Activities like the following help develop skills:

1 While the child watches, start setting a table for two for a tea party. Set one placemat and one set of saucer, cup, spoon, and plate. Have the child set the other place while he verbally explains what he is doing and why.
2 Point out sets and groups which have obvious 1:1 correspondence which obviously do not match. Have the child explain how and why they do or do not match.

In any activity, the emphasis must be on verbalization. Any other activity, such as physical manipulation, should remain incidental or only supportive of the need for verbalization.

CURRICULUM AREA:
Verbal Expression

LEARNING DISABILITY TYPE:
Visual-Auditory Association

Pre-School **E–3**

Problem-free behavior

The child can explain the characteristic held in common by several objects which may allow them to be grouped together as a set despite a lack of 1:1 correspondence. The child cannot only group but can state the rules or criteria used for grouping.

Sample task where deficit child may display difficulty

Worksheets which contain instances of objects which do not match a set are not easily explained by this child. After he has circled an item not belonging in a set, ask the child how he knew that particular item did not belong. His answer should be relevant and meaningful.

Do-it-yourself diagnostic activities

Show the child a picture of a group of similar objects along with a choice of numerals, one of which corresponds to the number of pictured objects. Ask the child to explain how to determine which numeral corresponds to the number of pictured objects, which cues are important for solving the problem, and so on.

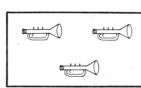

Non-arithmetic situations where similar behaviors are required

Inability to pass on directive information to others often hints of problems in this area. The deficit child finds it difficult and frightening to try to explain a set of directions to others. Therefore, he would rather be in the role of receptive follower than expressive leader.

Remedial objective for confirmed problems

The child will be provided with practice in verbally expressing the process of grouping objects (forming sets) on the basis of a single common variable.

Sample remedial activity

These activities help the child learn to describe how sometimes subtle commonalities between items cause them to belong to one group. You should verbally emphasize relationships the objects have to each other and encourage the child to do the same.

1 With a small group of children, play the game of "Telephone," by calling a child and describing sets portrayed in pictures. Use names of items that are similar (different flowers, birds, cars). Also play the

game having the children describe sets of objects placed in front of them, one by one.

2 Have the child tell you which object in a group does not belong with the others and to explain why. At the start, correct the child if he is incorrect and have him repeat the correct answer.

3 Cut out pictures of furniture, kitchen appliances, utensils, and tools. Encourage the child to group them and explain the grouping. Ask, "Which things go together and where are they found in the house?" Encourage the child to discuss the reasoning for the groupings. Give suggestions if necessary.

CURRICULUM AREA:
Verbal Expression

LEARNING DISABILITY TYPE:
Perceptual Motor Use

Pre-School **E–4**

Problem-free behavior

The child can explain how to do a perceptual motor activity related to arithmetic or describe the activity while performing it.

Sample task where deficit child may display difficulty

Ask the child to explain how to write a 5 on the blackboard while he is actually doing it. He should point out the relevant parts and movements necessary to produce a 5.

Do-it-yourself diagnostic activities

Observe the child while he explains to others how to play "Hopscotch," such as which foot should go on what numbers, how to recognize the numbers, what the player does next, and so on. Observational emphasis is on the quality of verbal expression.

Non-arithmetic situations where similar behaviors are required

Group creative play is difficult for a child with this deficit unless he plays a totally passive following role. Such a child would often rather play alone where questions about "What are you doing?" are not encountered. This child verbalizes to toys (such as dolls) less often than the child who adequately performs.

Remedial objective for confirmed problems

The child will be provided with practice in matching verbal expression to perceptual-motor behavior as it is related to arithmetic.

Sample remedial activity

Emphasis is placed primarily on the child's explanation matched to a performance rather than the performance itself. It is important that the child *tell* someone what is happening.

For example, in air writing the child can verbalize the developing shape of numbers. The appropriate description may be something like, "Start high and come down low," or "Start around and down then straight across," or "Around you go, halfway, and around again only halfway."

Another activity includes the child using a rope or string to form a straight line to make the number 1. Then he counts to 1, pointing to the rope-numeral. The child should continue to form all the numerals from 1 through 9 with the rope while orally counting the corresponding number of times.

CURRICULUM AREA:
Verbal Expression

LEARNING DISABILITY TYPE:
Spatial Orientation

Pre-School E–5

Problem-free behavior

The child can explain the nature of or characteristic used in dealing with temporal or spatial relationships.

Sample task where deficit child may display difficulty

Deficit children may have trouble giving correct answers to such questions as: "What does smaller mean?" or "How can you tell that the number is a six and not a nine?"

Do-it-yourself diagnostic activities

Refer to the Do-it-yourself diagnostic activity for Grouping with Spatial Orientation. (This may be done if the child was successful in his first encounter with this activity; otherwise, substitute from one of the other content areas.) Ask the child to explain to you or to another child what it means for an object to be standing up and how to identify an object in that orientation. Emphasis is on the quality of expression.

Non-arithmetic situations where similar behaviors are required

This child frequently encounters difficulty when asking for help with creative or constructive playthings. Thus, one often finds teacher-pupil dialogues like this:
"Please paste this on my sheet."
"Where?"
"There."
"Where, above or below the line?"
"There."
"Over here?"
"There."
"Where?"

Anything resembling the old Abbott and Costello routine about "Who's on first?" is a warning. The child needs help but doesn't have the necessary "help obtaining" vocabulary or verbal skills.

Remedial objective for confirmed problems

The child will be provided with practice in verbalizing concepts related to temporal, spatial, and orientational relationships.

Sample remedial activity

For adequate classroom functioning, the child must be able to verbalize concepts such as *when* and *where*. The use of the *term* should be stressed instead of allowing the pupil to use physical movements to make others understand what he means or wants. Activities may include:

1 Cut out a picture of a submarine or an airplane (or something that will illustrate the concept of *above* and *below*). Have the child tell a story about the position of the object. Be sure he uses the words *above* and *below*. If he doesn't, suggest them to him.

2 Use pictures to illustrate the concept of *inside* and *outside*. Again, have the child make up a simple story. Using a large picture (perhaps one of a field) and a small picture of an object (in this case, a cow) works well.

3 Use the concepts *before, after,* and *in the middle of,* using the same procedure as above.

CURRICULUM AREA:
Verbal Expression

LEARNING DISABILITY TYPE:
Verbal Expression

Pre-School **E–6**

Problem-free behavior

The child can explain the importance of being able to tell others what or how one is doing something.

Sample task where deficit child may display difficulty

When working as a member of an arithmetic group or sharing in a special project, ask the child to explain the importance of sharing information so the individual members of the group are able to work toward a common goal.

Do-it-yourself diagnostic activities

Have the children complete an arithmetic exercise. After completion, ask the child to explain to the other children how he solved the problem. Ask him to include every step in the solution to the problem. Also ask him why it is important that he include each step. This might be asked at a point when most of the other children are having difficulty understanding what was done. In this way, you can point out to the child doing the explaining that he needs to include more information.

Non-arithmetic situations where similar behaviors are required

Actively avoiding leadership roles, or total unwillingness to act as a classroom host to visitors, classroom representative, or messenger is a frequent tip off to the existence of a problem. This is the type of child who, upon being stopped while carrying a message for the teacher, cannot explain his mission, and ends up in the office with the teacher being paged for an explanation.

Remedial objective for confirmed problems	The child will be provided with practice in using his verbal skills to provide the input necessary for others to solve arithmetic problems, or to elicit verbal information from others necessary for the child himself to solve arithmetic problems.
Sample remedial activity	The child needs to be encouraged to take an active role in group discussions. Stress the importance of talking about ideas with others, and how the child can learn from listening to others, and how others can learn by listening to him. "Pop the Balloons" requires from two to twelve players and a blackboard and chalk. Draw a bunch of balloons on the board. In each balloon, write a word related to an arithmetic concept. Each child has a chance to "pop" a balloon by telling why the arithmetic concept is important to him and how he uses it. No reading is necessary for the child since you may do so.

CURRICULUM AREA:
Verbal Expression

LEARNING DISABILITY TYPE:
Closure and Generalization   Pre-School **E–7**

Problem-free behavior	The child can orally explain how closure or generalization conclusions related to arithmetic are achieved.
Sample task where deficit child may display difficulty	In a "counting off" exercise, require the child to know his number when his turn comes, and also to tell what his number will be in advance.

Do-it-yourself diagnostic activities

Ask the child to explain why learning about numbers is interesting, how he uses numbers at home, and how mothers and fathers use numbers around the house.

Ask the child to explain, without showing, how straight lines and circles are put together to make numbers.

Non-arithmetic situations where similar behaviors are required

Nondeficit children frequently volunteer information such as, "Guess what, I know how a rocket works," or "This is how water comes out of the faucet." Their information may be incorrect but their urge to share their creative problem solving is strong. Deficit children infrequently volunteer such information and also ask fewer questions relevant to such processes since question asking involves the risk of dialogue which might make difficult demands upon them.

Remedial objective for confirmed problems

The child will be provided with practice in verbal problem solving extending beyond a 1:1 correspondence with concrete objects or events.

Sample remedial activity

Closure and generalization behaviors are consistently required classroom activities. These demand that the child be able to express to others his reasoning in reaching a certain conclusion. In addition to the fear of giving a wrong answer, a child with this deficit behavior is also risking failure in verbalizing. Thus, verbalizing attempts as well as correct answers should be reinforced.

Show the child a set of pictures and begin a story relating to the pictures. Tell the child to complete the gaps in the story or add an ending.

CURRICULUM AREA:
Verbal Expression

LEARNING DISABILITY TYPE:
Attention

Pre-School **E–8**

Problem-free behavior

The child demonstrates awareness of the importance of verbal problem solving by focusing attention on critical verbal cues.

Sample task where deficit child may display difficulty

Ask the child to point out the "important" directing words in a sentence or repeat the critical words given in verbal instructions (for example, "I said to write your name *where* on the worksheet?").

Do-it-yourself diagnostic activities

With the children all in a group, read a series of sentences which are similar except for one key word. In each case, ask the children to explain which word is different or which is the key word. Start out by calling on the children in a set order, then switch from that order so that the child does not anticipate being next. Children may also be asked to verbally identify the key word in a series of directions.

Non-arithmetic situations where similar behaviors are required

What looks like disruptive behavior is often only inattention to critical verbal cues so that the child's responses to other than the focused stimuli are inappropriate motor behavior such as foot-tapping, humming, turning the wrong direction, etc. All are clues of possible trouble in this area.

Remedial objective for confirmed problems

The child will be provided with practice in employing attention strategies to oral speech (both receptive and expressive) related to arithmetic problem solving.

Sample remedial activity

Carefully choose appropriate cues for obtaining the child's attention. Strict adherence to the exclusive use of these cues for a period of time should be observed. Later in the child's arithmetic experience certain symbols and phrases will become important cues, hence, it is wise to start shaping this behavior now.

Children can be involved in "Important Number" games. In these games, children progress along a path if they respond to a number preceded by an important cue word (a color or animal name works well). Thus, 2 might be meaningless alone but is important if preceded by a color word, such as *red 2*. In actuality, these games are simple forerunners of common games such as "Simon Says."

More specific shaping can take place by teaching the deficit child to attend upon presentation of a stimulus word, such as *look*, preceding directions.

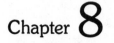

Chapter 8

Introductory Level Materials

Curriculum Areas	(1) Memory	(2) Visual-Auditory Discrimination	(3) Visual-Auditory Association	(4) Perceptual-Motor	(5) Spatial Orientation	(6) Verbal Expression	(7) Closure and Generalization
Vocabulary (F)	F1 p. 186	F2 p. 188	F3 p. 190	F4 p. 192	F5 p. 194	F6 p. 196	F7 p. 197
Relationships-Sets (G)	G1 p. 199	G2 p. 201	G3 p. 203	G4 p. 205	G5 p. 206	G6 p. 208	G7 p. 209
Operations (H)	H1 p. 211	H2 p. 214	H3 p. 215	H4 p. 217	H5 p. 219	H6 p. 220	H7 p. 222
Grouping (I)	I1 p. 224	I2 p. 225	I3 p. 228	I4 p. 231	I5 p. 232	I6 p. 234	I7 p. 236
Problem Solving (J)	J1 p. 238	J2 p. 240	J3 p. 242	J4 p. 244	J5 p. 245	J6 p. 247	J7 p. 248
Verbal Expression (K)	K1 p. 250	K2 p. 251	K3 p. 252	K4 p. 254	K5 p. 255	K6 p. 256	K7 p. 258

Learning Disability Types

Figure 8.1 Introductory level locator chart

CURRICULUM AREA:
Vocabulary

LEARNING DISABILITY TYPE:
Memory

Introductory **F–1**

Problem-free behavior

The child is able to recall newly learned vocabulary in direct relationship to the specific arithmetic use of each term.

Sample task where deficit child may display difficulty

Shown a one-step number sentence, ask the child to remember the labels for the different parts, such as, addend, plus, equals, sum, and so on.

Do-it-yourself diagnostic activities

Following a lesson about telling time or the use of the clock, the child can name, describe, or tell about the parts or functions of the clock which have arithmetic relevance if this area presents no problems. Hence, questions such as the following are diagnostically useful:

1 "What does the '3' on the face of the clock tell us?"
2 "What numbers do we find on a clock?"
3 "Which number is used when we talk about one-half of an hour?"

Non-arithmetic situations where similar behaviors are required

Though misnaming is an obvious clue to such deficits, the child having problems remembering labels usually quickly develops compensating mechanisms or substitute words. Using colloquial stand-by phrases such as "you know" and resorting to positional descriptions instead of labels (the "bottom number" instead of "subtrahend") is typical. Use of backdoor descriptions such as describing a glass as "only a little empty" instead of saying it is "almost full" can be a warning sign.

Remedial objective for confirmed problems

The child will be provided with practice in remembering and then correctly identifying use of arithmetic labels and terminology.

Sample remedial activity

Play "Memory Tic-Tac-Toe" or "Bingo." Give the child a plating board with nine compartments. Each compartment should contain an arithmetic word or symbol. Briefly show the child flashcards with similar words or symbols, one to a card. After the card is exposed, a brief waiting period follows varying from a second or two up to ten seconds. Then ask the child to point to the word or symbol he has seen. If the remembered identification is correct, the child is allowed to cover that word on his card with a marker or poker chip. The important variable here is memory; therefore, the words and symbols should be known or easily identifiable ones.

6	add	3
=	subtract	—
sum	+	two

CURRICULUM AREA:
Vocabulary

LEARNING DISABILITY TYPE:
Visual-Auditory Discrimination

Introductory **F–2**

Problem-free behavior

The child is able to discriminate between or match commonly used arithmetic terms and symbols whether heard or seen.

Sample task where deficit child may display difficulty

Ask the child to answer problem numbers two, four, five, and six, these numbers being dictated or written on the blackboard. The problem child may have difficulty in matching the dictated or written numbers to the correct problems on his worksheet.

Do-it-yourself diagnostic activities

Simple auditory or visual flashcard discrimination-match tasks are all that is needed. The child can be asked to respond by saying *alike* or *same* when two presented stimuli match. Then the task items can be administered at any level of difficulty appropriate for the situation. Auditory items might consist of pairs of words such as: six—six; add—subtract; or take away—take away.

Flashcards may consist of 3″ × 5″ cards divided into two equal halves, with printed words or symbols on each half. The directions and type of stimuli would be the same as for the auditory mode.

Non-arithmetic situations where similar behaviors are required

Deficit children often adopt vocabulary on the basis of poorly discriminated auditory input. Their resulting output clearly indicates this uncritical use, but only if listened to carefully. The old joke about a child praying, "Good

Mrs. Murphy," in place of "Goodness and mercy," is an example of this. The listener must be alert to catch the error.

Remedial objective for confirmed problems

The child will be provided with practice in matching and/or discriminating arithmetical symbols and words whether encountered visually or auditorially.

Sample remedial activity

Remedial activities should follow the "match-to-the-model" pattern. The child can be asked to do this at a very simple level, for instance, instructing him to find all the 6's on a certain page. Or, the problem can be more complex, such as saying to the child, "Addition problems always have a + sign by them. Circle those problems which say 'add' or 'addition' because that sign is there."

Auditorially presented problems are a little more difficult to practice since another individual (rather than a worksheet) must be consistently involved, unless some recording device is used. However, the child can practice discriminating whether or not operational directions in two consecutive statements are the same, and similar tasks can be used. The model would be something like: "When we say 'two *and* two are four' we know that we are adding because the 'and' between the two numbers tells us so. I am going to read you some more problems. You listen and *every* time it is an addition problem because the word 'and' is used, you say 'add' or raise your hand."

CURRICULUM AREA:
Vocabulary

LEARNING DISABILITY TYPE:
Visual-Auditory Association

Problem-free behavior

The child is able to match arithmetic terms to pictorially or otherwise presented relationships, functions, and operations, regardless of the context in which they appear.

Sample task where deficit child may display difficulty

Ask the child to correctly determine that the label "½" applies to each of these pictorializations.

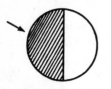

Do-it-yourself diagnostic activities

Ask the child to perform a task such as, "Draw a circle around the triangles."

▽ □ △ +

⬠ △ ▽ ✕

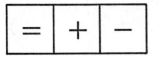

Non-arithmetic situations where similar behaviors are required

Remedial objective for confirmed problems

Sample remedial activity

Another task to require of the child might be, "Draw a circle around the signs which mean 'add.' "

If the child has difficulty switching from finding triangles to finding +'s, see the activities for Closure Difficulties.

At a more difficult level, the child may be asked to match visual displays with spoken vocabulary, such as matching a picture of the face of a clock reading "half-past ten."

Children experiencing association deficits in vocabulary present uneven levels of speech involvement according to the context. Familiar, long-experienced contexts yield normal amount of oral expression. But new contexts, where familiarity depends upon association rather than experience, results in far less spontaneous speech. Increased verbal shyness in new learning situations may warn of problems.

The child will be provided with practice in associating arithmetic vocabulary with correct symbols and operations.

Be sure the child is familiar with the vocabulary words you wish him to use. Give the child ample opportunity to pronounce the words. He cannot be expected to incorporate the words into more complex verbal context if he is unsure of the meaning or pronunciation. Present the child with a worksheet that shows the arithmetic term and an example.

$1 + 1 = \boxed{2}$ This is the *sum.*

$\boxed{3} + \boxed{3} = 6$ These are the *addends.*

$4 \boxed{+} 2 = 6$ This is the *plus* sign.

$4 - 1 = 3$ This is a *minus* sign.

Worksheet problems should involve associations, such as: "Draw a line from the circled part to its name."

$$1 + 1 = ②$$ plus
$$3 + ③ = 6$$ minus
$$4 + 2 ⊜ 6$$ addend
$$4 ⊖ 1 = 3$$ sum

Associations should be learned between numerals, pictorializations, symbols, and terms in all combinations.

CURRICULUM AREA:
Vocabulary

LEARNING DISABILITY TYPE:
Perceptual Motor Use

Introductory **F–4**

Problem-free behavior

The child is able to match vocabulary to perceptual-motor behavior or perceptual-motor behavior to vocabulary.

Sample task where deficit child may display difficulty

Using a model clock to teach time, upon direction, the child is able to place the "minute" hand on the 12 and the "hour" hand on the 3.

Do-it-yourself diagnostic activities

Supply the child with four equally long, slim cylindrical sticks (pencils or "popsicle" sticks could be used) and ask him to place them so that he makes a square. Then ask him to use as many of them as he needs to make a triangle. Next, ask him to make a plus sign, and then a minus sign, and finally, a times sign.

Clock-setting drills, such as those previously discussed are also useful.

Non-arithmetic situations where similar behaviors are required

The simple, everyday classroom experience of "Show and Tell" (whether carried out formally or intermingled with other classwork) can yield warning signs of this deficit. The clue is an inability to show what is told, or always choosing to tell instead of demonstrating or combining the two.

Remedial objective for confirmed problems

The child will be provided with practice in matching arithmetic vocabulary to overt perceptual-motor behavior and vice-versa.

Sample remedial activity

Many of the activities related to set terminology can involve use of perceptual-motor skills and can be used for the child who has these rather than grouping problems. For example, the following activities may be used:

1 Bundling sticks to represent groups of ten.
2 Using a place-value box where numbers are indicated by sticks or poker chips being placed in the ones, tens, or hundreds columns.
3 Using a place-value chart where the child must draw pictorializations representing those sets represented by different columns.

Sorting activities which require physical manipulations of vocabulary cards is also helpful.

CURRICULUM AREA:
Vocabulary

LEARNING DISABILITY TYPE:
Spatial Orientation

Introductory **F–5**

Problem-free behavior

The child is able to recognize and produce temporal, spatial, or orientational vocabulary appropriate to observed concrete relationships.

Sample task where deficit child may display difficulty

The child can correctly produce positional vocabulary, as in answering, "What word describes the position of the ball to the square in each example?"

 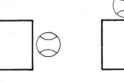 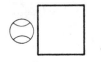

Do-it-yourself diagnostic activities

Superimpose object drawings on a clock-like circle. Ask the children questions such as:

1 "What word describes the cat's and dog's position?"
2 "The cat is _____ than the dog."
3 Is the ball or the drum on the right side of the circle?"

Non-arithmetic situations where similar behaviors are required

A common behavioral example of deficit learning in a child of this age is failure to learn to tell time, despite thorough knowledge of numbers and obvious interest in time concepts.

Remedial objective for confirmed problems

The child will be provided with practice in using and applying spatial, temporal, and orientational terms in arithmetic relationships.

Sample remedial activity

Remedial worksheets should require the child to match or produce the correct terminology to demonstrated relationships. For example:

Inside
Outside

1 Where is the ball? Circle the right word.

2 Which way is the arrow pointing?

3 The dog is sitting _____ the cat.

CURRICULUM AREA:
Vocabulary

LEARNING DISABILITY TYPE:
Verbal Expression

Problem-free behavior

The child is able to use arithmetic vocabulary in creating or solving simple word problems.

Sample task where deficit child may display difficulty

Ask the child to produce word problems which convey the same information as $2 + 2 = ?$ and $? + 2 = 4$.

Do-it-yourself diagnostic activities

Ask the child to describe in words the steps to take in building an arithmetic problem using pictures and symbols. For example, place on the table three pictures of a dog, a plus sign, and an equal sign. The child should describe this (either as a unit or step by step as you wish) as, "Two dogs and one dog are . . ." The procedure can be made as simple or as complex as the diagnostician wishes.

Non-arithmetic situations where similar behaviors are required

Marked contrast in computational (or any reasoning) tasks between those which offer concrete, visualized objects and directions, and those which are presented orally, sometimes indicates problems. Failure to remember oral instructions or confusion in following oral instructions may also be a clue.

Remedial objective for confirmed problems

The child will be provided with practice in creating word problems or in applying correct terminology to the solution.

Sample remedial activity

Remedial activities should follow a "say-it-with-words" format. Worksheets and drills should present number lines, symbols, and pictorializations which require translating. For example, the child should be required to construct word problems or correctly describe such total presentations as:

$$3 + 1 = 4$$
$$3 < 5 < 6$$
$$2 = \boxed{?} + \boxed{?}$$
$$00 + 00 = 0000$$
$$5 + \boxed{?} = 6$$

CURRICULUM AREA:
Vocabulary

LEARNING DISABILITY TYPE:
Closure and Generalization

Introductory **F–7**

Problem-free behavior

The child is able to verbally explain subparts of an arithmetic problem-solving process, or, given the initial step(s) of a problem solving sequence, the child can explain necessary subsequent steps.

Sample task where deficit child may display difficulty

Correct answers can be provided to questions such as:

1 "I have two boxes. Each box has several pieces of chalk in it. I wish to find out how many pieces of chalk I have in both boxes altogether. What should I do?"

2 "What does the + sign tell us to do?"

Do-it-yourself diagnostic activities

Present word problems to the child in which some element is missing that is necessary in order to solve the problem. Ask the child to tell you what other information is needed to answer problems such as:

1 "John has 3 balls. How many more balls does he have than Susan?"
2 "Susan has 4 pieces of candy. How much less candy does John have?"

If such questions prove too difficult, the diagnostician may want to see if the child can simply discriminate complete word problems from ones which are incomplete, such as:

1 "John has two crayons. Susan has one crayon. How many do they have together?" [complete]
2 "John has two crayons. How many do John and Susan have together?" [incomplete]

Non-arithmetic situations where similar behaviors are required

Leadership requires ability to generalize and produce closure and then to convey directions to others. Conversely, failure to assume any leadership roles in a child who is not otherwise shy, may be indicative of lack of self-confidence in these same two behaviors. Careful observation often will provide information about specific areas where these difficulties lie.

Remedial objective for confirmed problems

The child will be provided with verbal practice in explaining, describing, or solving subparts of total arithmetic problems.

Sample remedial activity

Remedial activities for this area should follow essentially the same format as in the preceding area, except that the child is asked to fill in and describe missing parts and to correctly describe how to complete initiated operations. For example:

$3 + 1 = 4$ "What do we call the 3 and the 4?"

$2 = \boxed{?} + \boxed{?}$ "How could we rewrite this using numbers or words in place of the squares?"

$5 + \boxed{?} = 6$ "What is the number which is missing?"

CURRICULUM AREA:
Relationships-Sets

LEARNING DISABILITY TYPE:
Memory   Introductory **G–1**

Problem-free behavior

The child can recall on demand rules (such as place values) and properties (such as shape and size) used to group elements into a set or sequence.

Sample task where deficit child may display difficulty

Following a demonstration lesson on how unlike objects may be grouped together on the basis of some common characteristic or function (such as different objects sharing the same characteristic of being toys), ask the child to identify the characteristic used to group objects used in the lesson.

Do-it-yourself diagnostic activities

After the child has been shown that the numeral 110 is made up of 0 in the 1's place, 1 in the 10's place, and 1 in the 100's place, ask the child to tell you what is in each place for other two- and three-digit numerals. The emphasis should be on the child's remembering the place values.

Non-arithmetic situations where similar behaviors are required

Although keeping a neat room seems to be a problem for all children, some may find it especially difficult due to having trouble remembering where things are properly stored—a basic relationships-set with memory interaction. School children who require extra labeling and pictorial cuing for everyday operations such as putting things away may be experiencing this type of difficulty.

Remedial objective for confirmed problems

The child will be provided with practice in recalling principles or rules used to sequence or group objects.

Sample remedial activity

Worksheets and activities should follow this sequence:

1 Establish a set using an explained rule.
2 Reiterate the rule.
3 Wait a brief elapsed time.
4 Make an additional inclusion/exclusion decision using the rule.
5 Require the child to identify the rule.

An example of this procedure follows:

1 "Let's put all the animals together."

2 "The drum is not an animal is it? The rule we used was that only animals were put together."

3 Wait ten seconds.

4 "Here is a flower. Should it go in the group?"

5 "No, you were right. The flower doesn't belong. Why? What is the rule we were using?"

CURRICULUM AREA:
Relationships-Sets

LEARNING DISABILITY TYPE:
Visual-Auditory Discrimination

Introductory **G–2**

Problem-free behavior

The child can correctly determine whether or not two ordered, combined, or separated sets are the same or different.

Sample task where deficit child may display difficulty

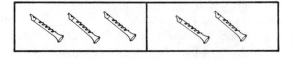

Ask the child to answer worksheet questions such as, "Look at the pairs of groups. All the things should be grouped according to the numbers of things in a group. Which pairs have the same number of objects?"

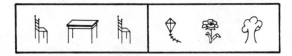

Do-it-yourself diagnostic activities

Present the child with paired sets of pictures with the task of determining if the two should be considered alike or different. Pictures should share a variety of characteristics upon which the decision is to be made, including such things as color, number, shape, or function.

Non-arithmetic situations where similar behaviors are required

The deficit child has difficulty combining such related but separate characteristics as shape and function. Therefore, he frequently fails to successfully or easily follow a direction such as, "Go get something else to cut this string. These scissors are dull." However, he is quite capable of following the direction, "Go get a knife." Being asked to group the class into two subgroups with children of equal heights in each would cause similar problems.

Remedial objective for confirmed problems

The child will be provided with practice in making alike-different discrimination of paired sets based upon a variety of observed characteristics.

Sample remedial activity

Remedial activities can include alike-different decisions in sets involving pictorializations, symbols, numbers, and so on. Practice should include working with (1) sets which are equal, (2) sets which are unequal, and (3) separating sets into equal subsets.

On a worksheet, direct the child to put a C in front of the sets if they are equal.

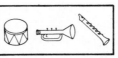

Next, ask the child to circle those items not belonging in the set.

CURRICULUM AREA:
Relationships-Sets

LEARNING DISABILITY TYPE:
Visual-Auditory Association

Introductory **G–3**

Problem-free behavior

The child can recognize and use common properties in separate groups to successfully combine the groups.

Sample task where deficit child may display difficulty

Present the child with three sets of pictures. In one set all the pictures are of toy cars. In the second set all the pictures are of wagons. In the third set the pictures are all of dolls. Say to the child, "The wagons and the cars can be put together to make one group. The dolls would not fit into that group. What are we using to decide which things can go together in a group? Can you think of anything which would let us put wagons and cars and dolls together in one group?"

Do-it-yourself diagnostic activities

Give the child toy coin money: 5 pennies, 3 nickels, 3 dimes, and 1 quarter. Ask the child to show you how many different ways he can group the coins to make 25¢. (He can tell how to do it or can manipulate the coins himself, since the emphasis is on his applying the concept that all the coins are money.)

Non-arithmetic situations where similar behaviors are required

The deficit child may have difficulty in being creative in play to the extent that new objects can be used in place of familiar ones. Thus, "rockets" must be *rockets; tissue tubes* or *ball point pens* are not easily or readily included in the play as substitutes for the real items.

Remedial objective for confirmed problems

The child will be provided with practice in recognizing and using properties to combine separate groups.

Sample remedial activity

Activities should provide an opportunity for the child to develop the concept of expanding a set. This entails the child recognizing the various characteristics of the elements. Practice should include working with associations like the following:

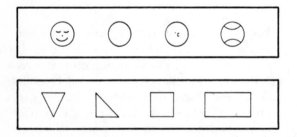

1 Can all these items be combined into one group? Why?

2 In what way are all these items alike? They may be made into one group or two. What characteristic would you use to make two groups? What characteristic would you use to make one group?

CURRICULUM AREA:
Relationships-Sets

LEARNING DISABILITY TYPE:
Perceptual-Motor Use   Introductory **G–4**

Problem-free behavior	The child can physically manipulate individual elements so as to combine, separate, order, or rearrange group relationships.
Sample task where deficit child may display difficulty	Ask the child to select blocks of appropriate color from a box of blocks to form requested color sets.
Do-it-yourself diagnostic activities	Supply each child with a long string and many beads of various colors, shapes, and sizes. Direct the child to make necklaces by stringing the beads according to different properties. The child's ability to identify and then *use* various properties for grouping should be apparent.
Non-arithmetic situations where similar behaviors are required	Most young children enjoy every opportunity to be of assistance in classroom housekeeping chores, such as picking up and putting away tools and materials. Deficit children may be less eager to volunteer such help since they may have trouble matching motor behavior to relationships-sets decisions and directions. They know quite well that both peers and teachers are quick to note and point out errors.
Remedial objective for confirmed problems	The child will be provided with practice in physically manipulating objects in the environment to form meaningful groups.

Sample remedial activity

Focus should be on developing the child's use of motor abilities and coordination for manipulating objects into given sets. In order to encourage the child to participate, the activities are presented in game form. Many sorting games can be invented. For instance, assemble red and blue poker chips, red and blue hoops (embroidery hoops work well), and red and blue sticks. Place all red objects in one pile and all blue objects in another. Tell the child to sort the three similar shapes—chips, hoops, and sticks—into three different piles. Reverse the procedure and have the child resort back to the original color piles.

Another game which can be used is beanbag tossing. The children can play as individuals or compete team against team. The beanbags can be tossed by different colors into different baskets according to some prearranged grouping rule.

CURRICULUM AREA:
Relationships-Sets

LEARNING DISABILITY TYPE:
Spatial Orientation

Introductory **G–5**

Problem-free behavior

The child can combine, separate, order, or group sets on the basis of temporal, spatial or orientational properties alone.

Sample task where deficit child may display difficulty

Ask the child to successfully complete the following task: "Circle all those numbers which are members of the 10's set with a red crayon. Circle all those numbers which are members of the 100's set with a yellow crayon. Circle all those numbers which are members of the 1's set with a black crayon."

49	2	847
111	139	321
322	46	7

Do-it-yourself diagnostic activities

Prepare a worksheet on which there is a series of numbers. Ask the child to circle all the numbers which come before 15 when counting from 1 to 25.

16, 1, 10, 5, 17, 21,

14, 41, 9, 3, 2, 22, 14

Non-arithmetic situations where similar behaviors are required

Any pairing of meaning with position may cause this type child problems. Therefore, such simple positional set concepts as understanding that the position of a wall lightswitch indicates whether it is off or on, or in translating two dimensional perspective pictures to obtain positional information (smaller figures are farther away, blocking out part of an object by another indicates which object is in front) may be situations where warnings of deficits may be observed.

Remedial objective for confirmed problems

The child will be provided with practice in establishing groups or sets based on spatial, temporal, or orientational properties.

Sample remedial activity

Simple blocks with numbers, letters, shapes, and objects on them provide many remedial opportunities. Blocks can be arranged numerically or alphabetically in horizontal, vertical, sequential, and other spatial, temporal, and positional arrangements. Children can provide their own model by creating an arrangement and then trying to replicate it.

CURRICULUM AREA:
Relationships-Sets

LEARNING DISABILITY TYPE:
Verbal Expression

Introductory **G–6**

Problem-free behavior

The child can orally define the properties or processes used in combining, separating, or ordering sets.

Sample task where deficit child may display difficulty

If the child has combined three wagons and two autos into a set of five conveyances, he can orally explain how this was done, and how the grouping principle was applied.

Do-it-yourself diagnostic activities

Present the child with a number of objects, two at a time, which have some common properties. Ask the child what property or in what way the two objects are similar so that they may be combined. For example, ask, "How are a dog and a cat (or a drum and a bugle) alike so that we might include them in a single group?"

Non-arithmetic situations where similar behaviors are required

Lack of *group* creative play may be an indication of problems. Creative play in itself demands that a child find new and novel ways to group things by bestowing them with imaginary properties. Blocks become automobiles and crayons become people. When done in a group, such play requires at least some verbal communication between participants to let each other know what arbitrarily assigned properties are involved and how seemingly unrelated elements have been formed into sets.

Remedial objective for confirmed problems

The child will be provided with practice in verbalizing the reasoning behind and steps in combining separate objects into groups.

Sample remedial activity

Use the same games, activities, and worksheets as described in the other relationship-sets sample remedial activities. In this case, however, require the child to describe, explain, and verbalize in an informal way regarding why and how things were done. Care should be taken to discourage rote repetition of memorized rules and to encourage informal discussion.

CURRICULUM AREA:
Relationships-Sets

LEARNING DISABILITY TYPE:
Closure-Generalization

Introductory **G–7**

Problem-free behavior

The child can correctly determine what property must be added to or subtracted from separate elements to allow them to be included in a set.

Sample task where deficit child may display difficulty

Ask the child to determine how many blocks must be added to each box of blocks to make them all become boxes of four blocks each.

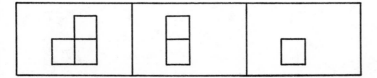

Do-it-yourself diagnostic activities

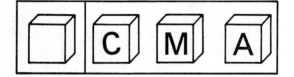

Games of "how can we fix this so that it can belong to the group" will help a teacher quickly spot a child's inability to add characteristics to or take characteristics away from an item in order to establish a grouping relationship. For example, asking the former question about the single block will require the child to see that a letter must be added to the side of the block to make it belong to the group. By varying the missing property, one can check even more specifically for ability to close or generalize with different types and levels of complexity in relationship properties.

Non-arithmetic situations where similar behaviors are required

Quantitative extrapolation may be very difficult for the child with problems in this area. Therefore, expanding routine situations to include another person (such as rearranging place settings to add an additional place at the table or subdividing toys to share with another child) may not be done easily.

Remedial objective for confirmed problems

The child will be provided with practice in moving beyond the obvious, concrete properties of objects in forming groups and sets.

Sample remedial activity

Worksheet activities are easily constructed. For instance, you may ask the child, "What must be done to the object in the circle if it is to belong to the group in the box?"

CURRICULUM AREA:
Operations

LEARNING DISABILITY TYPE:
Memory

Introductory **H–1**

Problem-free behavior

The child can recall the algorithms, processes, and manipulations necessary to addition and subtraction.

Sample task where deficit child may display difficulty

Ask the child to demonstrate that values carried or borrowed along with the resulting renaming involved in addition or subtraction can be remembered long enough to successfully complete a problem.

Do-it-yourself diagnostic activities

Using a set of 3″ x 5″ cards in three colors, place them in a variety of patterns, such as:

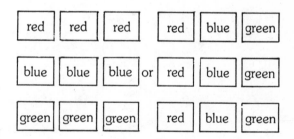

Instruct the child to study them for the rule used in their arrangement. Help the child determine the rule if he cannot arrive at it independently. Remove the model, then give the child a second set of cards in three different colors. Ask him to tell you the rule he would use in arranging these cards in a similar fashion. (Numbered or lettered cards might be used in place of colors but symbolization may present detraction from the main task.)

Non-arithmetic situations where similar behaviors are required

Operations are essentially only individual behaviors, performed according to some learned (memorized) sequential order. Game rules and directions are the same type function. Children who frequently do the wrong thing in games may be having trouble in this area. Often this can easily be seen in such behaviors as the child playing ball who successfully catches the ball and then momentarily stands there, looking perplexed, wondering what to do with it.

Remedial objective for confirmed problems

The child will be provided with practice in recalling the actual processes involved in addition and subtraction operations.

Sample remedial activity

Worksheets including exercises like the following will help. If using renaming instead of borrowing or carrying, have the child write the renamed number.

1 Each of these problems needs to have a number *carried over*. Write that number in the box. Turn the paper over and, without looking, write the answer again.

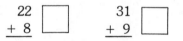

2 Each of these problems needs to have a number *borrowed*. Write that number in the box. Turn the paper over and, without looking, write the answer again.

3 Add these numbers, trace the arrowed line with your pencil, and then write the answer in the box at the end of the arrow.

2+2   1+6   9+7

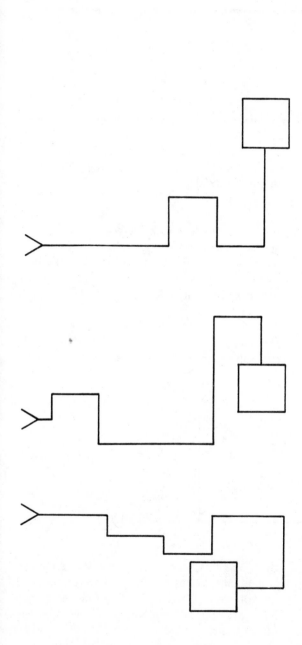

CURRICULUM AREA:
Operations

LEARNING DISABILITY TYPE:
Visual-Auditory Discrimination

Problem-free behavior	The child can determine if perceived addition and subtraction operations and/or solutions match a model.
Sample task where deficit child may display difficulty	Ask the child to check his own answer to an addition or subtraction problem against one which is arrived at by an inverse method. Also, he may be asked to check his estimation against a computed result.
Do-it-yourself diagnostic activities	Prepare a worksheet that requires the child to circle the item that matches the model.

$$
\begin{array}{c}
2 \\
+3 \\
\hline
5
\end{array}
\qquad
\begin{array}{c}
2 \\
+3 \\
\hline
6
\end{array}
\qquad
\begin{array}{c}
2 \\
+3 \\
\hline
5
\end{array}
\qquad
\begin{array}{c}
2 \\
+4 \\
\hline
6
\end{array}
$$

Non-arithmetic situations where similar behaviors are required	Everyone has seen a parade where someone is marching along, blissfully unaware that he is out of step. Children with problems in this area are often "out of step" or "out of phase" with others around them during classroom activities and show no more personal awareness than the person in the parade. Such behavior, consistently observed, offers a warning.

Remedial objective for confirmed problems

The child will be provided with practice in matching addition/subtraction operations and solutions to a model.

Sample remedial activity

Any activity which requires a child to match arithmetic operations against a model will be helpful. Correcting his own papers against a blackboard list or working with worksheet examples such as the following can be used.

Make your work look just like that in the box.

Is your answer the same as the one in the circle?

CURRICULUM AREA:
Operations

LEARNING DISABILITY TYPE:
Visual-Auditory Association

Introductory **H–3**

Problem-free behavior

The child can demonstrate his ability to discern the similarity of addition and subtraction operations required in arithmetic problems presented in varying forms.

Sample task where deficit child may display difficulty

Ask the child to demonstrate how word problems (four apples and four apples are how many apples) and number sentences (4 + 4 =   ) call for the same operation.

Do-it-yourself diagnostic activities

Prepare a worksheet similar to the example and ask the child to draw a line from the pictorializations to the matching number sentences.

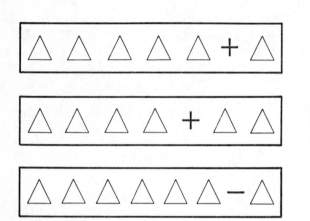

$$4+2$$

$$6-1$$

$$5+1$$

Non-arithmetic situations where similar behaviors are required

The deficit child may experience difficulty with almost any task which requires him to move from a demonstration or model to the real thing. In reading, for example, the child may adequately identify separated sounds in a phonics worksheet (ba-by), but have difficulty performing the same task in a regular reading assignment.

Remedial objective for confirmed problems

The child will be provided with practice in recognizing similarities based upon common operations rather than specific form.

Sample remedial activity

Use worksheet problems following this format:

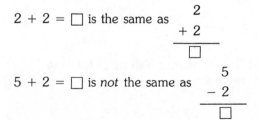

$2 + 2 = \square$ is the same as

$5 + 2 = \square$ is *not* the same as

Here are some more problems in pairs. Tell the child to put a big "C" in front of the two problems if they mean the same.

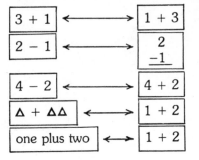

CURRICULUM AREA:
Operations

LEARNING DISABILITY TYPE:
Perceptual Motor Use

Introductory **H–4**

Problem-free behavior

The child is able to perform fine motor behavior necessary for problem solving in addition and subtraction.

Sample task where deficit child may display difficulty

Ask the child to write numerals and symbols required for counting, adding, and subtracting in number sentences and problem structuring and number lines. Remind the child to keep columns and rows sufficiently neat for computation.

Do-it-yourself diagnostic activities

Dot-to-dot drawing, coloring by number, drawing horizontal and vertical lines using a ruler, or other activities of this nature are useful in informal analysis and diagnosis.

Non-arithmetic situations where similar behaviors are required

The deficit child has trouble performing functions he may know quite well—to the extent that perceptual-motor performance often lags noticeably behind verbal expression abilities. Functional awkwardness in everyday tasks is an important cue. The slang phrase, *motor morons*, is sometimes used, but incorrectly so, since lack of intelligence is not a factor. This is plainly indicated by the child's thorough understanding of what he's supposed to do even when he can't do it—an especially frustrating experience which often leads to either withdrawal or silly over-acting attempts to play the clown.

Remedial objective for confirmed problems

The child will be provided with practice developing and using fine perceptual-motor skills necessary in performing addition and subtraction operations.

Sample remedial activity

Activities should require a child to physically produce or copy all forms of problem notation. Simple copying can be used, for example

or behavior can be shaped at a more basic level by introducing dotted line figures.

CURRICULUM AREA:
Operations

LEARNING DISABILITY TYPE:
Spatial Orientation   Introductory **H–5**

Problem-free behavior

The child is able to demonstrate understanding of spatial, temporal terms and positional orientations relevant for use in addition and subtraction computation.

Sample task where deficit child may display difficulty

Ask the child to correctly place the subtrahend to the right of the minus sign in a horizontal number sentence or on the bottom in the vertical subtraction problem.

Do-it-yourself diagnostic activities

The primary positional or spatial relationships necessary to operations at this level are sequential (before, after; front, back; over, under; above, below; and beside). By simply using blocks or any two objects which can be easily manipulated, demonstrate these relationships and ask the child to identify, explain, mimic, or create them. The process need not be complicated. Sometimes the two-dimensional nature of printed or written relationships is confusing to a child. By using models drawn on a blackboard this input can be checked.

Non-arithmetic situations where similar behaviors are required

Misaligned worksheets; difficulty in finding one's place in reading or in other work; or failure to correctly follow positional directions in gym, cafeteria, or elsewhere may all be warning signs.

Remedial objective for confirmed problems

The child will be provided with practice in being involved with and manipulating the spatial, temporal, and positional orientations prerequisite to addition and subtraction operations.

Sample remedial activity

Use tackboard cards with numbers and symbols on them which the child can manipulate to meet certain positional requests. For example, give the child the following cards:

$$\boxed{4}\;\boxed{5}\;\boxed{-}\boxed{=}$$

Instruct the child to "Put the 4 above the 5." "Put the numbers *beside* each other; the 5 *first* and the 4 *last*." "Put the minus sign between the 5 and the 4."

CURRICULUM AREA:
Operations

LEARNING DISABILITY TYPE:
Verbal Expression

Introductory **H–6**

Problem-free behavior

The child is able to ask for or orally present the data necessary for problem solving using the operations of addition and subtraction.

Sample task where deficit child may display difficulty

Ask the child questions such as, "If we want to find out how many books we have if we added together the books in Jane's house to the books in Bill's house, what questions would we have to ask Jane and Bill before we could do our adding work?"

Do-it-yourself diagnostic activities

Perhaps the simplest way to check this area is to provide the child with opportunities to participate in "fill-in" activities. Prepare a list of important data, such as:

- Mary has two sisters.
- John is five years old.
- Roberta has two apples in one basket and three apples in another.
- $5 + 1 = 6$

Then tell a story and stop when a piece of data is needed. Encourage the child to provide it. For example, "Tomorrow will be John's birthday. He will be one year older than he is now. He is now _____ years old so tomorrow he will be _____."

Non-arithmetic situations where similar behaviors are required

In an adult, the clue might lie in being seen as the "strong, silent type." This is not far from being true for the child as well. Any youngster who can easily do things (often to the extent of being playground leader and always first chosen on teams), but cannot or does not ever verbally instruct or lead others should be suspect.

Remedial objective for confirmed problems

The child will be provided with practice in verbalizing data necessary for addition and subtraction problem solving.

Sample remedial activity

Play "Ask For What You Need" games. Give the child some data bits on a card. Tell him in order to solve a certain problem he must ask for what is missing. The reverse side of the card should contain the missing part so the child can check the accuracy of his request. An example of this activity is:

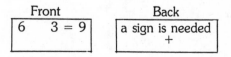

Front	Back
6 3 = 9	a sign is needed +

CURRICULUM AREA:
Operations

LEARNING DISABILITY TYPE:
Closure and Generalization

Problem-free behavior

The child can perform subparts of addition and subtraction operations or, given the initial step(s) of a problem solving sequence involving these operations, the child can perform necessary subsequent steps.

Sample task where deficit child may display difficulty

Ask the child to fill in or supply missing parts of a number sentence, such as, $1 + 3 = \square$, or complete operations initiated, such as, $2 + 2 = \square$, $3 + 1 = \square$.

Do-it-yourself diagnostic activities

Prepare a worksheet similar to the following which requires the child to fill in the box. When the type of missing part to be filled in changes often, the child with this disability will have difficulty. For example:

$$3 \; \square \; 1 = 4$$
$$2 \; \square \; 1 = 3$$
$$6 \; \square \; 3 = 9$$
$$2 \; \square \; 1 = 1 \; \longleftarrow$$
$$7 \; \square \; 3 = 4$$
$$7 + 3 = \square$$
$$7 + \square = 9 \; \longleftarrow$$
$$8 - \square = 6$$

These are particularly crucial points

Non-arithmetic situations where similar behaviors are required

Children experiencing deficits in this area may alert observers by showing rather rigid and stereotyped use of tools and work objects. Pliers, modeled as a tool for holding something, may not easily be seen as a tool which can help pull out a nail. Rulers, explained as instruments of measurement, may not appear to be helfpul in sharply creasing a folded paper. The problem is one of not being aware of partial or extended operations, not of being able to do them once demonstrated.

Remedial objective for confirmed problems

The child will be provided with practice in searching out and providing missing pieces of data or operations necessary to addition or subtraction problem solving.

Sample remedial activity

Give the child a model of a number sentence and follow it with similar number sentences with missing parts. For example:

$$\boxed{3 + 1 = 4}$$
$$\Box + 1 = 4$$
$$3 \ \Box \ 1 = 4$$
$$3 + \Box = 4$$
$$3 + 1 \ \Box \ 4$$
$$3 + 1 = \Box$$

After working with this completed model and sequential gaps for a while, the child may proceed to exercises without the completed model. Similar formats should be followed for each operation.

CURRICULUM AREA:
Grouping

LEARNING DISABILITY TYPE:
Memory

Introductory **I–1**

Problem-free behavior	The child is able to recall characteristics and properties of established measurement groups in order to use them in comparison judgments.
Sample task where deficit child may display difficulty	Ask the child to recall which measurement groups contain certain properties. For example, "Do inches measure distance?"
Do-it-yourself diagnostic activities	Talk with the child about measurements and have him complete sentences similar to the following:

- "When I want to tell how long something is, I measure with a (ruler)."
- "A ruler has numbers on it which are called (inches)."
- "Which is longer, a foot or a yard?"
- "Which is bigger, a nickel or a dime?"
- "I look at a (thermometer) when I want to know what the temperature is outside."

Non-arithmetic situations where similar behaviors are required	Inability to remember measurement properties will generalize to everyday experiences. As a result, common measurement terms will often be misused or inappropriately applied by the deficit child. Inability to meaningfully interpret measurement directions such as, "move that chair just one or two inches" can frequently be observed.

Remedial objective for confirmed problems

The child will be provided with practice in recalling the applied attributes of different measurement groups.

Sample remedial activity

Activities should include opportunities for the child to match characteristics and properties together from memory. Here are two examples of worksheet problems.

1 Draw lines between those things which fit together.

seconds   hours
quarts   pints
inches   feet

2 We measure distance in _____ and _____.

We measure time in _____ and _____.
We measure liquids in _____ and _____.

CURRICULUM AREA:
Grouping

LEARNING DISABILITY TYPE:
Visual-Auditory Discrimination

Introductory **I–2**

Problem-free behavior

The child can compare two or more groups for equality based upon heard, seen, or measured characteristics of the individual elements of the groups.

Sample task where deficit child may display difficulty

Ask the child to perform tasks such as: "Look at these groups. If all the separate pieces in the groups are the same length, put an equal sign between the boxes."

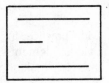 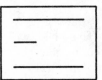

Do-it-yourself diagnostic activities

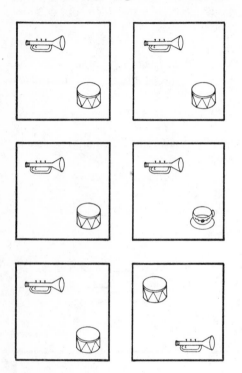

Prepare a worksheet on which the child is to mark whether each set of measured objects shown are the same or different. If they are the same, the child should make an = sign next to the set; if not, he should mark it ≠ .

Non-arithmetic situations where similar behaviors are required

The warning signs here are similar to those observed in the pre-school child; however, the grouping behaviors required of this age child demand more precise and meaningful discriminations. Instead of grouping concrete objects, such as scissors, this child may have to learn to discriminate between abstract groups of people (such as students or teachers from his school at a district rally). Therefore, failures become increasingly more threatening and a subtle warning of difficulty can sometimes be seen in overdepending on peers, parents, or teachers.

Remedial objective for confirmed problems

The child will be provided with practice in using fine characteristics of individual elements of a group to provide the basis for making group comparisons.

Sample remedial activity

Worksheet exercises like the following are helpful. Ask the child, "Are the two groups the same? Put a C in front of them if they are."

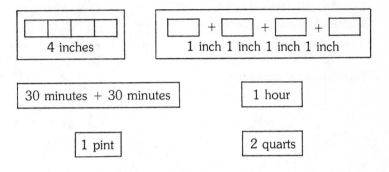

Use pictorialized, numerically notated, and word problem presentations. In the initial steps both groups should stay in the same model for example, pictorialization. At a more difficult level, modes may be mixed, such as:

CURRICULUM AREA:
Grouping

LEARNING DISABILITY TYPE:
Visual-Auditory Association   Introductory **I–3**

Problem-free behavior

The child can determine whether or not the heard or seen measurable characteristics of the elements of two or more groups are such as to allow direct comparisons or grouping together into a single set.

Sample task where deficit child may display difficulty

Say to the child, "Each box has a small thing and a large thing in it. Draw a circle around those things which can be called 'small.' "

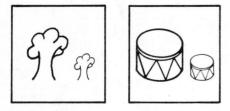

Do-it-yourself diagnostic activities

Prepare a worksheet on which the child must determine in each case which grouped measurement shown is the smallest or the largest. Ask questions such as:

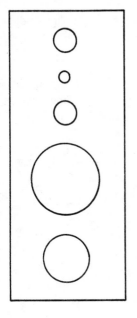

1 Which two are the same size?
2 Which one is the smallest?
3 Which one is the largest?

Non-arithmetic situations where similar behaviors are required

Again there is a similarity to the warning signs seen in readiness level children such as problems in understanding money concepts. At this level, however, the signs may be more subtle and may appear in more complexity, such as trouble with associating value or purchasing power with coin denomination and lack of discrimination in how to use or handle items of worth differently than those which are inexpensive.

Remedial objective for confirmed problems

The child will be provided with practice in distinguishing fine measurable characteristics of individual elements of groups which may allow a regrouping or rearranging on the basis of those elements.

Sample remedial activity

Since grouping at this level deals predominantly with measurement, exercises here should help the child learn the applied use of measurement in grouping. Therefore, exercises should include such activities as:

1 We want to group long lines together. Draw a circle around all the lines longer than 1". Here is a line exactly 1" long:

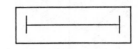

2 We want to put all circles smaller than a penny together. Which circles are smaller than a penny? Here is a circle the same size as a penny:

3 Which of these would you measure with a ruler?

4 Which of these would you measure with a measuring cup?

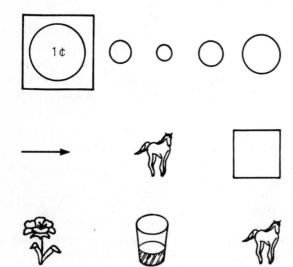

CURRICULUM AREA:
Grouping

LEARNING DISABILITY TYPE:
Perceptual-Motor Use

Introductory **I-4**

Problem-free behavior	The child is able to physically manipulate the tools and objects necessary for group comparison in measurement.
Sample task where deficit child may display difficulty	Ask the child to nest boxes, perform measurements, manipulate objects to be physically grouped or regrouped, or remove an object which prevents a collection of objects from being labeled a group.
Do-it-yourself diagnostic activities	Simply ask the child to demonstrate performance of this type by measuring sand, using a ruler, or handling play money. Practically the entire range of required motor activities can be quickly and easily explored in everyday classroom activity.
Non-arithmetic situations where similar behaviors are required	Problems in this area are easily generalized to situations outside the classroom. Problems with correctly putting bikes into bike-racks, putting away athletic equipment, and proper storage of clothes in lockers or cloakrooms are typical warning signs.
Remedial objective for confirmed problems	The child will be provided with practice in physically making group comparisons and measurements.

Sample remedial activity

It is usually quite easy to keep a child involved with remedial work in this area since children enjoy the active role involved. A simple remedial activity is to give the child a ruler and ask him to find things of a certain length, or give him a stop watch and have him count the number of cars which drive by in sixty seconds. As physical facility increases, more and more emphasis can be placed on grouping as a result of measurement. For example, the child may be told to put all the books taller than 8" on a certain shelf.

CURRICULUM AREA:
Grouping

LEARNING DISABILITY TYPE
Spatial Orientation

Introduction **I–5**

Problem-free behavior

The child is able to use temporal, spatial, or orientational measurements and judgments in the comparison of groups.

Sample task where deficit child may display difficulty.

Ask the child to group according to the spatial-orientational properties assigned to objects, activities, or events. Thus, the child can group together activities which take a long time, or objects which require certain types or amounts of space to receive them (thimbles require little space; elephants, a lot of space).

Do-it-yourself diagnostic activities

Use the same type of activities as suggested under Grouping and Perceptual-Motor Use, focusing on obtaining correct measurements, awareness of process necessary to obtain designated amounts, etc. In this analysis it may be helpful to demonstrate some activities and ask questions about them. For example, place a measuring cup full of water and three different containers in front of the child. Pour the water into the first container. Refill the measuring cup so the child can see it. Then pour the water into the second container. Repeat the same procedure for the third container. Then ask if one container has more or less in it or if they all have the same.

Non-arithmetic situations where similar behaviors are required

Inability to plan activities to fit a time-space (always starting a major project with only a few minutes time available) and poor conceptualization of activity-location relationships are possible warning signs.

Remedial objective for confirmed problems

The child will be provided with practice in using temporal, spatial, or orientational measurements to make grouping judgments.

Sample remedial activity

Some paper and pencil games lend themselves to remedial activity in this area. One of these is "Zoo Keeper." Essentially it consists of grouping animals by some spatial rule such as width and then making a progressively finer grouping decision based on another dimension such as size. To play this game, the child should have cards with names and/or pictures of animals on them and a zoo sheet. (An 8½ × 11 worksheet with boxes along one edge will be fine. Boxes are one of four sizes and shapes: (1) tall and narrow; (2) tall and wide; (3) short and narrow; and (4) short and wide. These represent cages.)

First, the animals are grouped with all the tall ones in one group and short ones in another. Then each of these are subdivided into wide and narrow animals, resulting in

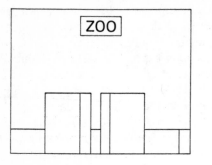

four groups total. Children are then allowed to decide where to house their animals in the zoo, drawing in and coloring the animals in the cages of their choice. Similar games can be played with dishes, toys, etc., instead of animals.

CURRICULUM AREA:
Grouping

LEARNING DISABILITY TYPE:
Verbal Expression

Introductory **I–6**

Problem-free behavior

The child can communicate either orally or in writing the process and results of measurement.

Sample task where deficit child may display difficulty

Ask the child to orally complete such analogies as:

1 A pint is little, a quart is _____.

2 An hour is long, a minute is _____.

Do-it-yourself diagnostic activities

Give one child $1.00 worth of play money coins. Have another child tell the first how much money he should give him in precise terms. For instance, the second child may request four dimes or six nickels, and so on.

Another activity might be requesting a child explain to another how to measure how tall a classmate is.

Worksheets on which there are a series of analogies concerning measurement are also effective. Use, for example, statements like the following:

1 One cup is big, ¼ cup is _____.
2 A quarter is big, a dime is _____.
3 A gallon is big, a quart is _____.
4 3 hours is short, 7 hours is _____.
5 4 o'clock is early, 9 o'clock is _____.

Non-arithmetic situations where similar behaviors are required

A most frequently encountered warning sign is the child's inability to answer the question "Why?" when asked to explain his actions. Actions which have contextual or group-related answers are particularly susceptible to this problem. The hint lies not in the deed as much as the inability to report it, explain it, or talk about it.

Remedial objective for confirmed problems

The child will be provided with practice in communicating the processes and results of measurement.

Sample remedial activity

Using pictures of animals, dishes, toys, etc., discuss the relative size of the objects. Or, discuss the compared size of two classroom objects (two pencils, for example) and then actually measure the objects and report the findings.

CURRICULUM AREA:
Grouping

LEARNING DISABILITY TYPE:
Closure and Generalization

Introductory **I–7**

Problem-free behavior

The child can identify missing elements in a group necessary to make it equal to another group.

Sample task where deficit child may display difficulty

Ask the child to answer such questions as: "How many nickels does it take to equal a dime?" or "How many pennies equal a nickel?" Also, pictorial problems may be used. Ask the child, "What must be added to the second group to make it equal to the first group?"

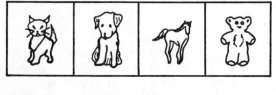

Do-it-yourself diagnostic activities

Prepare a worksheet and ask the child to tell you or draw in what must be added to the box on the right to make it the same as the box on the left.

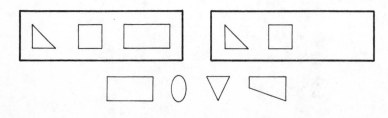

Non-arithmetic situations where similar behaviors are required

Rigid, consistent habit-bound behavior even in the face of obvious reward for doing something different or new may be a warning. To move beyond the concrete here and now is not a typical part of the deficit child's behavioral repertoire. New solutions to old problems are more frightening than rewarding; therefore, they are frequently resisted.

Remedial objective for confirmed problems

The child will be provided with practice in completing the steps in measurement grouping which will achieve equality in number, size, etc.

Sample remedial activity

Many worksheet examples can readily be found for this area. Pictures cut from catalogs or food ads can also be used. Sample problems may include:

1 How many more pennies will it take to make the two groups the same?
2 How many more hours until 12 o'clock?

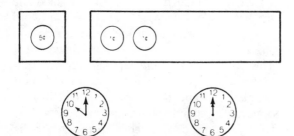

CURRICULUM AREA:
Problem Solving

LEARNING DISABILITY TYPE:
Memory   Introductory **J–1**

Problem-free behavior	The child is capable of remembering the problem solving possibilities of different operations as they are necessary for translation of simple problems into operational form.
Sample task where deficit child may display difficulty	Ask the child to translate an informal problem into an operations or computational format.
Do-it-yourself diagnostic activities	In a group activity, present some problems to the children that will require them to decide which rules they need to apply to solve the problems. For example, read them a word problem such as: "Mary had four ribbons and she lost one. How many did she have left?" Then ask how to write out the number sentence, where each number and symbol must be placed. Repeat this so each child has an opportunity to contribute and note especially failure of an individual child to remember the rule for a solution used shortly before.
Non-arithmetic situations where similar behaviors are required	The deficit child may need much more initial help and prodding in getting started in repeating a previously learned task. In gym, after hitting the ball during his first time at bat on a particular day, this child may be startled into the next step by everyone yelling, "Run!"

Remedial objective for confirmed problems

The child will be provided with practice in recalling the rules needed to guide formulation of simple arithmetic problem solving models.

Sample remedial activity

Use a set of flashcard problems stated in conversational or informal form. The child explores the problem and translates it into an established operational area or form. Correct answers on the back allow self-monitoring. For example, the following problem might appear on the front of the flashcard: "John has 1 bike. Sue has 2 bikes. How many bikes do they have altogether?" The back of the card should read: "This is an addition problem."

Every different problem type can be used and complexity can be increased or decreased as necessary. The technique can be expanded at later levels to include two- and three-step problems. Be sure to assist the child with reading or read the card for him so that difficulty with this aspect does not get in the way of the primary remedial objective.

CURRICULUM AREA:
Problem Solving

LEARNING DISABILITY TYPE:
Visual-Auditory Discrimination

Introductory **J–2**

Problem-free behavior

The child can solve simple comparison problems through the use of pictorialized data both with and without numerical notation.

Sample task where deficit child may display difficulty

Show the child figures such as these, and ask, "Are there the same number of children in each playground?"

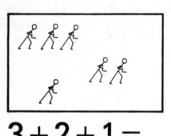

3 + 2 + 1 =

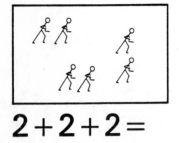

2 + 2 + 2 =

Do-it-yourself diagnostic activities

Prepare a worksheet on which the child is to indicate answers to problems presented both with and without numerical notation. The child should also be required to work through more involved problems, covering more than simple computational demands. Some of

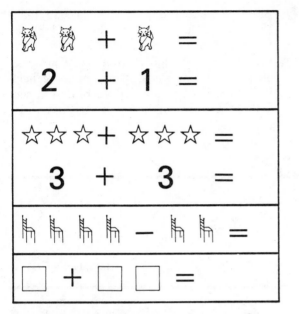

these should be presented verbally as well as visually.

Non-arithmetic situations where similar behaviors are required

Very young children often dress themselves in weird combinations of unmatched socks or inappropriate garments (slippers and winter coat) because they have not reached the developmental stage where appropriate clothing discrimination choices are expected or demanded of them. Seeing this same type of behavior (selection of tools for an activity in class) in an older child may warn of this general deficit area.

Remedial objective for confirmed problems

The child will be provided with practice solving comparison problems presented in a variety of formats.

Sample remedial activity

Remedial activities should take the child through these important stages of problem solving using discrimination:

1 Working with pictorialization of concrete objects.
2 Working with pictorialization with numerical notation.
3 Working with numerical notation alone.

All work should require the child to make like-different judgments of directly displayed factors using any or all of these three steps. For example, though a worksheet could deal entirely with one stage, it may be more helpful for the child to see the progression in separate problems.

CURRICULUM AREA:
Problem Solving

LEARNING DISABILITY TYPE:
Visual-Auditory Association

Introductory **J–3**

Problem-free behavior

The child can create appropriate word problems and then number sentences from visual or auditory input.

Sample task where deficit child may display difficulty

Given the following pictorialization, ask the child to provide the appropriate word problem and number sentence.

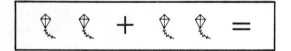

Do-it-yourself diagnostic activities

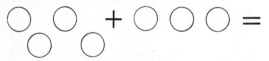

John has four marbles and three marbles. How many marbles does he have altogether?

Prepare a worksheet on which the child is shown a series of pictorializations and an accompanying word problem. The child is expected to write a number sentence from these stimuli.

_____ + _____ = _____

Non-arithmetic situations where similar behaviors are required

Children having problems in this area may warn us by many inappropriate behaviors unrelated per se to arithmetic. Asking the janitor a question which should be directed to the librarian or failing to see that a tablet edge can be used as easily as a ruler to draw a straight line are examples of association difficulties in everyday problem solving. Caution should be shown however since such difficulties may also reflect generalization problems.

Remedial objective for confirmed problems

The child will be provided with practice constructing arithmetic problem solving algorithms from typical auditory or visual data input.

Sample remedial activity

The remedial activity should help the child form connections between simple word problems and number sentences. The appropriate associations to be formed can be presented to the child in a model followed by asking the child to replicate the model (several times if necessary). The modeling exercise can start at an easy level so the child's interest is maintained. Word problems like the following are easy and can be used as models. These can be presented visually or orally.

Say to the child, "Jane has 5 cents and gave her brother 3 cents. Jane now has 2 cents. The number sentence for this problem would look like this: $5 - 3 = 2$. Now you read (or listen to) the next problem and write (or tell me) the number sentence that should go with it. Denise has 15 cookies and ate 3 at lunch. Denise has 12 cookies left. Write your number sentence here _____."

A game that can be played for practicing association between word problems and number sentences is "Problem Dominoes." Put the number sentence ($5 + 2 = 7$) on one-half of a card and put the word problem (I have 5 apples and 2 apples) on the other half. The cards are matched as in regular dominoes.

CURRICULUM AREA:
Problem Solving

LEARNING DISABILITY TYPE:
Perceptual-Motor Use

Problem-free behavior	The child can perform the necessary physical manipulations to do simple problem solving.
Sample task where deficit child may display difficulty	Ask the child to perform defined measurement tasks such as determining the number of cups of sand in a container.
Do-it-yourself diagnostic activities	Have the children play a game such as "Easy Money" which involves buying and selling things, thus involving manipulation of money, making change, etc., from what are essentially verbal problems. Some supervision by either a more advanced student or the teacher may be required.
Non-arithmetic situations where similar behaviors are required	As contrasted with the child having association problems, this youngster often will obtain the correct tool or instrument but then show confusion in using it. One may reasonably expect a first grader to know that a typewriter produces letters but not know how to make it do so. But when similar confusion exists over use of tools and instruments commonly employed by the child's peers, deficits of this type may be expected.
Remedial objective for confirmed problems	The child will be provided with practice perceiving and using motor movement relevant to simple problem solving.
Sample remedial activity	Remedial activities consist of simple practice in doing. The purpose of remediation in this area is not to practice problem solving but to

practice the motor skills used in problem solving.

A useful worksheet consists of a simple problem, portrayed in several forms, followed by steps asking the student to perform activities to arrive at the same solution. For example:

1 Measure 2 separate cupsful of sand into a bucket.
2 Measure 1 more cupful of sand into the bucket.
3 Now measure how much sand is in the bucket altogether by pouring it into the cup.

2 cups + 1 cup = 3 cups

2 + 1 = 3

CURRICULUM AREA:
Problem Solving

LEARNING DISABILITY TYPE:
Spatial Orientation

Introductory **J–5**

Problem-free behavior

The child can use the spatial or temporal relationships of pictorialized data to formulate and solve simple problems.

Sample task where deficit child may display difficulty

Ask the child to solve problems similar to the example.

Both boys started to work when the clock looked like this.

Bill finish when the clock looked like this.

Tom finished when the clock looked like this.

Who took the longest to do their work?

Do-it-yourself diagnostic activities

Worksheets may be used which contain elements necessary for problem solving. Such elements should include spatial or temporal relationships relevant to the problem solving process. For example, say to the child, "John is building a wall of blocks. He needs only one more block to finish it. Which of the pictured blocks should he use to fill the last hole?"

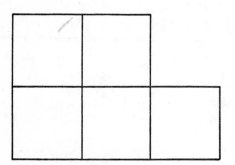

John's wall

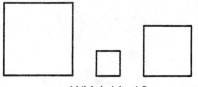

Which block?

Non-arithmetic situations where similar behaviors are required

An easily perceived warning of possible problems in this area can be observed in the child who gets "lost" in familiar surroundings. This child often takes the "longest way around" rather than seeing that more direct routes to familiar places in the school are available for his use. Calling attention to this problem often only results in more confusion and hesitancy in the child.

Remedial objectives for confirmed problems

The child will be provided with practice in problem solving related to measurement and spatial and temporal relationships.

Sample remedial activity

Using a stopwatch have the child perform a simple short task like coloring a geometric figure or putting blocks in a box. Have the child note the elapsed time. This procedure allows the child to have an idea of the length of time it is necessary to do a specific task.

You can also have the child measure personal articles or parts of his body like a finger or an arm. The child can use this information to compare length with other children's fingers or arms.

Sequential arrangement exercises using blocks of different lengths, cups of different sizes, etc., can also be used.

CURRICULUM AREA:
Problem Solving

LEARNING DISABILITY TYPE:
Verbal Expression

Introductory **J–6**

Problem-free behavior

The child can orally communicate the elements of and solutions to simple problems.

Sample task where deficit child may display difficulty

Ask the child to verbally explain how simple problem solutions were arrived at and the sequential steps involved.

Do-it-yourself diagnostic activities

Use a child who is doing well in operations and grouping activities as a demonstrator showing how relevant arithmetic problem solving steps may be performed. Other children, including the child to be diagnosed, can then be asked to describe or explain the demonstrated steps. It is possible for you to do the demonstrating, but some of the spontaneity of the situation will be lost and some observation opportunities may be forfeited.

Non-arithmetic situations where similar behaviors are required

Almost every teacher has experienced finding a youngster in the hall, standing there alone, quietly crying. The most frequent response is to ask, "What's wrong?" When the deficit child is faced with a problem solving dilemma, often not this traumatic, such a question by a teacher or peer is not apt to elicit a very meaningful response. Difficulty in knowing how to satisfactorily ask for help is a warning sign.

Remedial objective for confirmed problems

The child will be provided with practice in verbalizing the elements and solutions of arithmetic problem solving.

Sample remedial activity

Use pictorialized problems such as those suggested for problem solving and perceptual-motor use. Have the child follow through all the steps accompanying them by a verbal explanation. Such a procedure is easily translated into a game where the child tries to explain what he's doing well enough for the other children to be able to figure out what type of problem he is working on.

CURRICULUM AREA:
Problem Solving

LEARNING DISABILITY TYPE:
Closure-Generalization

Introductory **J–7**

Problem-free behavior

The child is able to complete problem solving processes where a piece of information must be supplied or where the process is open ended.

Sample task where deficit child may display difficulty

Ask the child to complete computations such as:

$$\Box + 3 = 5$$
$$4 - 3 = \Box$$
$$2 + 2 \Box 4$$

Do-it-yourself diagnostic activities

Using the blackboard or worksheets, ask the child to fill-in or complete unfinished problems. The diagnostician can easily control the areas and format being explored. If desired, the process can be made more abstract by moving to verbal rather than visual presentation.

Non-arithmetic situations where similar behaviors are required

Deficit children can often be observed to be "creatures of habit." Well-learned problem solving applications are performed satisfactorily and even with zeal. New situations or changes in context which require modification are not handled well. Hints of problems can be noted when a child repeatedly tries to apply old methods to new problems.

Remedial objectives for confirmed problems

The child will be provided with practice in arithmetic problem solving where he must assume responsibility for providing missing elements or data.

Sample remedial activity

A simple worksheet format is available which provides very constructive practice for the deficit child while keeping motivation high. It consists of providing the child with a series of incomplete problems in both word and number form. From a pool of data the child selects the appropriate missing data or elements and completes the problem. For example, the worksheet might state: "One table had three boxes on it. The other table had _____ boxes on it. Altogether there were how many boxes? 3 + □ = ?"
Another worksheet problem may require the child to look at a picture and fill in missing facts.

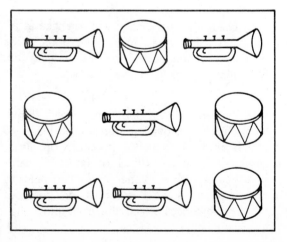

The children like to listen to the school band.
The band has _____ drums.
The band has _____ horns.

CURRICULUM AREA:
Verbal Expression

LEARNING DISABILITY TYPE:
Memory

Introductory **K–1**

Problem-free behavior	The child can remember the labels, symbols, and verbal expressions necessary to communicate simple problem formulation and solving.
Sample task where deficit child may display difficulty	Ask the child to supply word problem phrases or labels to match the symbols in a number sentence.
Do-it-yourself diagnostic activities	Provide the child with some 3×5 cards showing various operational steps, processes, number facts, etc. Ask the child to verbally identify or to explain what each card means.
Non-arithmetic situations where similar behaviors are required	The deficit child may generally display an inability to verbally pass on instructions or to carry a specific message to someone since these tasks involve the interaction of memory of exact terminology and verbal expression.
Remedial objective for confirmed problems	The child will be provided with practice recalling and using labels and expressions necessary to communicate problem solving and operational steps in simple arithmetic.
Sample remedial activity	Use the traditional "Show and Tell" format with children, providing phrases or labels to match number sentence symbols on flashcards. Or, use a "Wheel of Fortune" cardboard circle with a spinner which can point to any one of several symbols or parts of number sentences which the child must then verbally label.

CURRICULUM AREA:
Verbal Expression

LEARNING DISABILITY TYPE:
Visual-Auditory Discrimination

Introductory **K–2**

Problem-free behavior

The child can orally communicate how bits or sets of data, pictorialized or numerically notated problems, number sentences, or simple word problems are alike or different.

Sample task where deficit child may display difficulty

Ask the child to orally explain how measurements determine that an element does or does not belong in a set.

Do-it-yourself diagnostic activities

Ask the child to go through a number sentence, word problem or other pictorialized problem, element by element comparing it to identical elements in a model and explaining why it does or does not match. Children with problems will lose their place, make incorrect matches, or fail to see matches which are present.

Non-arithmetic situations where similar behaviors are required

Confusion in making his wants and wishes known can be a warning. Minor difficulties are portrayed in conversation like, "Is this the toy you want? No? Then tell me what's wrong with it? How is the toy you want different?" The deficit child will reply, "I can't."

Remedial objective for confirmed problems

The child will be provided with practice in verbalizing comparisons and in comparing verbalizations in arithmetic problem solving.

Sample remedial activity

Materials and games from almost any of the other areas of Visual-Auditory Discrimination can be converted for use in this area by requiring the child to add verbalization to the activity. As a matter of fact, using these materials helps the child focus on the verbalization problem since all should be easily within his ability if he has no other deficit areas.

CURRICULUM AREA:
Verbal Expression

LEARNING DISABILITY TYPE:
Visual-Auditory Association   Introductory **K–3**

Problem-free behavior

The child can orally communicate how various approaches to problem solving relate to each other.

Sample task where deficit child may display difficulty

Ask the child to orally explain how a word problem and a number sentence which convey the same information are alike.

Do-it-yourself diagnostic activities

Ask the child to verbally express how a portion of a number sentence would be expressed in a word problem or vice versa. Verbal information required can be as general or explicit as the diagnostic need warrants.

Non-arithmetic situations where similar behaviors are required

Problems here may be portrayed similarly to those seen in Verbal Expression With Visual Auditory Discrimination, except that the communication breakdown usually relates to the child's desire to have some prior encountered process applied to a new situation. Thus, a child who prefers fried to broiled meat will want to express a similar preference for french fries over boiled potatoes but have difficulty communicating the preference.

Remedial objective for confirmed problems

The child will be provided with practice in verbally expressing the comparison of elements and groups in arithmetic problem solving.

Sample remedial activity

Use any materials which display problems or data in different forms. Provide the child initially with a model of how elements of a problem solving situation are similar despite being in a different form (for example, words versus numbers) by verbally explaining some sample problems. Require the same verbalization of the child by moving him through these steps:

1 Comparisons where simple common elements are found.
2 Comparisons where simple common elements are not found.
3 Comparisons where more difficult common elements are found.
4 Comparisons where more difficult common elements are not found.

CURRICULUM AREA:
Verbal Expression

LEARNING DISABILITY TYPE:
Perceptual-Motor Use

Introductory **K–4**

Problem-free behavior	The child can orally direct or discuss the physical manipulations involved in simple arithmetic problem solving processes.
Sample task where deficit child may display difficulty	Ask the child to explain the physical tasks necessary to measure the number of cups of sand required to fill a pitcher.
Do-it-yourself diagnostic activities	Ask the child to play a "Tell Me What To Do" game with you. Start by saying, "I'm going to write out a number sentence which tells me to add two numbers together. The first number is 4. The second number is 3. Tell me what to do." The child should be encouraged to describe motor behaviors involved in writing computations, measurement, etc.
Sample remedial activity	Use the procedure outlines in Problem Solving and Verbal Expression, only have one child direct another in the physical manipulations which must be done. It is easy to evaluate performance by the degree to which other children can follow instructions. Having the responding children ask the director when his instructions are unclear will help shape his behaviors.

CURRICULUM AREA:
Verbal Expression

LEARNING DISABILITY TYPE:
Spatial Orientation

Introductory **K–5**

Problem-free behavior

The child can orally explain the role which positioning of numbers plays in formulating number lines and pictorial representation of data used in simple problem solving processes.

Sample task where deficit child may display difficulty

Ask the child to orally explain the correct placement of the subtrahend in vertical subtraction.

Do-it-yourself diagnostic activities

Using a felt board, magnetic numbers, or even paper cards and thumbtacks, ask a child to direct another person in the physical positioning of numbers, symbols, lines, words, etc., in arithmetic problem solving. It is easy to involve the child in any phase of spatial expression relevant to the diagnostic concern.

Non-arithmetic situations where similar behaviors are required

Expressed comprehension of mechanical operations ("The big rod on top is fastened to the little wheel underneath and makes it turn.") requires both of these functions. Therefore, deficit children rarely do well in explaining any such operation or process or even in directing others as to "where" to place an object, whereas both of these tasks are fairly routine for the non-deficit child.

Remedial objective for confirmed problems

The child will be provided with practice in verbally explaining the role of position and spatial relationship in arithmetic problem solving.

Sample remedial activity

Use worksheet examples like this:

1 $4 - 3 = 1$
"To put this in another form, should the 3 be on the bottom or top? Why?"

$$\begin{array}{r} 4 \\ -3 \\ \hline 1 \end{array} \qquad \begin{array}{r} -4 \\ \hline 1 \end{array}$$

2 $4 - 3 = 1$
"To put this in a vertical form, should the 3 be under the 4 or over the 4? Why?"

3 "In horizontal subtraction, where does the subtrahend go?"

The child is required to verbalize positional relationships both with and without visual models. All types of positional and sequential relationships can be used.

CURRICULUM AREA:
Verbal Expression

LEARNING DISABILITY TYPE:
Verbal Expression

Introductory **K–6**

Problem-free behavior

The child is able to actively participate in verbal discussion and corrective feedback exchanges related to simple problem solving processes.

Sample task where deficit child may display difficulty

Ask the child to explain and respond to questions about a computational problem and use the verbal feedback to make appropriate corrections.

Do-it-yourself diagnostic activities

Simple, informal, give-and-take conversations about arithmetic problem solving are an easy way to informally spot problems. The diagnostician can play "dumb" or take a deliberately wrong tack to explore the child's sensitivity to such things and his willingness to respond when both demand the verbal expression mode.

Non-arithmetic situations where similar behaviors are required

An easily perceived cue is available here. Children who do not verbally express themselves well and/or do not perceive the value of such expression seldom elicit or participate in arguments, debates, exploratory discussions or any verbal exchange which involves two-way communication and ability to produce spontaneous explanations or information.

Remedial objective for confirmed problems

The child will be provided with practice in arithmetic problem solving and strategy planning when the entire process is limited to the auditory-verbal mode.

Sample remedial activity

Remedial activities follow a format similar to that used in Nonwritten Problem Solving and Verbal Expression, except that visual cues and recording of progress are used. Problems should be explored, always in a group situation, and worked out together. Although it may seem repetitious, all remedial activities should go through the three steps of:

1 Talking about what you are going to do.
2 Talking about what you are doing.
3 Talking about what you have done.

Both child and instructor should participate to foster the dialogue concept.

CURRICULUM AREA:
Verbal Expression

LEARNING DISABILITY TYPE:
Closure and Generalization

Introductory **K–7**

Problem-free behavior	The child is able to verbally supply missing words or phrases or complete open-ended statements in simple verbal, nonwritten problem solving experiences.
Sample task where deficit child may display difficulty	Ask the child to verbally supply the missing information: "The two girls together have five apples. Mary only has two. Therefore, Nancy must have _____."
Do-it-yourself diagnostic activities	Engage the child in a "I'll Start It, You Finish It" activity involving open-ended and missing parts of sentences. Explore areas and operations progressively from simple to complex functions.
Non-arithmetic situations where similar behaviors are required	Deficit children may not mimic others' speech in role playing as much as non-deficit children. The deficit little girl, playing at being mother, may go through many accurate physical representations of the rule, but may not produce generalized appropriate speech as well.
Remedial objective for confirmed problems	The child will be provided with practice in verbally supplying missing symbols, words, data, or operations in arithmetic problem solving.

Sample remedial activity

Practice should involve all problem types and forms. Closure should be required to provide missing parts ($3 + \square = 5$) and generalization to complete unfinished work ($9 - 2 = \square$). Children should be allowed to work mentally or to use paper and pencil as they wish, but answers must always be in oral form. One way to foster this is to have the children work in pairs with one recording answers. Answers should be arrived at together and verbal concensus required before recording.

Chapter 9

Post-Introductory Level Materials

Curriculum Areas	(1) Memory	(2) Visual-Auditory Discrimination	(3) Visual-Auditory Association	(4) Perceptual-Motor	(5) Spatial Orientation	(6) Verbal Expression	(7) Closure and Generalization
Operations (L)	L1 p. 264	L2 p. 266	L3 p. 268	L4 p. 270	L5 p. 271	L6 p. 274	L7 p. 276
Rule Application (M)	M1 p. 278	M2 p. 280	M3 p. 282	M4 p. 284	M5 p. 286	M6 p. 288	M7 p. 289
Written Problem Solving (N)	N1 p. 291	N2 p. 293	N3 p. 295	N4 p. 297	N5 p. 299	N6 p. 301	N7 p. 302
Non-Written Problem Solving (O)	O1 p. 304	O2 p. 306	O3 p. 308	O4 p. 310	O5 p. 312	O6 p. 313	O7 p. 315

Learning Disability Types

Figure 9.1 Post-introductory locator chart

CURRICULUM AREA:
Operations

LEARNING DISABILITY TYPE:
Memory

Problem-free behavior

The child can recall the algorithms, processes, and manipulations necessary for multiplication and short division computation.

Sample task where deficit child may display difficulty

Ask the child to form correct multiplication and division algorithms for solving dictated problems. For example, when told to "divide 6 by 3" the child will translate such directions into 6 ÷ 3 or 3$\overline{)6}$.

Do-it-yourself diagnostic activities

A slight change in classroom format from dittoed worksheets to dictated problems which require the children to structure their own algorithms or select the proper processes or manipulations will allow the teacher to check for children who have difficulty remembering them. Cross-checking with incompleted worksheets, for example, a word-problem which must be rewritten in some other form, will allow one to rule out any difficulties encountered with the dictation process itself.

Non-arithmetic situations where similar behaviors are required

Children have many opportunities in the course of a school day to perform routine procedures which have been previously taught and which serve as a model only through memory. Error deviations from such procedures (such as checking out a library book) may be a signal of trouble in this area.

Remedial objective for confirmed problems

The child will be provided with practice recalling algorithms, processes, or manipulations appropriate to specific arithmetic problem solving situations.

Sample remedial activity

In everyday classroom situations the child must be able to remember arithmetic operation processes. As he reaches the Post-Introductory level he will be expected to use this ability outside the structured math lesson and in both classroom and out-of-school activities. Problems such as dividing class members into equal-sized teams or multiplying the number of students times 2 to see how many sheets of paper are needed for a particular project become important functional behaviors. Recall of operational processes must be virtually automatic.

To stress memory behavior, the teacher should have the child use the skill for practical classroom projects immediately after lessons where these things are learned. Gradually increase the time between the conclusion of the multiplication or division lesson and the practical usage of the arithmetic procedure. Include praise and encouragement for the child and do not focus on difficult tasks but upon recall skills.

A series of flashcard problems where the child must recall the correct process or algorithm to use is helpful for individual practice. The correct algorithm can be on the back side of each card to allow self-monitoring.

CURRICULUM AREA:
Operations

LEARNING DISABILITY TYPE:
Visual-Auditory Discrimination

Post-Introductory $L-2$

Problem-free behavior	The child can determine if perceived multiplication and short-division operations and/or solutions match a model.
Sample task where deficit child may display difficulty	Ask the criterion-level child to check his own work against a model for accuracy and note and correct discrepancies.
Do-it-yourself diagnostic activities	Self-marking activities prior to handing in papers of their own or asking children to sort already completed problems into pairs which are alike will help the diagnostician spot the child having difficulty. Children working in pairs, checking their work against each other, is a natural structure for providing situations where behaviors of this type may be examined.
Non-arithmetic situations where similar behaviors are required	Any failing to match to a model which involves activity should be noted since such failures indicate a breakdown in the ability to perform in harmony with discriminations. There are many opportunities to observe such behavior on the playground, in the cafeteria, in the library, filling out forms, etc.
Remedial objective for confirmed problems	The child will be provided with practice in matching to a model or discriminating non-matches with materials dealing with multiplication and division computation.

Sample remedial activity

Give the child models which are already paired correctly. Using these samples as models, the child can then be given simple problems to work, gradually moving to more difficult matching processes. The child must be provided with a model in each case. When the child fails a certain problem, explain what must be done to correctly match the model and immediately have him repeat the procedure.

For example, explain the following model to the child: $2 \times 4 = 8$ matches

$$\begin{array}{r} 4 \\ \times 2 \\ \hline 8 \end{array}$$

because the numbers and the operations symbol are the same. Then ask the child to match the rectangle with the correct circle:

$$\boxed{1 + 3 = 4}$$

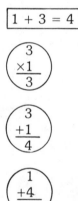

Matches can become increasingly complex as necessary.

CURRICULUM AREA:
Operations

LEARNING DISABILITY TYPE:
Visual-Auditory Association

Post-Introductory **L–3**

Problem-free behavior

The child can discern the similarity of multiplication and short division operations required in arithmetic problems presented in varying forms.

Sample task where deficit child may display difficulty

Ask the child to draw a circle around the number sentence which fits with certain word problems. For example, "Twelve divided by four equals three."

1 $4 \div 12 = 3$
2 $12 \div 4 = 3$
3 $3 \div 4 = 12$
4 $4 \div 3 = 12$

Do-it-yourself diagnostic activities

Dictation activities where the child must translate word problems to number sentences are a useful activity in which to spot children having problems. Such activities can be centered around a game format where the students are playing roles. For example, say to the class, "I'll be mission control and you be astronauts. I'll read out problems about the amount of fuel needed to get to the moon just like I was talking over the radio. You copy them down in numbers and work them out and call me back on the radio when you have the answer."

By shifting problem format and the responding student (astronaut), the teacher can systematically search for children having problems or double check a child already suspected of having a problem.

Non-arithmetic situations where similar behaviors are required

Children with deficits in this area may operate quite satisfactorily in routine, normal, and familiar contexts. However, when faced with having to apply a regular routine to a new situation they run into problems. Unusual breakdown in routine behaviors in new situations is a warning sign.

Remedial objective for confirmed problems

The child will be provided with practice in equating multiplication and division problems regardless of the format in which they occur.

Sample remedial activity

During a school day a child may encounter a new situation and have to apply available knowledge in solving the problem. The deficit child cannot easily use learned problem solving skills to tackle new problems. In arithmetic skills, a system of direct feedback can help the child become confident in using his knowledge in new situations and in recognizing similar forms of the same arithmetic process. The use of flashcards with a number sentence on the front and a word problem (with identical meaning) on the back can be used for such a self-directing feedback system. The cards can also be used in the reverse (word problem on front, number statement on back). Be sure to supply the child with models or demonstrations of how to use the materials.

There are 4 boxes.
Each box has 2 crayons.
How many crayons altogether?

Front

$$4 \times 2 = \boxed{?}$$

Back

CURRICULUM AREA:
Operations

LEARNING DISABILITY TYPE:
Perceptual-Motor Use

Post-Introductory **L–4**

Problem-free behavior

The child is able to perform fine-motor behavior necessary for computation in multiplication and short division.

Sample task where deficit child may display difficulty

Ask the child to write out multiplication and division problems with appropriate horizontal and vertical neatness and proper alignment.

Do-it-yourself diagnostic activities

Have children prepare their own worksheet by copying from a posted model or a blackboard example. Or, on prepared worksheets, provide only part of the necessary aligned structure and format necessary for problem solving. Require the child to produce it himself. An easy way to do this is to present problems in one orientation (such as horizontal) and require the child to rewrite them in the other.

Non-arithmetic situations where similar behaviors are required

This is one of the easiest areas in which to see warnings of possible deficits. Craft and hobby activities and a host of other fine-motor tasks require behaviors similar to those demanded in the arithmetic operations of this level. Fine-motor problems almost always generalize, thus, problems in one area should suggest the high probability of problems in another. The child knows what to do, but has trouble doing it.

Remedial objective for confirmed problems

The child will be provided with practice in using fine-motor skills to provide neatness and alignment necessary for computation in multi-plication and division.

Sample remedial activity

Make sure the child has no gross-motor coordination problems before requiring fine-motor control necessary in the horizontal and vertical positioning of multiplication and division problems. If fine-motor coordination is the only difficulty, a good starting exercise for remediation is air writing or sand writing. The child should practice orienting himself to the correct positions of the numbers first, either horizontal or vertical. Work on one direction at a time to avoid unnecessary confusion.

If these two techniques are easily mastered, worksheets requiring completion of incompleted figures and following dot-to-dot exercises are useful.

CURRICULUM AREA:
Operations

LEARNING DISABILITY TYPE:
Spatial Orientation

Post-Introductory **L–5**

Problem-free behavior

The child is able to demonstrate understanding of spatial, temporal terms and positional orientations relevant for use in multiplication and division computation.

Sample task where deficit child may display difficulty

Say to the child, "Multiplication problems can be turned around and yet you will still get the answer. For example, 4 times 8 can be written 4×8 or 8×4, yet the answer is still 32.

Turn each of these multiplication problems around."

1 2 × 6 = 12
2 6 × 9 = 54
3 3 × 1 = 3
4 4 × 5 = 20
5 7 × 2 = 14

Do-it-yourself diagnostic activities

Using magnetic or felt-board numbers, ask the child to arrange pairs or short sequences of numbers and symbols in varying spatial, temporal, or positional orientations. For example, using a 3, and a 5, and a × sign, the child could be directed to:

1 Make a multiplication problem where the 5 comes first.
2 Make a multiplication problem where the 5 comes last.
3 Put the multiplication sign between the 3 and the 5.
4 Put the numbers in the correct position for doing vertical multiplication.

Non-arithmetic situations where similar behaviors are required

One of the easiest ways to observe this behavioral area outside of arithmetic activity is in the child's general handling of directions on any worksheet or activity involving positional tasks. For a deficit child, a simple direction to "Put your name in the top, right corner," may be a difficult task.

Remedial objective for confirmed problems

The child will be provided with practice in applying spatial, temporal, and positional terms and concepts to multiplication and division computation.

Sample remedial activity

The child must have an understanding of the different positional relationships involved in the mechanical operations of multiplication and division to do successful computation. There are a number of different areas which may need remedial work. One may be the commutative property of multiplication; another, the horizontal and/or vertical orientation of division and multiplication problems.

A remedial activity for commutative properties might consist of a model with a simple problem beneath it:

Model

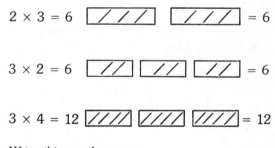

$2 \times 3 = 6$ ⬜ ⬜ $= 6$

$3 \times 2 = 6$ ⬜ ⬜ ⬜ $= 6$

$3 \times 4 = 12$ ⬜ ⬜ ⬜ $= 12$

Write this another way:

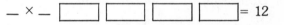

$\_ \times \_$ ⬜ ⬜ ⬜ ⬜ $= 12$

A remediation activity involving directionality of the division and multiplication operations should also consist of a model, with emphasis on orienting the child to the correct direction with cues. The teacher can gradually remove the cues. For example:

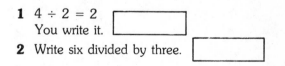

1 $4 \div 2 = 2$
You write it. ⬜

2 Write six divided by three. ⬜

3 Write eight divided by two. ⬜

CURRICULUM AREA:
Operations

LEARNING DISABILITY TYPE:
Verbal Expression
Post-Introductory **L–6**

Problem-free behavior

The child is able to verbally obtain or provide the data necessary for or obtained from problem solving using the operations of multiplication and short division.

Sample task where deficit child may display difficulty

Ask the child to verbally communicate about designated products, quotients, multiplicands, divisors, etc., such as being able to answer the question, "What is the quotient in this problem?"

$$8 \div 2 = 4$$

Do-it-yourself diagnostic activities

Play a "Do-A-Problem" game with an individual child or group of children. Provide a set of data on individual sheets or written on the blackboard. Then say, "Let's do a problem about this." The displayed information contains all the data necessary to compute an answer for a question such as "How many eggs does the farmer have?" But the data is not systematically arranged and the teacher asks leading questions such as, "How many baskets with eggs in them are there?" "How many eggs in each basket?" and so on.

Non-arithmetic situations where similar behaviors are required

Simple question and answer conversations with a child about how to do something can provide much information in this area. The topics do not need to be academic but should involve some specific operations, such as how to use a screwdriver or how to put a stamp on an envelope. The observer should be alert for communication difficulties of either an expressive or receptive nature.

Remedial objective for confirmed problems

The child will be provided with practice in verbally requesting or providing information and data to be used in multiplication and division problem solving.

Sample remedial activity

Using chalk, draw a 4 × 4 square pattern on the floor with a variety of multiplication and division problems, one in each square. One part of each problem has a circle around it, for example: $4 \times 2 = \textcircled{8}$ The child tosses a beanbag in a compartment and then must read the problem aloud and correctly identify and/or explain the circled part to score a point. The player with the most points at the end of the game wins.

Individual worksheet problems of the same nature may be constructed for repetitive individual practice.

$6 \div 3 =$ 2	$6 \otimes 3 =$ 18
$6 + 3 =$ $\textcircled{9}$	$6 - \textcircled{3} =$ 3

CURRICULUM AREA:
Operations

LEARNING DISABILITY TYPE:
Closure and Generalization   Post-Introductory **L–7**

Problem-free behavior

The child can perform subparts of multiplication and short division operations, or given the initial step(s) of a problem solving sequence involving these operations, the child can perform necessary subsequent steps.

Sample task where deficit child may display difficulty

Ask the child to complete worksheet tasks such as these:

1 $2 \times \square = 6$
2 $\square \div 3 = 2$
3 $4 \times 5 = \square$
4 $3 \div 1 \square 3$

Do-it-yourself diagnostic activities

"What Did I Leave Out?" games will elicit the necessary diagnostic behaviors. You can provide a computational model, constructing it step-by-step. Children can be first asked to note *when* some important step has been omitted or is incomplete, and then can be asked to fill-in or provide the missing part. Children can play leader by starting an algorithm (translated from a word problem) which another child then finishes.

Non-arithmetic situations where similar behaviors are required

Children like to "jump in and help" and such behavior is part of their normal behavioral repertoire if they are given any reinforcement at all. The child having difficulties in this area may show either an unusual reluctance to be a helper, or may do so with marked inappropriate behavior since the closure or generalization aspects are not well perceived.

Remedial objective for confirmed problems

The child will be provided with practice in solving each separate sub-sequence of the multiplication and division computation process.

Sample remedial activity

In preparing any type of remediation activity for a closure and generalization problem, first make certain that the child understands and can successfully complete the operations with all the given subparts. If the child has these entering abilities, the remediation activities should begin with problems that denote where a part might be missing, but give the problem as a whole. For example: $2 \times \square = 8$.

Then proceed to give a model and present easy problems, gradually increasing in difficulty, with subparts missing or with just the beginning steps given. For example:

$\square \times 2 = 4$

$4 \div \square = 2$

On a worksheet, the child will be required to fill in the missing number or sign for each of the following:

1 $2 \square 3 = 6$
2 $4 \div \square = 4$
3 $10 \times 10 = \square$
4 $5 \square 2 = 10$
5 $24 \div \square = 12$

CURRICULUM AREA:
Rule Application

LEARNING DISABILITY TYPE:
Memory   Post-Introductory **M–1**

Problem-free behavior

The child can recall the specific facts, elements, or sequence of an arithmetic algorithm or rule when faced with a problem solving situation requiring its use.

Example task where deficit child may display difficulty

Ask the child to solve problems such as this: "JoAnn has 8 cookies. She wants to share them with her friend so that each of the 2 of them have the same number of cookies. To be sure she divides the cookies correctly she wants to work out the division problem using a number sentence. Which number should go in each box?"

□ ÷ □ = □

Do-it-yourself diagnostic activities

It is easy to sit down with an individual child and check for adequate memory of rules to apply in various problem solving situations. To avoid making such a question and answer session overly frightening or threatening, it is best to start out in a "multiple-choice" format and gradually move to dependence on complete recall. Therefore, preliminary questions should take a format such as: "Does the 8 go here or there?" Step-by-step, this can evolve to more difficult forms: "Where does the 8 go?" "Put each number and symbol in its correct place."

Non-arithmetic situations where similar behaviors are required

Deficit children are unable to recall rule structures which guide standardized behavior.

Because of this, their behavior is often "unstandardized," unpredictable, or inappropriate to the norm. A common place to observe the effects of such apparently capricious behavior outside of arithmetic tasks is in games, particularly those that are highly structured, such as board games. Other children often interpret such inappropriate behavior as cheating. But, even if such a charge is not leveled against the deficit child, he is apt to find such games unreinforcing since he has difficulty following play or doing the right things to win.

Remedial objective for confirmed problems

The child will be provided with practice in remembering elements of arithmetic algorithms when faced with problem solving demands.

Sample remedial activity

The typical classroom situation frequently demands that the child remember rules, processes, and directions. The teacher can best remediate an arithmetic deficit of this sort by modeling and presenting situations which require use of arithmetic algorithms appearing further and further separated in time from the formal lesson. This should be a gradual procedure with increased time lapses occuring only when the child has successfully accomplished recalling the rule after a shorter period of time. The modeling for remediation may initially consist of giving the child the correct procedure and working the problem out for him, then having the child solve a problem in a similar format but with different numbers. For example, with the child, solve the following problem: "John has 12 books and wants to share them equally with his 3 friends. How will John do this and how many books will each of his friends get? Answer: John will divide the 12 (books) by 3 (friends) and each friend will get 4. $12 \div 3 = 4$."

Now direct the child to solve this problem without your help: "Nancy has 10 books and wants to share them equally with her 2 friends. How will she do this and how many books will each of her 2 friends get?"

Gradually change the situation, but give models when the child falters on a problem. As skill of application increases, model algorithms should be varied randomly and models used less and less until total recall of all necessary rule application is achieved.

CURRICULUM AREA:
Rule Application

LEARNING DISABILITY TYPE:
Visual-Auditory Discrimination

Post-Introductory **M–2**

Problem-free behavior

The child can make "same" or "different" discriminations in either the auditory or visual mode based upon the application of a learned rule.

Sample task where deficit child may display difficulty

Perform an exercise similar to the following: "Quarts, pints, and gallons all measure volume. Inches, feet, and miles all measure distance. Listen carefully to these two measurements I will read aloud and tell me if they are measuring the same or different types of things."

1 2 quarts—3 feet

2 2 pints—4 gallons

3 5 inches—1 mile

Do-it-yourself diagnostic activities

Diagnostic activities should involve both auditory and visual opportunities to match input to a stated rule. Care must be taken that the child is not required to produce associations as part of the task. Matches may be more complex than 1:1 relationships, but the governing rule should be clearly stated. For example, presented with a two-compartment box and pictures cut out of a magazine, tell the child: "This barn (the box) has two rooms. The red box is for animals. The blue one is for machines. Match the pictures to the right rooms and put them where they belong in the barn."

After a simple beginning such as this problem, subsequent tasks should involve arithmetic rules more and more until the total decision making base is an arithmetic rule.

Non-arithmetic situations where similar behaviors are required

Like many others, the interaction of this content and L.D. problem area has parallels outside of arithmetic. Problems in these parallel areas may signal a warning. For example, a child may have trouble mixing colors to match a color wheel in art because of failure to adequately learn or apply color-mix rules.

Remedial objective for confirmed problems

The child will be provided with practice using arithmetic algorithms and rules in making "same as" or "different" comparisons.

Sample remedial activity

Remediation should start at a simple problem solving level where the rules are simple and uncomplicated and the child will achieve success easily. For example, show the child a display of various geometric shapes. Then tell him the *rule:* Triangles have three straight sides. Ask the child, "Which of these figures are triangles?"

The problem becomes more complicated when an additional step is involved. For example, the *rule:* The brick layer can only use bricks which are squares or rectangles. Squares and rectangles have four straight sides and four equal angles. Which of these bricks can the brick layer use? Which must he not use?

CURRICULUM AREA:
Rule Application

LEARNING DISABILITY TYPE:
Visual-Auditory Association   Post-Introductory **M–3**

Problem-free behavior

The child can make inclusion/exclusion grouping decisions regarding separate elements whose commonalities depend upon application of a learned rule or algorithm.

Sample task where deficit child may display difficulty

Ask the child to solve problems such as: "These figures are different sizes and shapes. Can you think of a rule about shapes or sides or angles which tells you which ones belong together in the same group? If you can, put an X in each of those which you would group together."

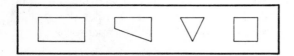

Do-it-yourself diagnostic activities

The diagnostic task here is somewhat similar to that of Rule Application with Visual-Auditory Discrimination. Worksheets, accompanied by some discussion, are the easiest way to spot problems. The format should be something like that shown in the example. Questions to the child might include:

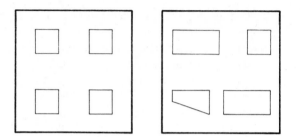

1 Are these two groups the same in some way?

2 How did you know? What rule did you use to decide?

Non-arithmetic situations where similar behaviors are required

The ability to use a rule to help tell someone how to handle a variety of new experiences tends to build self-confidence regarding such situations. Normal children of this age should be showing signs of increasing self-confidence in doing new things, sharing new experiences, adopting through applying the past to the present. The deficit child is apt to view such experiences as frightening or threatening, or at least something to approach with caution. Unusual reticence in approaching new experiences or in trying out old skills in new contexts may hint of problems in the child who displays little unusual reticence or caution in familiar contexts.

Remedial objective for confirmed problems

The child will be provided with practice in applying rules or algorithms to determine whether there are commonalities which can be used to group apparently different elements.

Sample remedial activity

Use progressive problems where a problem is presented and then a rule sought. Both the subtlety of the common elements and the complexity of the rule should be slowly increased as the child's skills improve.

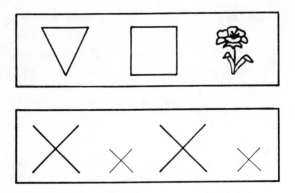

In the first example, tell the child two of the three figures belong in a group. Ask him what rule was used to group them. In the second example, tell the child to use the rule of equal size to put the figures into two groups.

CURRICULUM AREA:
Rule Application

LEARNING DISABILITY TYPE:
Perceptual-Motor

Post-Introductory **M–4**

Problem-free behavior

The child can demonstrate understanding of a learned rule through physically grouping, arranging, separating, or combining elements in an arithmetic problem solving situation.

Sample task where deficit child may display difficulty

Ask the child to arrange numbers on a magnetic board in the correct algorithm for solving a given multiplication or division problem.

Do-it-yourself diagnostic activities

"Listen Then Do" games are useful here. Tell the class, "We are going to put numbers together to do a (multiplication or division) problem. First I'll tell you (or write on a blackboard) the numbers and what they are. Then you write them down on your paper the right way according to the rules we've learned. For example, in a horizontal division problem where 2 is the divisor and 6 is the dividend, you would write '6 ÷ 2 = ' on your paper." The full range of physical manipulations relevant to grouping, arranging, etc., as required by structured rules in arithmetic operations can be explored.

Non-arithmetic situations where similar behaviors are required

As in the case of the interaction of Operations with Perceptual-Motor Use, common activities involved in crafts and hobbies are good places to look for warning signs. The problem may surface in the child showing that the rule is known (for example, the glue goes on the rough side), but failing to put it to use. Or, the reverse may be displayed—behaviors of adequate motor quality but demonstrating inadequate rule application.

Remedial objective for confirmed problems

The child will be provided with practice in physically applying arithmetic rules relevant to grouping, combining, or separating elements of a set.

Sample remedial activity

Remediation should be consistently conceived with having the child physically perform activities which result from the application of a rule. These include sorting, ordering, correctly constructing algorithms, arranging, etc. Worksheets should always require that work data be rearranged or transcribed into proper position. For example, instuct the child to arrange these numbers in a column and then add them: 4, 2, 7, 6, 3.

CURRICULUM AREA:
Rule Application

LEARNING DISABILITY TYPE:
Spatial Orientation

Post-Introductory **M–5**

Problem-free behavior

The child can apply learned rules to arithmetic problems involving shape, symmetry, congruence, or temporal order.

Sample task where deficit child may display difficulty

Given the rule that all triangles have three and only three sides, the child must then correctly identify triangles among any set of geometric shapes.

Do-it-yourself diagnostic activities

The diagnostician is interested in the ability of the child to apply a learned rule. Analysis of the child's behavior involves two steps:

1 Does the child know or remember a certain rule or realize that it is to be applied here? Although this is primarily a memory or perhaps an attention task, it is a necessary entering behavior.
2 Given the rule, can it be applied?

Worksheets are an easy way of handling step two. For example,

- Rule: Squares have 4 right angles and 4 equal sides.
- Problem: Which of these figures are squares?

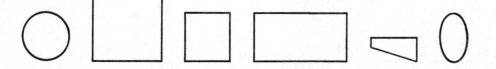

Non-arithmetic situations where similar behaviors are required

Many school rules involve application of permissions and prohibitions to time or location situations. (For example, children are told, "You may read any of the magazines on the special shelf without asking permission during the 15 minutes before lunch or bus time.") Deficit children send up warning signals by displaying total confusion. They ask for permission when it is not necessary, or proceed without approval when they should not. They may be accused of being careless or of not listening when neither may be the case.

Remedial objective for confirmed problems

The child will be provided with practice in applying arithmetic rules to problems involving shape, symmetry, congruence, or temporal order.

Sample remedial activity

The teacher who is planning remedial activities for a child with this deficit behavior must provide adequate visual examples of the rules. The arithmetic rules concerned with spatial orientation can easily be turned into creative play activities. Again, it is important to start at a simple level so the child (1) will understand what he is expected to do so a proper learning set is developed, and (2) is provided a starting point where he will easily achieve success. A simple temporal rule to start with might be the changing of the seasons. This can easily be adapted to an art project by having the child draw pictures depicting how the four different seasons of the year affect tree colors. The child should then explain the "rule" or how the seasons relate to color change.

Similar problems in applying spatial, temporal, positional rules may be presented in areas such as: time (clock hand positions and time of day); money (size of coins and relative value); and geometric shapes (angles, number of sides). Always move from stating the rule to increasingly difficult applications of it.

CURRICULUM AREA:
Rule Application

LEARNING DISABILITY TYPE:
Verbal Expression   Post-Introductory **M–6**

Problem-free behavior	The child can orally state or explain the rule relevant to an arithmetic problem solving task.
Sample task where deficit child may display difficulty	Ask the child to explain how commutativity permits flexibility in the algorithm of multiplication, for example, $3 \times 5 = 15$ or $5 \times 3 = 15$.
Do-it-yourself diagnostic activities	The diagnostic activities and worksheets for the five previous areas associated with rule application can be used here by simply carrying them one step further and asking the child to orally explain a rule applied to do a task. For example, if the child has correctly identified which figures are squares, he may be asked, "How do you know? What is the rule used to decide?"
Non-arithmetic situations where similar behaviors are required	Children having problems in this area have difficulty telling why they did or should do something. That the rule is present and can be successfully applied can be seen in their actions, but if a deficit is present, their inability to discuss these actions is apparent. Such problems are apt to generalize outside of arithmetic areas.
Remedial objective for confirmed problems	The child will be provided with practice verbalizing arithmetic rules.

Sample remedial activity

The teacher should encourage the student to engage in informal conversation before the remedial lesson so that verbal expression becomes typical behavior generalizing across situations. Remedial activities could consist of flashcards with a rule relevant to an arithmetic problem solving task on one side and an example of the rule on the other side.

Have the child read the rule, study the example, and then state or explain the rule that goes with the example. Be sure that the emphasis is placed on applying, not rote reciting, of the rule involved.

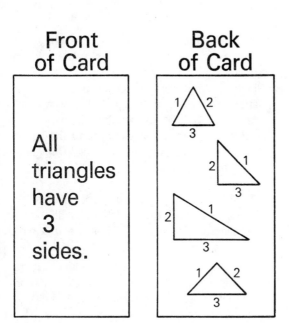

Front of Card

All triangles have 3 sides.

Back of Card

CURRICULUM AREA:
Rule Application

LEARNING DISABILITY TYPE:
Closure and Generalization

Post-Introductory **M–7**

Problem-free behavior

The child can correctly choose and apply a rule relevant to a presented arithmetic problem solving task, or, when presented with a rule, he can correctly identify the type of problems where such a rule may be applied.

Sample task where deficit child may display difficulty

When given a word problem the child can correctly select and use the appropriate multiplication or division algorithm necessary to create a numerical problem ready for computation.

Do-it-yourself diagnostic activities

This area, too, is really only a slightly more complex extension of others related to rule application, and again, some of the same diagnostic materials can be used. Form of presentation, order, and queries accompanying the material need to be altered, however, to fit this area. Using the example of the squares in the previous section, the child might be asked different questions:

1 "Here are some different figures. We want to find out which ones fit together according to shape. What is a rule which we might use to do this?"

2 "We have rules which tell us certain things for sure. For example, we know that a square always has 4 sides the same length, and 4 right angles. What are some ways we might be able to use a rule like that?"

Non-arithmetic situations where similar behaviors are required

Children with deficits in this area turn out to be rigid literalists about rules. Thus, they can be observed carefully looking both ways before crossing the street but running through the parking lot; whispering in class but yelling in the hall. There need be no evidence of rebellion or rule-testing; merely a failure to generalize rules to more than the single literal example situation.

Remedial objective for confirmed problems

The child will be provided with practice in choosing and applying rules to match a problem or identifying the range of problems to which a rule may be applied.

Sample remedial activity

Use examples of common problems in all forms: number sentences, pictorializations, and word problems. Require that the child choose a rule to be applied in solving a certain problem. The rule may be a grouping rule, or an algorithm, or a number fact, etc., but application must be shown. Flashcards may be used where the child is required to produce the rule for a displayed problem or when displayed a rule, to produce a sample problem where it can be used.

CURRICULUM AREA:
Written Problem-Solving and Expression

LEARNING DISABILITY TYPE:
Memory

Post-Introductory **N–1**

Problem-free behavior

The child can retain inputed data sufficiently long to record it, or having read or written it, can retain it sufficiently long to apply it.

Sample task where deficit child may display difficulty

Ask the child to record dictated data in either random or specific algorithm form.

Do-it-yourself diagnostic activities

Check for problems in this area by dictating selected parts of worksheets. Children can be given sheets with portions left blank to be filled in by this method. When the sheets are corrected, they can be analyzed for this problem as well as for normal purposes.

Non-arithmetic situations where similar behaviors are required

A simple clue is the child's failure to remember written directions once they are removed from sight. The memory difficulty usually appears in the form of partial or inaccurate recall rather than total blanks, and may be observed in a wide variety of circumstances.

Remedial objective for confirmed problems

The child will be provided with practice in remembering data bits long enough to use or apply them.

Sample remedial activity

Simple memory drills are about the only way to work directly on this problem. The material to be recalled should be of arithmetic nature and should be presented to the child in increasing amounts and with lengthening delays between presentation and recall. Circled data bits on worksheets, flashcards, or almost any type of written or spoken arithmetic material may be used. Exact control of the time factor can be easily achieved by using prerecorded cassette tapes where the teacher reads a phrase to be remembered. For example, record the words, "Five plus two." Wait a predetermined length of time and then say, "Write it down." Wait a few seconds and say, "Did you write down five plus two?" Such cassettes can be used over and over and can easily be filed according to elapsed time and difficulty of material.

CURRICULUM AREA:
Written Problem-Solving and Expression

LEARNING DISABILITY TYPE:
Auditory-Visual Association

Post-Introductory **N–2**

Problem-free behavior

The child can correctly perceive and/or record in written form similarities and differences between data elements of an arithmetic problem solving task.

Sample task where deficit child may display difficulty

Ask the child to discriminate whether the numerical aspects of two word problems are the same or different and record them accordingly. An example may be: "Are the two multiplication problems in these two sentences the same? Write down the parts of these two problems which are the same."

1 How many apples are there if we have 4 baskets, each holding 2 apples?

2 How many children are in the bus if each of 4 seats has 2 children?

Do-it-yourself diagnostic activities

Use worksheets with problems similar to those shown in the example.

1 These two groups are the same. Each group has the same number of squares as the other. How many squares are there in each group? _____. Each group has the same number of straight sides. There are how many straight sides in *each group?* _____.

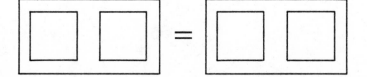

2 How are these two multiplication problems alike?

1 Four times two equals?

2 There are four boys. Each boy has two dogs. Altogether, how many dogs do they have?

Write them down in a number sentence so they look just alike.

1

2

Non-arithmetic situations where similar behaviors are required

Children with problems in this area can frequently be seen to have difficulties in using written labels or in noting whether or not they are reacting discriminatively to written directions. Thus, searching for an item on the basis of a written label (Find the book entitled *Rockets to the Moon*.) can cause these children problems.

Remedial objective for confirmed problems

The child will be provided with practice in perceiving amd recording differences and similarities in the data elements of arithmetic problems.

Sample remedial activity

An interesting bingo-type game can be used for remedial work in this and the following area. Children are given a "bingo" card or a worksheet on which there are printed problems. A set of cards contain other problems in the same general format which contain common data elements. Children attempt to match problems on their sheets to those presented on the card. This can be done in groups or individually and has high interest value for most children.

CURRICULUM AREA:
Written Problem-Solving and Expression

LEARNING DISABILITY TYPE:
Auditory-Visual Association

Problem-free behavior

The child can perceive or record in written form characteristics of data or informational elements which allow or disallow grouping because of common properties.

Sample task where deficit child may display difficulty

Give a worksheet like the following to the child:

"These things have all been grouped together. Draw a line to the word which best tells why all three groups belong together."

round

three

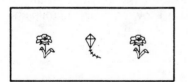

alike

Do-it-yourself diagnostic activities

Use worksheet problems such as these:

1 The objects in each group all belong together for a certain reason. Underline the correct reason: Shape   Size

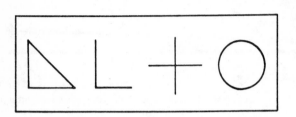

2 Write down why they are the same shape or size. Hint: Are they all square? Are they all the same size?

Non-arithmetic situations where similar behaviors are required

Successfully using written association requires that the child not be bound to specific stimuli, but operate instead upon the classes or sets to which the stimuli belong. If unable to operate with such freedom, the child may be perceived as a *literalist* in using written words. The child can find matching written labels (scissors—scissors), but has difficulty with broader labels (paper cutting tools).

Remedial objective for confirmed problems

The child will be provided with practice in perceiving and recording associated elements of problems which allow or disallow grouping.

Sample remedial activity

Use the same "Bingo" game format as in the previous sample remedial activity. In this instance, however, data elements of the problem may not match, but some other elements are held in common and the child's worksheet notes those elements.

CURRICULUM AREA:
Written Problem-Solving and Expression

LEARNING DISABILITY TYPE:
Perceptual-Motor Use

Post-Introductory **N–4**

Problem-free behavior	The child can demonstrate fine-motor behavior, eye-scanning, and perceptual-motor coordination necessary to reading and writing as used in arithmetic tasks.
Sample task where deficit child may display difficulty	Ask the child to trace down a column of figures keeping his place with his finger as he checks it for accuracy against a model.
Do-it-yourself diagnostic activities	Children love to serve as helpers to the teacher and here is a place where the child suspected of having problems can be routinely observed. Copying sets of figures, arranging magnetic numbers, writing assignments on the blackboard, and similar activities provide opportunities to observe this fine-motor behavior.
Non-arithmetic situations where similar behaviors are required	Children often give clues to their self-perceived difficulties in this area. They may do this by asking for reassurance that they are "doing" right in following "written" instructions, or in asking for clarification of how to follow written instructions, for instance, "Have I done (or am I doing) this right?" Such behavior may easily generalize beyond arithmetic areas.
Remedial objective for confirmed problems	The child will be provided with practice in using fine-motor behaviors relevant to reading and writing of arithmetic problems.

Sample remedial activity

Remedial exercises for this area must be concerned directly with reading and writing of arithmetic. Worksheets can involve both aspects at once by requiring the child to read and follow directions for fine-motor performance. For example:

1 Find the numbers in boxes and copy them in the circles.

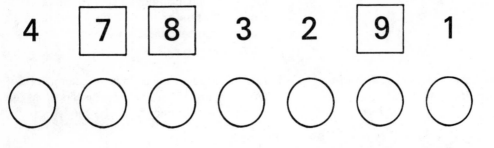

2 Some of these numbers have lines under them. Copy the underlined numbers into a column and add them.

2 4 3 5 1

+ _____

3 Here are some numbers scattered around. Arrange them in a row.

____ ____ ____ ____ ____

Now arrange them in a column. ____

____

____

____

____

CURRICULUM AREA:
Written Problem-Solving and Expression

LEARNING DISABILITY TYPE:
Spatial Orientation

Post-Introductory **N–5**

Problem-free behavior

The child can successfully solve and present information about arithmetic problem-solving tasks involving temporal, spatial, or orientational properties, while operating entirely in the written mode.

Sample task where deficit child may display difficulty

Ask the child to perform a worksheet task such as: "Put an X through the smaller of each pair."

pint	quart
foot	inch
four	two
minute	hour

Do-it-yourself diagnostic activities

This area can be checked by demanding totally individual work related to spatial orientation restricted to written material and then contrasting it with similar problems performed in groups and using other modes of presentation. Preliminary diagnostic hints may be obtained by watching individual children express preference for a written versus an oral or partly oral approach. The deficit child will fairly consistently prefer modes which are easier for him, and in this case, given a preference, he will usually shy away from written problem solving.

Non-arithmetic situations where similar behaviors are required

Adults who experience difficulty here have trouble filling out forms! Names are put above the line when they should go below, addresses are put in the wrong boxes, etc. Children display similar problems or confusion in following written instructions on worksheets, games, hobby sets, etc. As with the Perceptual-Motor Association and Use area, reassurance is sought with usually direct reference to spatial or temporal aspects: the right *place,* or the *right* time.

Remedial objective for confirmed problems

The child will be provided with practice in solving and presenting information about temporal, spatial, or orientational problems in the written mode.

Sample remedial activity

Since this area is dealing with the written mode, it is important to try to avoid verbal-auditory input. The easiest way to do this is to provide the child with worksheets which require him to pursue directed temporally or spatially oriented problem-solving tasks and then to record the obtained data. Such activities can involve any one of a number of areas. For example:

"Use a ruler to measure this line. How long is it? Write the answer in the box *below* the line."

_____

☐

CURRICULUM AREA:
Written Problem-Solving and Expression

LEARNING DISABILITY TYPE:
Verbal Expression   Post-Introductory **N–6**

Problem-free behavior	The child can translate verbal arithmetic information into written form or the reverse.
Sample task where deficit child may display difficulty	Ask the child to read his written number sentences aloud or convert orally presented algorithms into written number sentences.
Do-it-yourself diagnostic activities	Have children play "Secretary" or "School" games wherein individuals take turns dictating, recording, and reading or transcribing their notes. Problems in translating from one mode to another will be easily seen.
Non-arithmetic situations where similar behaviors are required	Generalization to and from non-arithmetic areas is obvious here. Inability to convert any written or spoken communications to the opposite mode, regardless of the context, should be a warning sign. Children with problems cannot, for example, accurately write down a telephone message.
Remedial objectives for confirmed problems	The child will be provided with practice in translating verbal arithmetic information into a written form or from one written form to another.
Sample remedial activity	Remedial activities should consist of translation exercises (oral to written, written to oral, written to written) of increasing complexity. Deficit

children should regularly be asked to read their answers and to copy down spoken directions. Worksheets should demand progressive steps such as:

Directions (to the child): "Listen. I will read some numbers. Copy them down here.

————————————▶ ——— ——— ———

"Now, arrange them in a column here.

————————————▶
————————————▶
————————————▶

"Add them. Write your answer here.

————————————▶ —————————

"Now, hold up your hand and when I call your name read your answer aloud."

CURRICULUM AREA:
Written Problem-Solving and Expression

LEARNING DISABILITY TYPE:
Closure and Generalization   Post-Introductory **N–7**

Problem-free behavior

The child can finish in written form uncompleted arithmetic problem solving sequences or explain the necessary steps prerequisite to arriving at a solution in a written problem.

Sample task where deficit child may display difficulty

Given a written word problem (divide nine by three), ask the child to read it and then explain how to go about solving the problem.

Do-it-yourself diagnostic activities

Worksheets using only word problems will help the diagnostician spot this area of difficulty. It is fairly easy to discern whether or not it is the written form which is causing the difficulty by giving the suspected deficit child identical problems to do which are presented in number sentence or oral format.

Non-arithmetic situations where similar behaviors are required

Just as younger children with closure-generalization problems have difficulty in dot-to-dot exercises, children at this level have trouble with written word/sentence completion games or tasks. "Fill in the Missing Letters" games are no joy to this child and will usually be avoided. Such tendencies to shy away from or do poorly in such activities can be observed in many different facets of school word and play.

Remedial objective for confirmed problems

The child will be provided with practice in completing, in written form, unfinished arithmetic problems.

Sample remedial activity

The teacher needs to be sure the child has a firm foundation concerning the complete arithmetic process before expecting him to be able to finish an incomplete problem. The remediation activity should provide the child with first, a completed example of a written arithmetic problem, and then various forms of the same problem with parts missing (but with answers supplied). For example:

> Seven multiplied by three equals twenty-one.
> ( ) multiplied by three equals twenty-one. 7 or seven
> Seven multiplied by three equals ( ).
> 21 or twenty-one

Once the idea is mastered, similar problems with blanks or omissions are presented. The child first completes them in written form and then, on demand, explains how he has finished the uncompleted model.

Problems may be in any written format: number sentences, pictorializations, word problems, etc.

CURRICULUM AREA:
Non-Written Problem Solving and Expression

LEARNING DISABILITY TYPE:
Memory   Post-Introductory **O–1**

Problem-free behavior

The child can recall and orally communicate to others information relevant to solving arithmetic tasks involving up to two-step problems.

Sample task where deficit child may display difficulty

Ask the child to explain the rule for laying out a proposed problem, for example, "What is the rule for which number comes first when composing a division number sentence?"

Do-it-yourself diagnostic activities

There is an old children's game (typically played on the front steps) called "Stairs." Using riddles or various questions, children advance up the stairs by giving correct answers. A similar game may be used for diagnostic purposes in this area. Each arithmetic rule which the teacher feels relevant should be written in a question form on a 3 × 5 card. Children draw cards and advance up the steps as they give correct verbal answers. By choosing certain cards for individual students to answer, the diagnostician can easily explore specific areas with an individually selected child.

Non-arithmetic situations where similar behaviors are required

A child's everyday world is full of situations where rules must be applied: what to do when the fire alarm rings, where to go to see if someone has turned in a lost article, how to identify one's own school bus, etc. Although children having problems in this area may be able to satisfactorily apply such rules once presented, they will evidence a deficit in being able to recite such rules upon demand.

Remedial objective for confirmed problems

The child will be provided with practice in remembering sufficient arithmetic vocabulary to do unwritten computation and to communication relevant arithmetic information to others.

Sample remedial activity

As presented in other memory areas, the practitioner must be sure the child has a firm understanding of the rules he must remember to apply. If, during an introductory activity, the child appears to have good comprehension of the rules, continue remediation by increasing the time between when the lesson is given and an application in a two-step arithmetic problem solving task. At first the duration between the lesson and usage should be very short, but with successes, the time interval should be increased.

The "Bingo" game format can also be used in this area. A series of questions are prepared on 3 × 5 cards. The cards are also color-coded with one of three basic colors. Cards are selected at random or in an order to match the diagnostic questions. Successful answers allow a child to cover a similarly colored square on his answer sheet.

blue	red	yellow
red	yellow	blue
yellow	blue	red

The "Stairs" game which is used in the informal diagnostic activities for this area can also be expanded for remediation. In every case though, the importance of remembering should be stressed to the child so a set for remembering is created.

CURRICULUM AREA:
Non-Written Problem Solving and Expression

LEARNING DISABILITY TYPE:
Auditory-Visual Discrimination   Post-Introductory **O–2**

Problem-free behavior

The child can provide or elicit information about arithmetic problems involving alike/different judgments and decisions, or without written notation, solve and communicate the results of such problems.

Sample task where deficit child may display difficulty

Ask the child to *mentally* solve problems such as, "Do triangles and squares have the same number of sides?"

Do-it-yourself diagnostic activities

The only way to check this area is to ask the child to perform under non-written constraints. Problems presented should cover both the receptive and productive aspects. For example:

Receptive: "Work this problem in your head. How much is three times four? Is it the same as four times three?"

Production: "If we want to know if two figures are the same, what would we need to know about them?"

Non-arithmetic situations where similar behaviors are required

Children having problems do not ask or cannot answer questions about similarities and differences in general. Such reluctance to become involved in dialogue may result either in stilted, restricted behavior, or the opposite—behavior which might have been more precisely appropriate had questions been asked. This child may sit, unoccupied, or leave without permission rather than ask if his status is the same as another child's who has been given permission to do extracurricular activity. Upon being challenged, the child may be seen to be unable to frame verbal questions or responses.

Remedial objective for confirmed problems

The child will be provided with practice in verbally communicating about arithmetic "alike-different" problems.

Sample remedial activity

Remediation activities must be in the auditory-verbal mode so two people, or one person and a recorded program, must be involved. The format for question and answers, in an increasingly difficult progression, always follow one of the two forms:

1 "I am going to name (list, describe, etc.) two things (problems, objects, numbers, divisions, etc.). You listen and tell me if they are alike or different."

2 "We have a cardboard square and would like to find another cardboard square to go with it. Our friend has a piece of cardboard he says we can have. What questions should we ask our friend to find out if his piece of cardboard is square?"

CURRICULUM AREA:
Non-Written Problem Solving and Expression

LEARNING DISABILITY TYPE:
Auditory-Visual Discrimination

Post-Introductory **O–3**

Problem-free behavior

The child can provide or elicit information about arithmetic problems involving inclusion/exclusion judgments and decisions based upon common properties or attributes governing the grouping together of different elements or sets or elements, or without written notation, solve and communicate the results of such problems.

Sample task where deficit child may display difficulty

Ask the child to *mentally* solve problems such as, "What is there about triangles which make them more like squares than circles?"

Do-it-yourself diagnostic activities

As in the previous area, diagnostic analysis must be totally limited to non-written material, since this area deals with associating common elements rather than making a 1:1 identical match. Questions asked should include requests for the child to note both similarities and differences, and then to state how chosen elements are used to group elements into sets. Again, the ability of the child to both provide and elicit material should be checked. A sample question series checking the child's ability to provide information might read like this:

1 How are cars and bicycles alike?
2 How are they different?
3 What is a way you might set up a group which would allow both cars and bikes to be included?
4 What is a way you might set up a group which would allow bikes to be included but wouldn't allow cars to be included?

Non-arithmetic situations where similar behaviors are required

Children with problems in this area are not very good "idea" people in group situations when they must present their ideas. Their unwillingness to verbally project ideas may sometimes be seen in compensation behaviors which cause them to develop into excellent followers—good at putting ideas to work, but reluctant to suggest answers or to challenge ideas on the basis of whether or not they fit the situation.

Remedial objective for confirmed problems

The child will be provided with practice in verbally communicating about arithmetic grouping and set problems.

Sample remedial activity

Use the same general approach as when dealing with Non-Written Problem-Solving and Visual Auditory Discrimination. The format of the questions must be changed to force the child to deal with association and sets rather than simple discrimination. Questions and answers series should always progress through the steps noted under the informal diagnostic activity for this area. In essence, such a series covers these steps:

1 Recognition of cues for set inclusion.
2 Recognition of cues for set exclusion.
3 Using inclusion cues to group.
4 Using exclusion cues to deny grouping.

Some incidental learning, helpful in later generalization of the skill, will take place if these four steps are called to the child's attention in everyday situations. For example:

1 Milk and cocoa are both drinks.
2 Milk is cold while cocoa is hot.
3 Milk and cocoa can be grouped together if we are using "drinks" as our rule.
4 Milk and cocoa cannot be grouped together if we are using "temperature" as our rule.

CURRICULUM AREA:
Non-Written Problem Solving and Expression

LEARNING DISABILITY TYPE:
Perceptual Motor Use

Post-Introductory **O–4**

Problem-free behavior	The child can orally direct or discuss the physical manipulations necessary for data collection, computation, application, or estimation activities involved in up to two-step arithmetic problem solving.
Sample task where deficit child may display difficulty	Ask the child to physically direct you or others in the laying out of numbers and symbols in an algorithm on the blackboard.
Do-it-yourself diagnostic activities	Using the same format as in the "Do-A-Problem" game (see Informal Diagnostic Activity for Operations with Verbal Expression), ask the child to direct another child or you in performing some physical manipulation. Children may be encouraged to use only speech if they are told to pretend that they are talking over a radio and cannot be seen, only heard.
Non-arithmetic situations where similar behaviors are required	Clues are obvious here. This child may have difficulty in any area where physical actions or deeds must be described, discussed, or related. The child has difficulty, usually easily observed, in explaining how to do things. Seldom will he be seen as a leader in physical activities where verbal directions are necessary. This child would greatly prefer leading "Follow-the-Leader" to leading "Simon Says" games.

Remedial objective for confirmed problems

The child will be provided with practice in verbally communicating about the physical manipulations necessary for data collection and computation in arithmetic.

Sample remedial activity

To work most effectively, remedial activities in this area require more than one person. However, some children will be willing to play both the "Teller" and "Doer" roles while working alone. The major difficulty in such instances is that while subvocal or silent problem solving are an important part of the area, they are impossible to monitor; thus, the child is denied shaping feedback.

A useful technique is to create a "Look, Think, Tell, and Help" game. A number of stimulus items are prepared on cards. These can consist of standard algorithms:

$$\begin{array}{r} 2 \\ +2 \\ \hline 4 \end{array}$$

or operations not yet completely structured:

two plus two equals four

is the same as

2 2 = 4

Where does the + go?

The child looks at the problem, thinks about what has to be done physically to solve or replicate it, orally directs someone else what to do, and if necessary, after a short wait, physically demonstrates his own directions.

The first step can also be "listen" rather than "look," followed by a request for directions, for example, "Where do I put the division sign in six divided by two equals three?"

CURRICULUM AREA:
Non-Written Problem Solving and Expression

LEARNING DISABILITY TYPE:
Spatial Orientation

Post-introductory **O–5**

Problem-free behavior	The child can provide or elicit information about arithmetic problems involving spatial, temporal, or positional relationships, or without written notation, solve or communicate results of such problems.
Sample task where deficit child may display difficulty	Require the child to mentally solve, without visual aids, a problem such as, "When it is six o'clock, is the hour hand pointing up or down?"
Do-it-yourself diagnostic activities	This area lends itself to a "Quiz Show" test of ability to provide or elicit the relevant spatial information. Children can pair up into "Host" and "Player" and use prepared questions to elicit oral responses. Other children can sit as panelist judges or group participants.
Non-arithmetic situations where similar behaviors are required	Asking the problem child for directions on how to get to a particular place or for information concerning something that has happened may cause deficit behaviors to show. Children unsure of themselves in this area may display a warning sign by always resorting to nonverbal aids—pointing, drawings, demonstrations, and so on.
Remedial objective for confirmed problems	The child will be provided with practice in verbally communicating about spatial, temporal, or relationship arithmetic.

Sample remedial activity

Again, the important strategy is to be sure this child stays in a non-written mode during remedial activities. Games similar to "Twenty Questions" are useful here. Start by telling the child: "Imagine that I am looking at a geometric figure. Try to find out what shape it is by asking me the right questions."

The roles may be reversed by asking the child to imagine a figure (or if necessary, give him a pictorialization). The remediator then asks questions like: "How many sides does it have?"

Other spatial and temporal areas may be explored by questions like: "I see a clock. Ask me the right questions to find out what time it is," or "I see four dogs walking in a line, one after another. One of them has a very long tail. Ask me the right questions to find out which dog has the long tail."

CURRICULUM AREA:
Non-Written Problem Solving and Expression

LEARNING DISABILITY TYPE:
Verbal Expression

Post-Introductory **O–6**

Problem-free behavior

The child is able to actively take part in verbal trial-and-error arithmetic problem solving, logical thinking, or estimation of solutions without use of written notation or aids.

Sample task where deficit child may display difficulty

Ask the child to participate in verbal discussions about the appropriateness of an answer to a stated problem. A sample question might be: "Do you think there would be more inches in a foot or more inches in a yard?"

Do-it-yourself diagnostic activities

Children enjoy participating in "What If?" discussions, for example, "What if whales could fly?" This approach can easily be shaped to include topics and situations relevant to verbal trial-and-error arithmetic discussions. By serving as moderator and discussion leader, you or the diagnostician can easily include opportunities to observe specific verbal expression behaviors in certain children.

Non-arithmetic situations where similar behaviors are required

The clues which may be seen in this area are very similar to those encountered as non-written problem solving interacts with memory. The major difference lies in the child's inability to explain problem solving action rather than in relating the rule involved. As noted in the other area, opportunities to observe such problems are frequent although the opportunity for dialogue may have to be introduced.

Remedial objective for confirmed problems

The child will be provided with practice in participating in purely verbal arithmetic problem solving.

Sample remedial activity

Remedial activities in this area require at least one person in addition to the child. With the experienced remediator, problem solving can proceed on an ad lib basis. However, it is useful to have prepared materials ready for aides, teachers, and in some cases, even other students to use. An easy way to do this is to write short travel or adventure stories which have problem solving situations in them that must be completed by the reader without using written cues. For example:

1 Mary's barn has places for hourses to stand. Each place will hold two horses. There are three of these places in Mary's barn. How many horses would Mary

have to buy to fill all these places? Try to work out the answer without using a pencil.

If this stage is too advanced, simpler steps can be tried. The same story and data could be used, but several progressive questions could be asked:

1 Is this a multiplication or division problem?
2 How can you tell?
3 What do we need to know to solve a multiplication problem?
4 What are the two numbers called?
5 What are the factors here?

CURRICULUM AREA:
Non-Written Problem Solving and Expression

LEARNING DISABILITY TYPE:
Closure and Generalization   Post-Introductory **O–7**

Problem-free behavior

The child is able to provide or elicit verbal information missing in an arithmetic problem solving sequence, or that which is necessary to complete an open-ended problem-solving task, or verbally project potential solution application in such problems.

Sample task where deficit child may display difficulty

Ask the child to verbally complete open-ended, non-written problems such as, "How much is eight divided by four?" or "How many threes does it take to make nine?"

Do-it-yourself diagnostic activities

This area can be checked by translating any typical open-ended or incomplete number sentences or word problems into an orally presented and orally answered format. The type of facts and operations covered and the degree of complexity involved should be varied considerably to pinpoint type and level of any problems observed. Questions might include ones of this type: "I would like to know if a four-sided figure is a square. I know it has four right angles. What else would I need to know?"

Non-arithmetic situations where similar behaviors are required

Closure or generalization require an individual to move out into problem solving activities either without total information being on hand or else to accept responsibility for finding or providing the necessary missing data. A child with problems in this area will often provide highly contrasting problem solving behavior, including the non-written area, when all necessary data are at hand as opposed to the incomplete data situations. Familiar situations, even with new problems, are much more comfortable for the child with problems in this area.

Remedial objective for confirmed problems

The child will be provided with practice in asking for or providing verbal information necessary for arithmetic problem solving.

Sample remedial activity

Play "I Would Like to Know," or "If We Wanted to Know" games where an open-ended or incomplete problem solving situation is established which requires solving under the non-written constraints. Here are some examples:

1 I would like to know how many pints of milk are in a 2-quart bottle. How could I find out?

2 If we wanted to know how many times three goes into twleve, how would we find out?

3 If we wanted to know where to saw a board to make it fit a hole in our wall, how would we find out?

4 I would like to know if I can put pens, crayons, and pencils all in one drawer and call them all by one name. How do I find out?

Appendix

Material Locator Charts

Curriculum Areas	(1) Memory	(2) Visual-Auditory Discrimination	(3) Visual-Auditory Association	(4) Perceptual-Motor	(5) Spatial Orientation	(6) Verbal Expression	(7) Closure and Generalization	(8) Attention
Number Recognition (A)	A1 p. 100	A2 p. 102	A3 p. 105	A4 p. 107	A5 p. 109	A6 p. 111	A7 p. 113	A8 p. 116
Counting (B)	B1 p. 118	B2 p. 120	B3 p. 122	B4 p. 125	B5 p. 127	B6 p. 130	B7 p. 131	B8 p. 134
Grouping (C)	C1 p. 136	C2 p. 138	C3 p. 140	C4 p. 142	C5 p. 143	C6 p. 145	C7 p. 147	C8 p. 149
Relation-ship Vocabulary (D)	D1 p. 151	D2 p. 154	D3 p. 156	D4 p. 158	D5 p. 160	D6 p. 162	D7 p. 164	D8 p. 166
Verbal Expression (E)	E1 p. 167	E2 p. 170	E3 p. 172	E4 p. 174	E5 p. 176	E6 p. 178	E7 p. 179	E8 p. 181

Learning Disability Types

Figure A.1 *Preschool readiness locator chart*

Curriculum Areas	(1) Memory	(2) Visual-Auditory Discrimination	(3) Visual-Auditory Association	(4) Perceptual-Motor	(5) Spatial Orientation	(6) Verbal Expression	(7) Closure and Generalization
Vocabulary (F)	F1 p. 186	F2 p. 188	F3 p. 190	F4 p. 192	F5 p. 194	F6 p. 196	F7 p. 197
Relationships-Sets (G)	G1 p. 199	G2 p. 201	G3 p. 203	G4 p. 205	G5 p. 206	G6 p. 208	G7 p. 209
Operations (H)	H1 p. 211	H2 p. 214	H3 p. 215	H4 p. 217	H5 p. 219	H6 p. 220	H7 p. 222
Grouping (I)	I1 p. 224	I2 p. 225	I3 p. 228	I4 p. 231	I5 p. 232	I6 p. 234	I7 p. 236
Problem Solving (J)	J1 p. 238	J2 p. 240	J3 p. 242	J4 p. 244	J5 p. 245	J6 p. 247	J7 p. 248
Verbal Expression (K)	K1 p. 250	K2 p. 251	K3 p. 252	K4 p. 254	K5 p. 255	K6 p. 256	K7 p. 258

Learning Disability Types

Figure A.2 Introductory level locator chart

Curriculum Areas

Learning Disability Types

	(1) Memory	(2) Visual-Auditory Discrimination	(3) Visual-Auditory Association	(4) Perceptual-Motor	(5) Spatial Orientation	(6) Verbal Expression	(7) Closure and Generalization
Operations (L)	L1 p. 264	L2 p. 266	L3 p. 268	L4 p. 270	L5 p. 271	L6 p. 274	L7 p. 276
Rule Application (M)	M1 p. 278	M2 p. 280	M3 p. 282	M4 p. 284	M5 p. 286	M6 p. 288	M7 p. 289
Written Problem Solving (N)	N1 p. 291	N2 p. 293	N3 p. 295	N4 p. 297	N5 p. 299	N6 p. 301	N7 p. 302
Non-Written Problem Solving (O)	O1 p. 304	O2 p. 306	O3 p. 308	O4 p. 310	O5 p. 312	O6 p. 313	O7 p. 315

Figure A.3 Post-introductory locator chart

REFERENCES

Aukerman, R. Reading in the mathematics classroom. In R. Aukerman, *Reading in the Secondary Classroom*. New York: McGraw-Hill, 1972.

Bannatyne, A. Programs, materials and techniques. *Journal of Learning Disabilities*, 1974, *7*, 333–343.

Bartel, N. Problems in arithmetic achievement. In D. Hammill and N. Bartel (Eds.), *Teaching children with learning and behavior problems*. Boston: Allyn and Bacon, 1975.

Bateman, B. Learning disabilities—yesterday, today, and tomorrow. *Exceptional Children*, 1964, *31*, 167–177.

Brown, V. Learning about mathematics instruction. *Journal of Learning Disabilities*, 1975, *8*, 476–485.

Burns, P. Arithmetic fundamentals for the educable mentally retarded. *American Journal of Mental Deficiency*, 1961, *66*, 57–61.

Callahan, L. and Robinson, M. Task-analysis procedures in mathematics instruction of achievers and underachievers. *School Science and Mathematics*, 1973, *73*, 578–584.

Chalfant, J. and Scheffelin, M. Central processing dysfunction in children: A review of research. *National Institute of Neurological Diseases and Stroke Monographs*, 1969, No. 9.

Connolly, A., Nachtman, W., and Prichett, E. *Keymath Diagnostic Arithmetic Test*. Circle Pines, Minn.: American Guidance Service, Inc., 1971.

Cowgill, M., Friedland, S., and Shapiro, R. Predicting learning disabilities from kindergarten reports. *Journal of Learning Disabilities* 1973, *6*, 577–582.

Cruickshank, W. Arithmetic vocabulary of mentally retarded boys. *Journal of Exceptional Children*, 1946, *13*, 65–69, 91.

Cruickshank, W. Arithmetic ability of mentally retarded children: I. Ability to differentiate extraneous materials from needed arithmetic facts. *Journal of Educational Research*, 1948, *42*, 161–170.

Cruickshank, W. Arithmetic ability of mentally retarded children: II. Understanding arithmetic processes. *Journal of Educational Research*, 1948(a), *42*, 279–288.

Cruickshank, W. Arithmetic work habits of mentally retarded boys. *American Journal of Mental Deficiency*, 1948(b), *52*, 318–330.

Doll, E. Neurophrenia. *American Journal of Psychiatry*, 1951, *108*, 50–53.

Dunlap, W. and House, A. Why can't Johnny compute? *Journal of Learning Disabilities*, 1976, *9*, 210–214.

Freidus, E. The needs of teachers for specialized information on number concepts. In W. Cruickshank (Ed.), *The teacher of brain-injured children: A discussion of the bases for competency.* Syracuse, N.Y.: Syracuse University Press, 1966.

Gagne, R. *The conditions of learning.* New York: Holt, Rinehart, Winston, 1970.

Gagne, R., Mayor, J., Gartens, H., and Paradise, N. Factors in acquiring knowledge of a mathematical task. *Psychological Monographs,* 1962, *76,* No. 7.

Gearheart, B. *Learning disabilities: Educational strategies.* St. Louis, Mo.: C.V. Mosby, 1973.

Hainsworth, P. and Siqueland, M. *Early identification of children with learning disabilities: The Meeting Street School Screening Test.* Providence, Rhode Island: Crippled Children and Adults of Rhode Island Inc., 1969.

Hammill, D. and Bartel, N. (Eds.) *Educational perspectives in learning disabilities.* New York: John Wiley, 1971.

Hollister, G. and Gunderson, A. *Teaching arithmetic in grades I and II.* Boston: D.C. Heath, 1954.

Johnson, D. and Myklebust, H. *Learning disabilities: Educational principles and practices.* New York: Grune and Stratton, 1967.

Johnson, S. *The marginal child: Workshop proceedings.* Plattsburgh, New York: State University of New York at Plattsburgh, 1962.

Johnson, S. and Morasky, R. *Learning disabilities.* Boston: Allyn and Bacon, 1977.

Kaliski, L. Arithmetic and the brain-injured child. In E. Frierson and W. Barbe (Eds.), *Educating children with learning disabilities.* New York: Appleton-Century-Crofts, 1967.

Kirk, S. *Educating exceptional children,* 1st ed. Boston: Houghton Mifflin, 1962.

Kirk, S. Behavior diagnosis and remediation of learning disabilities. In Proceedings of the Conference on Exploration into the Problems of the Perceptually Handicapped Child, First Annual Meeting, Vol. 1, Chicago, April 6, 1963.

Kirk, S. Learning disabilities: The view from here. On progress in parent information, professional growth, and public policy. Selected papers, Association for Children with Learning Disabilities. San Rafael, Calif.: Academic Therapy Publications, 1969.

Kirk, S., McCarthy, J., and Kirk, W. *Illinois Test of Psycholinguistic Abilities,* rev. ed. Urbana, Ill.: University of Illinois Press, 1968.

Lerner, J. *Children with learning disabilities: Theories, diagnosis, and teaching strategies.* Boston: Houghton Mifflin, 1976.

Mackie, R. *Special education in the United States: 1948–1966.* New York: Teachers College Press, 1969.

Mann, P. and Suiter, P. *Handbook in diagnostic teaching.* Boston: Allyn and Bacon, 1974.

Meeker, M. *The structure of intellect: Its interpretation and uses.* Columbus, Ohio: Charles E. Merrill, 1969.

Meier, J. Prevalence and characteristics of learning disabilities found in second grade children. *Journal of Learning Disabilities,* 1971, *4,* 1–16.

Myers, P. and Hammill, D. *Methods for learning disorders.* New York: John Wiley, 1976.

Myklebust, H. and Boshes, B. Minimal brain damage in children. Final report, United States Public Health Service Contract 108-65-142, United States Department of Health, Education and Welfare, Evanston, Ill.: Northwestern University Publications, 1969.

National Advisory Committee on Handicapped Children. *Special Education for Handicapped Children. First Annual Report.* Washington, D.C.: United States Department of Health, Education and Welfare, 1968.

Otto, W. and McMenemy, R. *Corrective and remedial teaching: Principles and practices.* Boston: Houghton Mifflin, 1966.

Peterson, D. *Functional mathematics for the mentally retarded.* Columbus, Ohio: Charles E. Merrill, 1973.

Piaget, J. How children form mathematical concepts. *Scientific American,* 1953, *189,* 74–79.

Reisman, F. *A guide to the diagnostic teaching of arithmetic.* Columbus, Ohio: Charles E. Merrill, 1972.

Resnick, L., Wang, M., and Kaplan, J. Task analysis in curriculum design: A hierarchically sequenced introductory mathematics curriculum. *Journal of Applied Behavior Analysis,* 1973, *6* (4), 679–710.

Roach, E. and Kephart, N. *The Purdue Perceptual-Motor Survey.* Columbus, Ohio: Charles E. Merrill, 1966.

Schroeder, L. A study of the relationships between five descriptive categories of emotional disturbance and reading and arithmetic achievement. *Exceptional Children,* 1965, *32,* 111–112.

Smith, D. and Lovitt, T. The differential effects of reinforcement contingencies on arithmetic performance. *Journal of Learning Disabilities,* 1976, *9,* 21–29.

Smith, R. *Clinical teaching: Methods of instruction for the retarded,* 1st ed. New York: McGraw-Hill, 1968.

Smith, R. (Ed.) *Teacher diagnosis of educational difficulties.* Columbus, Ohio: Charles E. Merrill, 1969.

Smith, R. *Clinical teaching: Methods of instruction for the retarded,* 2nd ed. New York: McGraw-Hill, 1974.

Smith, R. and Neisworth, J. Fundamentals of informal educational assessment. In R. Smith (Ed.), *Teacher diagnosis of educational difficulties.* Columbus, Ohio: Charles E. Merrill, 1969.

Sontag, E. Specific learning disabilities program. *Exceptional Children,* 1976, *43,* 157–159.

Stevens, G. and Birch, J. A proposal for clarification of the terminology used to describe brain-injured children. *Exceptional Children,* 1957, *23,* 346–349.

Strauss, A. and Lehtinen, L. *Psychopathology and education of the brain-injured child.* New York: Grune and Stratton, 1947.

Strauss, A. and Werner, H. Disorders of conceptual thinking in the brain-injured child. *Journal of Nervous and Mental Disease,* 1942, *96,* 153–172.

Valett, R. *The remediation of learning disabilities.* Belmont, Calif.: Fearon, 1967.

Walbesser, H. and Carter, H. Behavioral objectives. *The slow learner in mathematics: 35th yearbook.* Reston, Va.: National Council of Teachers of Mathematics, 1972.

Wallace, G. and Kauffman, J. *Teaching children with learning problems.* Columbus, Ohio: Charles E. Merrill, 1973.

Wilson, J. Diagnosis and treatment in mathematics. In P. Knoblock (Ed.), *The teaching-learning process in educating emotionally disturbed children.* Syracuse, N.Y.: Syracuse University Press, 1967.

Index

Index